# THE ONCE IN A LIFETIME

## A NOVEL

by
# SHARYL LIDZHAN

PRINTED IN PETALING JAYA 2022

sharyllidzhan@gmail.com

ISBN: 978-981-18-3596-4 (Paperback)
ISBN: 978-981-18-4742-4 (Hardcover)
ISBN: 978-981-18-4743-1 (E-book)

Any references to historical events, real people, or real places are used fictitiously. Names, characters, and places are products of the author's imagination.

Front cover image by Sharyl Lidzhan.
Book design by Aeyshaa @aeysha_bookdesign.
E-book design by Aeyshaa @aeysha_bookdesign.

Printed by Merce Associates Sdn Bhd.

First printing edition 2022.

1.

"We have to talk," Lyna said as she sat at the dinner table, a world unto herself. Alex squirmed in his seat, his eyes darting around the room in an attempt to minimise the dull throb rising from his stomach as those words were uttered. He looked across the table at Lyna, and even as the bubbling discomfort in his gut raged on, he felt at peace.

But Alex couldn't remember how he met her. Or at least, that was the official party line.

They met online.

Through a pimp.

Yes.

She had been an escort, a whore working in a digital brothel of the VUCA world. Her stage name at the commercial sex forum Sammyboy was, "Frida," who was a "twenty-three-year-old Polish mix, smooth like silk, sex like tiger, and teacher grade BBBJ." The post about her had her in white undersized lingerie she had inherited from the last whore. Arms raised, armpits in full glory, legs apart, and lips pouting. And Alex had fallen for it. Maybe it had been the soft, retro filter, her toned armpits, or even her pasty white skin. But it had been enough for him to get in touch with the digital pimp, "Mr Pimp," and pay a hundred and sixty dollars for a forty-five-minute session with Frida. The sex had been at the Orchard Rendezvous Hotel, complete with room service, was good, but the chemistry between the two of them, both on and off the bed, was electric, to say the least.

In real life, Lyna had a body built for all manners of sin and pleasure; she towered over most men and intimidated what was left of them. Her sinuous, off-season physique was a road map of strength and endurance, scarred by the arts of pleasure. Alex loved the way her lips pursed and pouted as she spoke, also in the way her hips swayed as it sat on top of a pair of athletic, weapon-like legs that never seemed to end. Her pixie-cut hair made her look non-threatening, and her eyes were like calm pools of clear blue, ominous and waiting for a poor fool to wade into it before a whirlpool of rage appeared to drown the poor soul. Blessed, or cursed, a voracious, almost libertine appetite, she would make the divine Marquis de Sade blush with her words just from the naughty glint in her eyes. Flawed as she was, she had a good heart behind her rack of 34Cs, from which came forth the gentlest of souls that would nurture and nourish a caveman beast right out of barbarism.

The highlight, however, was how instinctive they were for each other's pleasure. They both knew which buttons to press, lick and slap, and when to do all of that. If fucking were an Olympic sport, these two libertines would be a shoo-in for the gold medal and world record holders in the doubles event.

He loved how her skin turned pink, almost reddish after an orgasm or a hot shower, giving her a healthy, almost ethereal glow. He loved how her body fit perfectly with his, and how when he cuddled with her, the warmth of her flesh melted whatever worries he had for the day.

She loved how his voice went several octaves lower after fucking, giving him an intense baritone voice that always re-ignited the smouldering embers of her lust into a blazing fury. She loved the sweaty, masculine musk mixed with his perfume that emanated from his flesh, a scent so alluring, she often felt like licking him all over, all night long.

It was not long before he forked out another hundred and sixty dollars to see her, and another hundred and sixty, and another. Sometimes, he would just pay her for her time, just so he could take a shower with her and to lie in silence, in her arms. Once, he paid her three hundred and twenty dollars just to rant and rave about work, friends and for her to listen to his diatribe, offer him cigarettes and expensive room service beer. It became a very expensive shower to have, a most costly cuddle, and an exorbitant rate for a listening ear, with or without the booze. It was a sweet deal for a whore nonetheless, having an easy, steady stream of money coming in without having to fuck him. However, somewhere along this line of Alex's often intense emotional outpouring of angst and malaise, they came to adore each other and became friends, with real, albeit budding, feelings for each other. Alex had been happy to keep paying for her listening ear and to ravage her body, but they had nurtured the relationship to a point where money was not an issue for both of them anymore. They were happy to just be with each other, as they both saw the futility of it, and decided to talk and fuck, off the books.

So they became fuck friends, friends with benefits. They saw each other so much that they even toyed with the idea of moving in together, but the thought of renting a place did not appeal to both their pragmatic sensibilities. However, as months went by and with her visa running out, they received a massive stroke of luck, when she was offered a five-year expatriate package to work at a shipbuilding company in Tuas, which included, among other perks, rent-free accommodation. It was actually another one of her other clients who offered her the job, thinking that her pretty face would make for an excellent front for his company. Also thinking he too could fuck her off the books by virtue of being her boss, but that was not to be so as she soon made it clear that she was only for Alex. It brought her a lot of grief in the early months of the new job rife with challenges in the form of lewd comments and harassment often led by her scorned former client and now boss.

But she did not care one bit.

All she saw was that she had a stable job, very regular hours and a stable, decent income. But most importantly, she would be able to see and fuck Alex anytime she wanted. Alex thought the same and was beside himself with joy, because being with Lyna, or whatever this was called, was the closest thing he had come to being in a real and stable relationship. Even as they did not clearly define the boundaries, they were happy with it being that way because all they knew was that they wanted to be in each other's arms and company as much as possible. The fucking became an icing on the cake.

However, as months went by, the drudgery and stress of regular work soon took a physical and emotional toll on them both, and they moved from being good friends who fucked, to being foul-weather friends who fucked. They became friends who only saw and talked to each other when either one was feeling down having had a bad day at the office.

Well, there was not much talking involved, really.

Just a lot of fucking.

Back in the hole-in-the-wall restaurant in Telok Ayer, Lyna went on, snapping him back to reality, "I need to go back home to Lviv. Mother is sick. I think she is dying," she said, doing her best to be cold and devoid of emotion. "She has been sick for a while now, something to do with her heart, I'm not too sure. But don't worry, I won't be long, and I will be back here soon enough," she assured the increasingly emotionally-fragile Alex.

Alex whined, "Damn it, Lyna, how long will you be away for? Will you come back?" His voice almost broke in a falsetto, quivering like a feather blown in the wind.

"Why are you so whiny? I didn't fuck you all this time just to see you turn into a sappy man-child. I told you, I will be back, don't worry," she snapped as she slapped the table hard, catching the attention of other people at the restaurant. But almost immediately, she felt a pang of guilt slapping her across the face. She might be a tough little cat with retractable steel claws and fangs in her vagina, but it was different with Alex. With Alex, she felt an overpowering need to nurture him, to protect him.

Some might even say to love him.

And it was not too much of a stretch to see why because, as foul-weather friends, they had evolved to be each other's emotional balance in times of great imbalance and disruption. They were each other's countermeasures deployed before or when shit hit the fan. They were each other's crime scene clean-up crew, washing away the blood spatter and the decomposing soup that was the corpse of their emotional well-being, before the cops came and investigated. So she felt that it was unfair for her to up and leave all of a sudden, even if it was for that short while.

Maybe.

Or not.

Who knew?

"I'm sorry, babe, you know how important my family is to me. But you also know how important you are to me, and how important this is for us. So I promise you, okay, I'll come back for you," she assured him as she took his hand, kissing and licking his palm.

But how far she could keep her promise, Alex couldn't tell.

And neither could she.

Petulant and surly as he had become of late, he had no choice but to somewhat believe her, and as much as he wanted their fleshly pursuits to continue, he knew that this could very well spell the beginning of the end for them.

Lyna knew too.

But they were not one to be talking about emotions. That was one of the first rules of fuck buddies: to leave emotions at the door, fuck like bunnies, and to be in heat only for each other. According to them anyway.

Just as he began to mentally prepare himself to be out hunting the stale-beer-smelling, smoky watering holes in the urban tundra for what he often referred to as 'physical therapy,' Lyna thought up of a seemingly brilliant idea. An idea in the form of a tasty little Russian treat named Anna, a fresh marketing consultant hire who came from St Petersburg to the grimy tropical climes of Singapore. She thought Anna could distract Alex during her absence, to lessen the pain of a possible break-up, a human shaped Vicodin tablet for Alex to chew on if he felt the pain of Lyna's absence.

"You want to pimp out your colleague to me? What makes you think I'll like her, or that she wants to? Or…"

"Don't worry, she's just like me," she interrupted him. "And I'm sure she will take good care of you and love you like me. Just show her around the island, feed her, keep her company, do fun activities with her, and it'll be fine. Maybe even better than it has been with me," she said to him, almost like an eloquent pimp marketing her wares.

Alex noticed one thing that stood out from all of her drivel — that it was the first time Lyna used that word. *Love.* Their ears pricked and reacted, albeit subtly, at the mention of the word. Lyna was surprised she used it, Alex too, but he was expecting and hoping for it to be so.

"Do you blame her?" Alex would say with a cocky sneer on his face and a tilt of the head. It was more like humour used to mask the longing he was starting to feel for Lyna. Yes, he missed her already, and that was when she was still sitting opposite him. He couldn't imagine how it would be when she was really gone, despite the fact that he was very happy that Lyna had used the word 'love' in the same sentence as 'us' and in describing their relationship.

But he buried it.

They both did.

Lyna was being pragmatic. Maybe this country was rubbing off a lot more onto his precious little trollop than he ever realised.

As much as he was, at the very least, nonchalant at the prospect of being pimped again, he was never one to turn down a good chance for fresh pussy. He didn't want to care about connection, nor chemistry. This Anna was to be a stop-gap measure, a band aid applied on an increasingly fatal haemorrhage of the jugular vein that was their dysfunctional relationship, the Paracetamol taken to relieve a raging viral fever.

So Lyna had asked Alex to show Anna around and be a friend for her after she arrived. Anything that developed out of that was purely up to them both, and Lyna wanted nothing to do with it. And it was only weeks after Lyna left, that, Alex, starved for company and desperate for social contact, finally asked Anna out for dinner and drinks.

The air was light in the bar called Buyan at Duxton Hill, the tension almost palpable, and there was an urgent need for Alex to grind through the date in order for him to reach the appropriate moment for the golden question. As smooth as he was, he found it difficult to connect with Anna. Even with the alcohol flowing, it was starting to be a laborious chore maintaining conversation. Like trying to plug a leak with his fingers and a new leak kept appearing, and he had only so many appendages left to finger the wall. Nevertheless, the prospect of smooth, pink pussy was too difficult to ignore and he powered through the awkwardness.

"You know, this is weird. Here we are, at a place eating beef stroganoff, drinking Polish vodka and American bourbon, served by Filipino waiters, wearing clothes made in China and with an Australian rock band playing on the sound system," Anna said, trying very hard to wag the irony in the dog's face. Alex tried hard to remain interested as her perky breasts and a hint of nipple peeking through her top kept his attention. Almost just as he tried hard to maintain eye contact, helplessly trying to tread water in the deep end of the pool of her green eyes.

"Yeah, almost as ironic as an English-speaking Russian girl from St. Petersburg working for a Chinese company and having dinner with me," he quipped, half hoping it would cause offence.

But there was something about Anna that Alex just couldn't place. Maybe it was her bleached blonde locks falling lazily across her forehead, her deeply soulful, yet innocent eyes. Maybe it was the slightly upward smirk that she wore naturally on her luscious blow-job lips, giving her an almost chilly and condescending look. Maybe it was the deep, smouldering tone of her voice that, when coupled with an accent that was a patois of a regional Russian village, sprinkled with French and English? Or was it her statuesque posture that kept her upright and poised on any occasion?

No.

It was her perky breasts which jiggled and jumped as she laughed out loud at his deadpan jokes. It was her smooth, long legs that went on for days where, in certain lighting, highlighted the tiny, fine baby hair on her thighs. It was her seemingly strong sinuous arms of postmodern feminism and sexuality. It was the sensuous fold of her armpits that he would love to live inside of for weeks on end. The strong girl who lifted and did HIIT, yet yearning for both tenderness and a good ass-reddening spanking.

And in certain lights, she even looked like Lyna.

But unlike Lyna, the chemistry and connection between Alex and Anna was far from electric, but there was just enough electricity to fire up their loins. And after dinner and a few vodka shots later, coupled with copious amounts of awkward shameless flirting, they both found enough in themselves and the right frame of mind and body to go home and hit the sheets together, and they found themselves on an unplanned staycation at the RELC International Hotel at Orange Grove Road.

Things started predictably well, despite the almost weird fact that she insisted they showered, separately, before getting to more foreplay. Alex didn't care too much though, because the shower was a time for him to melt into the walls and enjoy being alone. Not that he wanted to do that now anyway. Not with a flaming mound of woman flesh waiting for him in the other room.

After a quick shower where he washed and soaped the parts he hoped Anna would go to with her mouth, he soon found himself in her bed and kissing her passionately. They kissed each other deeply with an intensity that would set the world afire. Their sloppy kisses would gross people out if they were listening, or set fire to the most jaded of loins. They didn't care that teeth got in the way of their kissing, with its sometimes uncomfortable clash of incisors. He found a comfortable spot in the very small breathing room between pleasure and pain to work her up to a raging blaze of sexual frenzy. It was as if Anna was trying to suck his tongue from out of his mouth, and even as he felt the pain of it, he didn't care, because he got to do the same thing to her. And she liked it. They both did.

To hell with clothes, as they tore each other's bathrobe and towel off. To hell with makeup as he gently licked and ravaged every inch of her face and her smooth pinkish body with his tongue, leaving a trail of saliva on her that glistened sensuously in the light. He took his time, breathed in her scent from every inch of her skin, and generously planting a combination of kisses, light suction and tongue all over her, leaving behind a trail of wet mouth-shaped splotches on her body.

The wet trails of pleasure.

He took his time to tease and explore the areas surrounding her genitals, lightly kissing, licking and gently blowing on her inner thighs, a move that sent her visibly quivering.

Or cringing.

He wasn't sure.

He took a few seconds to closely admire her smooth, slight stubble on her vagina, with his nose and mouth painfully close to making contact with the trembling flesh. She grabbed the back of his head, unable to withstand the tease anymore, but he resisted, adding fuel to the already raging sexual frenzy. Finally, he opened his mouth, let loose his tongue from its cage, and supped on her womanhood. Waves of pleasure pounded her relentlessly as her muscles trembled and shuddered involuntarily as she reached her sexual nadir. There was a deep gasp, he looked up, saw that her belly was sucked in so deep, he could almost see her spine. It was as if rigor mortis had set in as she tensed her muscles and her pink nipples, reddened and engorged with blood, stiffened to the point of bursting, before an almighty, guttural growl was unleashed and her body simultaneously exploded, which soon reduced her to a moist ball of quivering flesh.

Her climax endured for almost an eternity, and with the sight of Anna shaking uncontrollably from in between her legs, Alex felt like it was a job well done. Good as that feeling was, his body reacted by relaxing instead of being at its peak of sexual performance. He quickly restarted his body, a few tugs, and a short movie in his head about a screaming, sweaty porn star taken from behind, and he was ready to go. One of the very few times he decided to forgo receiving oral pleasure, he decided to unleash his highly proverbial viper into her Eden. He didn't want to take any more time to work her up into another frenzy and wanted to ride and prolong her breaking and crashing wave of pleasure. As she lay in bed, still deep in the throes of her climax, he picked her up, flipped her over into doggy-style. With the chugging guitars blazing in his ears, the thumping bass in his heart and the pounding drums in his hips, and the fury of a rock and roll circus marching along in his head to the beat, he penetrated her, slow, deep, rough.

Relentlessly.

Alex, standing on the floor, with Anna bent over at her knees at the foot of the bed, he ravaged her reddening genitals with his penis but, amidst the primal grunts, dripping sweat and the heavenly sound of hard flesh on wet flesh, something went wrong. She had started creaming, lots of creaming, to the point that his pelvis was wet from her secretions. He could feel her juices building up on his shaft, oozing and trickling down his scrotum. He looked down to see his manhood covered in white, viscous fluid. The very thought of this being caused by his penis almost overwhelmed his senses. He slowed down his fucking, closed his eyes and breathed in the moment when, almost true to cosmic form, that was where it literally turned sour, because that was when he noticed a smell.

The smell.

The smell was like semi-dried, cheap cement baking in the sun that had some rotten fish or eggs, or both, swimming in it! The infernal smell flew on decayed wings attached to putrefying flesh and steaming hot faecal matter, ambushed his olfactory senses, and embedded themselves in his nasal cavities. If everything had a colour, he would certainly see a plume of green mist lingering around their genitals, rising in a direct and coordinated assault to his face, nose and brain. In a concerted effort to plough through the sex and determined to salvage some form of pleasure from what was fast becoming a rotting corpse, he reached out to his pants pocket, fished out his pack of cigarettes and lighter, lit up, and started smoking just to kill the smell.

But the rancid odour fought valiantly against the fast-developing haze of cigarette smoke. It seemed weak and feeble in the foetid and rank air that was now enveloping the both of them. Alex soon felt a wave of nausea building up, and he audibly gagged. He stopped whatever action and movement that was happening below the waist, body tensing up, coughed out loud, and almost puked.

He actually did.

A little bit.

In his mouth.

And there was nothing like the taste of half-digested chicken and sauce swirling in your mouth and throat to kill even the most thunderous of boners.

And it did.

His once raging boner shrivelled away in a whimper as he went limp.

It was as if she knew. She too stopped. All the blood that flowed to her nipples, stiffening them, the same oxygenated blood that nourished her and covered her in a fresh crimson hue, now all flowed and pooled around her face in embarrassment. There he was, standing upright, while his penis hung shamefully low, a condom hanging desperately for dear life, cigarette in his mouth, puffing smoke endlessly in a futile attempt to kill the smell, and she, calmly and soundlessly, got out of bed. Without even looking at Alex, she grabbed a towel and disappeared behind the toilet door for a long shower.

It must have been almost an hour that went by before she got out of the shower, and in the meantime, Alex had been self-servicing. There he was, lying in a pool of his own juices mixed with Anna's fluids, cigarette still in mouth, and still gagging in the green mist of the rotten fish and eggs smell, before it hit him. Of how repugnant this must have looked and how disgusting this was.

But he did not care.

He just wanted to get off, again and again, to numb the pain of yet another failed attempt of making a connection with another person.

He longed to be back in the warm, loving arms of Lyna again, where things appeared more beautiful, where it smelled nicer and where colours were more vibrant, and good memories lingered in the air instead of this green mist of doom.

A violent pang of emotion slowly descended on him as he ran out of orgasms to have for the night and he toyed with the idea of fucking Anna again. But he didn't realise that by then, she had already dressed and left the hotel room. So, alone again, Alex lay in dread.

A dread that came in the form of Anna and the day she would call him up again to revisit their tryst. Not like the day would actually come anyway, after the abortion of a one night stand this turned out to be.

# 2.

S he raised her head, pulled her eyes away from her laptop, and finally breathed. Her eyes adjusted to the soft orange lighting in the bar and savoured the smell of stale beer and a moist bar counter that hung heavily in the air. Closing her eyes, she breathed in deeply as she took in the screeching vocals of Miljenko Matijevic belting out the popular ballad 'She's Gone.' The walls in the dimly lit, cavernous bar bled gin and tonic, as stories of regret, despair and love plastered over each brick and wood panel. Hazy, alcohol-filled memories clung onto the furniture, rolling on the floor like dogs as Carol took another deep breath that centred her.

She felt at home.

In a dingy dive bar, because everyone spoke in the same accent as she did, shared very similar experiences, and most importantly, knew her order and got it right every time. A pint of Guinness and a plate of extra spicy fried rice with a sunny side up. Chevy's has long been a sanctuary for Carol, a cool respite from the heat, the chaos of the corporate world, and the discordant cacophony of the city. Nestled in a quiet corner near Haji Lane, it was a place where everything was familiar like it was stuck in time, from the vintage posters she found very familiar to the songs she grew up listening to. The staff, unchanged since the bar first opened its doors to the public years ago, had become her friends, her therapists and her confidantes. There was Alicie, a classy, distinguished woman in her fifties who went around the bar ensuring that no glass was empty. Then there was Felicia, a tattooed bartender and chef who made a mean plate of fried rice, Carol's favourite. And there was Natasha, a dangerously curvy and feisty bar wench who never seemed to smile, but who could also be very affectionate with the regulars. She seemed to have a soft spot in her heart for Carol. They were three strong young women when they decided to set out on their own to run a bar the way they wanted to and be successful on their own terms. Maybe that was why Carol loved this place and found a home in it. These women had encouraged and nurtured her whims, fancies and vices, banished her doubts and rubbished her fears, listened to her stories and most importantly, had never judged her.

As long as she paid her bill at the end of the night.

The bar had been good to her, had protected her well from the blows that rained down from work and life, but unfortunately, never from leering men.

It wasn't that she didn't like it. In fact, she enjoyed the attention paid to her by men. She just wished they were much better at it than they thought they were.

"One more pint, Carol?" Natasha asked.

"No thanks, Nat, I'm alright. But I could do with a whiskey sour though."

"Oh, starting early today, are we?"

"No, just a small celebration after finishing this monster of a report."

"Okay, darling, coming right up."

Still in her corporate office garb, she felt uncomfortable as one would, and she preferred to be out in what she called pyjama sessions, drinking beers and cocktails in her track pants and her overly stretched-out, Threadless t-shirt. But she needed the garb. It made her feel powerful, in control and fearless in the male-dominated world of finance consultancy. Not like she needed to be the corporate superwoman anyway, but it put her in a powerful state of mind to conquer the world and take no prisoners. Taking measured sips of her whiskey sour, savouring each victorious drop of the cocktail, she contemplated whether it was going to be a solo night or one where she would choose someone to come home with her.

*Shall I have dick tonight? Or will the Hitachi do?*

*Do I even have time to get off tonight? Yes, I do, I am done with what I need.*

*Do I need to clean the house? Do I need to do laundry?*

*No, I don't. Maybe I'll just watch Colbert and Trevor Noah tonight.*

*Wait, do I need to schedule more appointments for the week?*

*No, I don't. And do I have work activities planned for the rest of the week?*

*Alright, I'm actually done for the week.*

*Maybe I'll just read a bit of Dostoevsky tonight, a bit more whiskey in bed sounds nice.*

And as she sat there, swimming in her multitude of thoughts, trying to wind down after a hard day's work of meeting clients and selling them a future they didn't really want, she noticed another corporate type across the bar, trying to make eye contact with her.

He smiled.

She instinctively smiled back but regretted it immediately.

*Ah, fuck, shouldn't have done that. I just wanna chill out here alone. Maybe he didn't see it.*

*Damn it, too late, he's walking over. Don't gussy up, Carol.*

She had five seconds to subtly size him up.

*Okay, he looks clean. But fair, pasty clean doesn't really mean clean, right?*

*But the hair. Why do all men here think that what looks good on David Beckham will look good on them?*

*Okay, at least he doesn't look like he has an STD on his face.*

*But he should just shave his face — what is that scraggly caterpillar on his lip?*

*Big arms, probably a gym freak. Strong shoulders, not bad.*

*Good forearm action going on there.*

*I do like a crisp white shirt though.*

*Legs. Where the fuck are his legs? They're like toothpicks!*

*One word. GORILLA!*

*Wait a minute. Is that stale Adidas eau de toilette? What is he, fourteen?*

"Hi. Are you here alone?" he said in a shaky voice but covered up by his boyish smile. His yellow, coffee-stained teeth peeked through his dry, chapped lips.

*Oh, I am so NOT kissing that.*

And with that, she had already decided not to fuck him.

"Do you see anyone here with me?" she replied dryly.

"Oh. Anyway, I'm Jared."

"I'm Joanne," she replied. She always gave a fake name to men she didn't really like. Joanne was her go-to name. She even had a fake career for Joanne. Joanne was a Feminism and Cultural Studies lecturer at National University of Singapore. She found it easier to have a fake identity because it allowed some distance between her and that persona, some breathing room for her to be out of the blast radius should there be an emotional fallout.

*Damn it. I should have just said, 'And I am not giving a fuck,' heh. Never mind, let's just see what he has to say.*

"So, Joanne, what do you do?"

*Why do men here always follow up with that question?*

"I am a Feminism and Cultural Studies lecturer at NUS. Yourself?"

"That's interesting," he said. "I'm a financial analyst at Great Eastern. I manage a thirty million dollar diversified portfolio that covers options, warrants, futures, unit trusts and many other financial instruments. Of course, the thirty million are my clients' money, but I find that I have to manage them and their expectations more than I manage their money. Know what I mean? So it is very hard work, and my time is pretty much taken up by all that because managing those funds can be very tricky, especially in a time like this when so many sectors are downsizing and money is not going anywhere. And I could do with less emotional outbursts from the clients, you know. Nevertheless, the economy should pick up soon, and the money's very good for my position and I can afford the things I couldn't afford before."

"Yeah, I see...."

"Yeah, so business has been very good, and I bought an apartment for myself, a bachelor pad, in Tanjong Pagar, so that I won't have to commute as much. It's a very new development in the city on a very high floor, and has a three-hundred-sixty-degree view of the city, and it's spectacular at night. I also bought an Audi TT recently – I know, what for, right? – seeing that I don't have to commute to work now. But you can say it's more of a vanity purchase than anything, also because my boss prefers that I drive a European car as opposed to a Japanese or Korean car. God forbid, I get a Chinese car. Haha. It's the image that I have to keep up in this industry, know what I mean? The power suit, the big watch, the apartment in the city, the fancy car. It give potential clients the security that their money is being managed by someone successful, even if it's only an image of success," he rattled on.

*Maybe I'm supposed to be impressed by all this?*

"That's nice..."

"I initially wanted to get a C-Class Mercedes, but I didn't want to look that old. You know? Because only older executives or business owners get a Mercedes, because it gives the impression that he is someone stable and comfortable. And my ex-girlfriend insisted on getting one. Something to do with class and status symbol. We couldn't agree on that, and we ended up fighting a lot. So I dumped her. Who in the world, at my age, gets a damn Mercedes, right? So I gave her the ultimatum, and she thought I was bluffing. Well, I wasn't bluffing. So we split. This was four months ago, and I feel free! We had been..."

*Oh God, he won't stop! And who the hell dumps someone over vehicular choices?*

"...together since we were in uni at Harvard Business School. We met at a mixer one night and we just never left each other's side after that. She pretty much moved in with me soon after, and it was just the two of us all the time, you know? We spent our first holiday as a couple together in L.A. So you can say I have never been around the block, you know what I mean? She's also an analyst...."

*Yeah, and I bet she talks as much as you do. How the hell did she get a single word in their conversations?*

Her internal monologue raged on.

"…and she's good at it too. But enough about her. I like coming to this bar, you know. It has such a quaint and vintage feel to it, unlike the high-end bars I usually go to in the business district, you know, The Bank and Artemis Sky Bar. Plus it's cheap here too; usually I'd have to pay over twenty dollars for a cocktail. Not that I drink many cocktails anyway, I prefer the more manly type drink, like beer and tequila. I can't drink much also because I go to the gym a lot to stay in shape, because this doesn't just happen, you know," he sniggered as he pointed to his biceps. "I've been trying out…."

*Well, apparently, your chopstick legs did happen though.*

Carol struggled to maintain some semblance of interest in what was rapidly becoming a car crash of a bar pick-up.

"…the Virgin Active gym right by the OUB Centre in Raffles Place, you know the one? It's pretty good, and for two hundred fifty per month for membership, I'd say yeah, it's pretty good. I try to get there about three to four times a week to pump some iron bait because I use it as time to think, you know? Every time I lift weights, I can focus and clear my mind. Sometimes I go to their yoga classes too just to change things up a little bit, and I can say that I'm quite bendy now. It helps with my job too because it can be a very high pressure –"

"Okay, okay, Jared, is it? Listen, okay, listen, stop talking," Carol said. "I know it's hard for you guys to squeeze out a relationship within those first few minutes of meeting someone, but tonight, no, okay? It is not appreciated, and you're boring AF. Don't you have anything else to talk about other than yourself? I don't care, and it does not interest me. There is nothing about what you said I find remotely interesting. So, you know what, honey, go back to your seat, and reflect on what just happened here, and then don't tell me about it, okay, cupcake?"

*Oh no.*

*Maybe that was too harsh. I should say something, right?*

*No, I shouldn't, because who the fuck is he that he needs his ego to be nurtured by me?*

*Maybe I should get him a drink.*

*Maybe I should apologise.*

*No, I should just ignore him now and let him stew in his own insecurity.*

Taken aback by the harsh bluntness, Jared's face was a mask of distress as he stammered, "Oh. Okay. Yeah, I talk way too much when I'm nervous. Can I start over?"

"No," Carol firmly said.

"At least let me buy you a drink?" he said, trying hard to salvage whatever that was left of his ego and this train wreck.

"No," Carol repeated.

"Bitch," Jared muttered under his breath, but loud enough for Carol to hear, as he turned away and walked back to his seat across the bar. And she didn't mind at all being called that. She had been called names far worse than that, with 'dusty thunder cunt' being one of the most creative ones she ever heard. But she believed that it was the price she had to pay for being strong, honest and principled.

Natasha, who had been watching the exchange, said, "You okay, luv? Would you like another drink?"

"No, I'm alright, Nat. In fact, I'll just have the bill, gonna call it a night, thanks."

She glanced at Jared while she waited for Natasha to bring the bill, and she saw him stewing in his own insecurity. He appeared to be seething at the rejection that had been handed to him on a filthy plate. His face was red with embarrassment, or was it rage?

*I really hope its rage.*

Or maybe it was the pint of beer he chugged down to drown the memory of being rejected. She could almost see smoke rising out of his ears, and his nostrils flaring in rage. He was drumming his fingers on the bar so hard and loud, he might break his nails. Oh, his nails, his long, unkempt dirty nails that were black from the build-up that collected under as he scratched his head and face, or wherever else he scratched.

*Look at that. It is so NOT manly, let alone sexy.*

Then, a moment of bravado came over him as he slammed his pint on the bar counter, marched right up to Carol, and fished out a handful of blue fifty-dollar notes from his pockets. He threw it on to the bar counter and said, "Here's money. Plenty more where that came from. It should be enough for you to spend tonight with me right?"

Carol was stunned.

"You want to buy me, and you think a few fifty-dollar notes will do it?" she asked incredulously.

"Yes, so how much would it take for you to spend the night with me?" he asked, as if it was a normal thing to do.

Even Natasha was getting worked up, and she was dangerously close to the point of jumping over the bar, broken bottle in hand, going right into Jared's eye. But she knew Carol had this.

And that she did.

"Okay, firstly, what makes you even think that was a good idea? In which world do you think that throwing money at a woman would impress them? In this day? At this age?" she calmly asked. Instead of waiting for an answer, she launched into a full Socratic line of questioning. "Does this ever work? Do you think any woman with self-respect would fall for this? Do you think that two hundred fifty dollars is going to impress me? Do you know how much I make in just one day on my job? What did you really think will happen next? Do you really think that women see cash as an aphrodisiac? And if so, do you really believe that is the kind of woman worth spending time and money on? What would you do if some guy did the same thing to your sister? Or your mum? Or aunt? Would you tolerate that?"

Jared didn't know what to do or say. He was expecting one of two things: Carol to be highly offended, throw a hissy fit, and walk out, just so he could tell his friends that that there was this "girl who can't handle me so she walked out," or that she'd be very impressed by all this and actually would spend the night with him. But what he wasn't prepared for was this line of probing questions asked calmly, almost coldly. He was confused. He eyes darted every which way but at Carol, and she knew that she had almost gotten him to question his morals and his existence.

But he doubled down and said, "Hey, you should be flattered, okay, that I want to spend my money on you!"

That threw Carol, and even Natasha, into a fit of rage. Time to slam the final nail in his coffin, and there was a part of her that wanted to break him and see him cry.

"What? I should be flattered that you treat me like a whore? Would you do this to your mum? Or your sister? Give them money just so they will spend time with you? If I were to call them now, and tell them about what you have done, do you think they will be happy at what you just did? And which one do you think is more insulting? The fact that you offered me money to spend time with you, or the fact that you offered me two hundred fifty dollars? Two hundred fifty! I can't even buy a new phone with that. Is that the level of respect you have for women? Is that the same level of respect you have for your mum?"

At that point, Carol grabbed the handful of fifty-dollar notes and threw them in his face, and she watched as they fell to the floor. She burned her eyes into his soul and watched as he scrambled on his hands and knees to pick the notes off the grimy bar floor.

That was the moment where she felt she won.

She gathered her things, paid her bill and walked out of the bar triumphant. With Tomayasu Hotei's 'Battle Without Honour or Humanity' playing in her head, she slung her pack on her shoulders without looking back, and she strutted out with the swagger of victory. But there was still something gnawing at the back of her head. As the hot city air hit her outside the bar with a heady stench of cigarette ash, exhaust fumes and stale kitchen, with the humidity embracing her tightly, causing a thin film of sweat to form around her un-caring face and her body, that gnawing became stronger.

Doubt.

*Maybe I shouldn't have said those things to him.*

*I should have been more compassionate, right?*

*I could've just walked out of there and saved him the embarrassment and saved me the trouble of making that speech.*

*But why must men be so dumb? Who the hell uses cash to pick up women?*

*Is it because I dressed up like a corporate whore?*

*Do I look cheap in this outfit?*

*I should have been a bit more tactful, I think.*

*But why should he deserve my compassion and my tact? Dude clearly has no respect for women.*

As she got into the cab that droned home, going past the familiar buildings, the inside of the cab intermittently bathed in bright city lights flickering almost in time with the sticky beats oozing out of the speakers, she continued to question herself and her actions. It was difficult to find a comfortable space in the small breathing room between being blunt and honest, and being compassionate and honest. She had to be almost everything and everyone, on top of being good at everything just to be nudged into the realm of slightly competent. And it was something that Carol struggled with internally every day while maintaining an ice-cold composure amidst the chaos of work and trying to maintain some semblance of a social life. And all of that while having to endure the verbal barbs coming from people around her, people who she thought she could trust, even other women, who would call her names and ascribe characteristics to her without even knowing her to begin with.

*Sometimes I wish I could meet a man who isn't annoyingly stupid.*

*Someone with a healthy respect for women, a man's man, you know, and not some sheltered momma's boy man-child.*

*Someone who isn't afraid to bang me like a drum at night, yet wakes up early the next morning to make breakfast.*

*Someone with one foot in pragmatism, the other in a pool of idealism and with his eyes on happiness and success.*

*Not a boyfriend nor a husband but a partner to build an empire with.*

*An equal who is not afraid to challenge me and push me.*

"Miss? Miss! We're here, that'll be twenty-eight fifty, please," the cab driver barked.

She paid and walked back to her apartment, the silence of the town ringing in her ears. The sound of her heels echoed loudly through the empty corridors. In a distance, a dog barked and whined as a light breeze passed through the trees, a pleasant caress of wind compared to the cold, harsh air-conditioner in the cab. The austere concrete ignored her presence as she fished out her keys from her bag.

She paused for a moment, as if to reflect.

*Ah well, I still have a home, a job, my health and family I can count on.*

*Most importantly, I still have my Hitachi Magic Wand, so that'll do for now*

She shivered with delight and anticipation at the multiple orgasms she would have with the Hitachi.

# 3.

After a particularly challenging day in school, Alex found himself at Harry's in Tampines Grande to unwind and let off some steam. It had been a bad day at work, and for an educator, bad days at work really affected them. Some took it personally, like Alex. Largely because he invested an inordinate amount of energy and emotion in managing the students as well as teaching, inspiring and motivating them and some of whom could often be very ungrateful.

Two stiff drinks and a quick flirt with the average-looking, middle-aged waitress later, Alex felt suitably relaxed and his focus was back to the big picture, whatever that was for him at that point, because he himself wasn't sure. He still saw Lyna in the big picture of his future, but that painting was fading fast as the sands of time eroded the details and wore down the subtle brush strokes and colours. Even as Alex was resigned to the fact that they might never see each other again, it was not something he wanted to do yet. She used to be in his thoughts all day, but now that faded painting was his vision in times of loneliness. Like a broken watch with broken hands and a disfigured face, yet the gears still dutifully turned.

Just as he was ready to leave the bar, out of the corner of his eye, he saw a somewhat familiar sight scurrying into the bar. He ignored it for a while, but he soon saw it make a beeline toward him. Alex got his face out of his papers, took a deep breath and saw that it was an old army buddy, Long, who was making deliveries in the area.

"Well, shit on me, it's you!" Long exclaimed very eloquently. He had longer hair than Alex remembered that covered his ears and made him look like a fat, not-so-smart, unphilosophical, but just-as-handsome Bruce Lee.

"Well fuck me! *Long!*" Alex cried out.

They both shook hands, caught up and proceeded to knock back a few. Never mind that Long was on the clock because as he proudly proclaimed, "So what, I am the boss, I can do whatever the fuck I want!" A few phone calls and a quick trip around the paperwork he had to do, and it was done. They were now free to reminisce about the time when they were skinny, fit and invincible.

"Remember that time in Taiwan, we found the ninja van in the jungle that didn't sell snacks, but had a mattress and a girl on it in the back of the van? Remember who ended up fucking her?" Long said, squeezing the story out in between fits of laughter. Alex vaguely remembered the story, but not in the same funny way Long did. Alex felt revolted, actually, at how a seemingly young girl had been prostituted to soldier boys who had been in the jungle and not washed for five days by someone who could very well be her uncle or dad.

"Remember that time in Thailand the sergeant-major gave us a lecture on how pink nipples meant the girl was a virgin, and that brown or black nipples meant that they have been suckled on by a thousand men?" Alex recalled to rapturous laughter. The bar was theirs to be wild in, and the waitress blushed at the stories told out loud, voices amplified by the pints of Guinness they both had knocked back.

As the sky began to take on an orange hue and the sun retreated into the distant horizon, and fired up after several pints, Long suggested they go to a more jumping joint. This joint was too yuppie for his blue collar sensibilities, apparently. The business crowd in their ties, tailored shirts and ill-fitting pants had rocked up and cast judging eyes at a shabbily dressed Long and wondered how the hell this guy was able to afford drinks in this bar. Alex, tired from the day, but also fired up from the pints, agreed.

Long called his off-duty delivery driver to take his van and drop both of them off at the Golden Mile Complex, also known as Little Thailand. It was a mall still stuck in the 80s, with coffeeshops and restaurants serving Thai cuisine. At the many mini-supermarkets there, all were hawking almost-fresh vegetables, herbs and spices from the land of smiles, giving the mall a pungent, leafy smell. There were rumours that the walls in the toilets there were peppered with glory holes, with strange men coming and going at all times of the day. It was also common to come across a blind drunk person there even in high noon. And with a sprinkling of tour agencies, hairdressers, massage parlours, several discount stores and remittance shops, it was not a mall that normal people would hang out in, let alone shop at.

But by night, the place transformed into a most dazzling place of sin, with the restaurants opening its doors for the executive and hipster dinner crowd, dragging with them the odd backpacker or three off the beaten tourist paths. Also opening their doors were the many Thai discos, or what was locally termed "hanging flower joints," a club or a disco where the ladies would be paraded on stage or walk about the bar, asking the customers to buy garlands of flowers for them to wear. Each garland cost anywhere from ten dollars to a whopping five thousand, and of course they would receive commission from the sale of the flowers. And the amount of attention, service and affection the lady gave the customer was in proportion to the price of the garland he paid. It was essentially some form of prostitution but a more organised, and a lot less fleshly, because the client was technically only paying for the lady's time. Whatever carnal activities that took place after the bar closed at 2 a.m. was entirely up to them.

Alex, being relatively new to the scene, was excited to be there. He had just gotten the rotten vagina episode out of his system, and while still yearning for Lyna's return, he was more than happy to be indulging in fleshly pursuits. Not like Lyna would care anyway. *She must not,* he thought. *She won't,* he convinced himself, and despite the fact that he still masturbated thinking about the times he and Lyna fucked, and how she was the first person she thought of in his post-orgasm mess, and how much he missed her, he buried it deep in him. *It cannot be,* he kept saying to himself.

Long led the way to a pub where he, a normal logistics supply chain manager in a smelly company T-shirt and cheap pants, transformed into a king!

"Darling!" cried one.

"Oooohhhhh, Tony!" cried another.

Tony.

That must be the boss name he gave himself. But it wasn't like he needed a boss name anyway, because from the way the staff and the women were tripping over themselves to serve him and be in his company, he was totally the boss.

The service staff led them to the almost-private area of the club, with a comfortable but worn sofa, a coffee table and a cannon of Martel Cordon Bleu fresh from the bar and four towers of beer. Alex enjoyed the sight of the staff fussing over them, helping them pour their drinks, serving bar snacks.

"Okay, here's the plan, we stick to the beer okay, and we let the girls finish the Martel. We need to focus on getting them drunk, not us," Long said.

"Got it," Alex said, just happy to be getting free booze and attention for the night.

There was something that was different about Long in the club. He appeared to be more self-assured, more confident, and he had this swagger about him like he owned the place, and it would be of no surprise to Alex if he did own the place. Everyone knew him, everyone wanted to talk to him, and everyone wanted to have drinks with him. Even in his sweaty logistics company T-shirt and stained cargo pants, and a pair of work boots that had seen better days in the 90s, he strutted around the joint like a golden peacock everyone wanted a piece of.

And then, the ladies of the night came by.

They came in full force and fervour, with one girl in a dress that was too tiny to be seen in public, plonking herself on Alex's lap, and another sticking her warm and wet tongue in his ear. Another slid her cold hand under his shirt, making him shudder with delight while one he couldn't see grabbed his ankles, lifted them up and massaged his calves. He felt very overwhelmed by all this but thoroughly enjoying the attention nevertheless, and as the night wore on, he sat back, relaxed and throwing back pints of beer from the tower. He was just enjoying the sights and sounds and the plethora of skimpy ladies flittering about the bar clinking their glasses with his in the hope of getting him to be their client for the night. Or at least to entice him enough to buy a garland from them, of which they would keep part of the proceeds as commission.

It could have been the weekday, or the fact that he still thought of and missed Lyna, but he was not interested at all in any of the skimpy dresses, the dangerous curves and the fleshly feminine musk that emanated from the ladies. He seemed to be in his own world, a world where he was cohabitating with Lyna and they both led normal lives, going to their jobs in the morning, kissing each other goodbye, making dinner, snuggling and watching TV before fucking in bed as they drifted into sleep. Or waking up at five in the morning and having morning sex before making breakfast and getting ready to go to work.

It was a pocket of the past, a wonderfully intimate and domesticated memory that moved around the edges of his consciousness, something that he felt strongly but was unable to grasp it tightly as it had no definite shape or form. It was an intricate and complex memory that could only be seen in the corner of his eye, so he pushed it away from him, knowing that it was only a memory and something to be forgotten as soon as a more pleasurable sensation presented itself.

Back in the club, Alex never had to pay for sex, although in some way he *was* paying for it. But the attention he often craved was being given to him sevenfold that night in the club. He felt like he was in Rome and behaved like the Romans did. And in the corner of his eye, he saw Long, deep in the lady-of-the-night's throat and hands grabbing every piece of fleshly real estate she had on her, while another was grabbing his crotch as she lifted his shirt and licked his nipples.

Scanning the club, and amidst the loss of interest the ladies were showing him, he saw this one lady by the deejay console who caught his eye.

She was dressed rather simply for a working lady at the club. A simple, white spaghetti-strapped top, and he noticed her collarbone. It protruded, leaving a chasm of skin that looked like it could be used as an ashtray, or a spit bucket.

*Or a cum bucket,* he thought playfully.

With tattoos crawling down from her neck to her arms, she looked dangerously sexy. She had a huge tattoo splashed across her upper chest, but all he could see was a splotch of black and a pair of owl eyes. It was quite a turn-on for him though. Her bright, innocent eyes were nicely enhanced by what looked like a stick-on tattoo at the corner of her left eye, framed by the perfectly manicured, plucked and weaved eyebrows. Standing still with her brown salon-styled hair made her stand out from the relentless cacophony of bright lights, loud music and the gyrating bodies. She wore skinny jeans that accentuate her lithe, supple legs. She looked like she did not have an ounce of fat in her body, nor muscle. She was like a walking sludge of skin, bone and water. As slim as she was, she was pretty stacked, with perfectly round breasts that seemed too perfect to be natural, with her alabaster pale, glittery cleavage displayed in all its glory. Just as he started to size her up, she came around, sat next to him, and introduced herself as Fern. They clinked glasses, and they began their conversation. Well, it was not much of a conversation, but more of shouting into each other's' ears whenever they wanted to say something to each other. But they had a nice enough time, and in between cigarette breaks, they managed to conjure up a meaningful enough chat to be honest with each other. He told her of his story, she told hers.

The night rumbled on in a thumping, discordant mixture of bass beats, auto-tuned vocals and strobe lights that jarred his senses. Soon, Alex had enough and he wanted to go home.

More for the fact that he had to teach a class in about five hours.

It was good timing for him; Fern had started to get clingy and needy. Nevertheless, he indulged her for a few more minutes, and that was as far as it went, until she asked him to go home with her, no charge, because she really liked him.

Funny how things worked.

He managed a successful pick-up without even trying, and that never ever happened to him. He usually had to try very hard, and even strike out several times before things would start to be successful. So, not one to turn down a free meal, he said okay and asked her where she stayed at, to which Fern replied that it was literally across the road from the shopping mall.

And so it began.

After saying goodbye to an almost unconscious Long, Alex and Fern walked out of the bar, arm in arm. And under the harsh, bright fluorescent lights of Golden Mile and the lift lobby, he noticed something weird about how she looked. She had way too much makeup on, and her face was a different shade than her neck! But always one to believe in the merits of powering through, as well as the fact that their tongues were already making their way down each other's throats, Alex was convinced this was going to be a good score. They finally arrived at her flat across the road on Beach Road, and even with the fact that she had two different shades on her face, he pressed on.

His thundering boner might have had a say in the decision he made.

No, it had *all* the say in the decision.

It was a decision that he would regret and would haunt him for the next few weeks.

So back at her flat, Fern took a breather from the initial foreplay as she wanted to take a shower.

Alone.

While it did seem odd at first, it wasn't an issue for him. So he went to wait for her, naked, on her bed. And she went into the shower for twenty minutes and came out ready for some Alex-love!

But there had to be something in the water, or swamp water, it seemed. Or the toilet she bathed in, because the woman who went in and the thing that came out looked like something spat out at Chernobyl.

She was a woman who had no eyebrows.

Gone were the perfectly manicured eyebrows he saw in the club, and she looked like an alien who just had uranium oxide for lunch and was feeling the radiation effects of it at dinner. She had all of three eyelashes after she plucked her false eyelashes out, and her face had suddenly became flat.

There was no character in her face, just like a tub of old, melted vanilla ice cream on a hot afternoon with wrinkles. And it was devoid of colour and expression.

Her eyes, which had been bright, innocent with a tinge of kink, were now soulless balls of black tar, and what was worse, they looked like they had moved an inch closer to each other, making her look like someone who needed to be back in her cell for evening count and a dose of suppressants by midnight.

It seemed that the shower not only washed off her face, but also most of her hair, as her long, thick, luscious, brown, salon-crafted hair was gone and all that was left were practically twelve strands of rusty copper wires hanging off a diseased flap of excess skin from what was a formerly grotesquely obese person.

In about twenty minutes, she had morphed from a shiny shimmering angel in the night into an ancient underwater crone a minion of Cthulhu himself.

Lying in her bed, she came crawling and purring awkwardly, and Alex's survival instinct kicked in. As she got on top of him, he played along for a bit, forcing himself to kiss her deeply as they engaged in the grand dance of love. He closed his eyes to reciprocate the intensity and passion that Fern was showing him, but in reality, he just did not want to see her. Her mouth repulsed him deeply, and he shuddered at the primary exchange of fluids from the oral orifice. But he faked it all, barely. Looking away from her face, he saw that she still had the rocking body, so he went to town with his hands. He caressed, fondled, grabbed and smacked whatever flesh he could get his hands on. His mind was still on Lyna, how she would ride him, how sweaty she would get, and the layer of sweat that he so often drank with pleasure. He thought of how Lyna smelled during sex, the musk of sweat and pheromones mingling with the subtle scent of her Chanel perfume.

He must have looked distant, and Fern, staring down at him with her soulless eyes, asked, "Are you okay?"

"Yes, yes, just a bit tired na, just now I drink many, many beer na," he replied.

"Okay, then I will work very hard na to make you no tired, okay?" she said as she winked at him. He swore something fell out of her eyelids as she winked and went into his mouth. Soon, the foreplay became more intense, and, leaving a trail of saliva, or slime for all he knew, Fern made the trip down south on him, and that was his opportunity.

Just as she was pleasuring his member, and amidst the moans and groans, he soon pretended to fall asleep. As good as she was, and as pleasurable as it was to him, he knew this was his only chance. So with only his boner betraying him, he closed his eyes and willed his body to stop reacting to her arts of pleasure.

He even threw in a snore to make the slumber look more authentic. The room fell into an abyss of silence punctuated by his spurious snores, and soon, a deep sigh heavily laced with sorrow. And, with an eye half open, he could see the disappointment plastered all across her face. She got dressed and lay beside him with her back facing him.

Spending the night there was not an option for Alex. And the sheets were starting to smell like a sour musk, reminding him of Anna. With new motivation, he really needed to leave and therein lay a major problem. How did he get the fuck out of the house? And with Fern right next to him to boot?

He devised a plan.

He woke up with a start, gasped deeply and loudly as if awakened from a nightmare, and he pretended to collect himself and told her that he needed to pee. Fern, back still facing him, grunted. Under the pretext of hanging the clothes he wore in the living room, he gathered them and got out of the bedroom. Soon, with swift, silent, and decisive movements, Alex got dressed and with the speed and stealth of a retired ninja, Alex bolted out of the flat and didn't even bother to take the lift. He flew down the steps of the ten storeys, not looking back. For fear of seeing her slithering after him with tentacles waving wildly, murder in her eyes!

Spent from the ordeal, but with his senses still jarred and over-stimulated from the club and the events that unfolded earlier, he didn't feel like he could go home and fall asleep. Even if he did, he would probably oversleep and get in trouble at work. Taking a sick day was out of the question because he took pride in not falling sick. So Alex didn't even bother going home, instead, went to Mustafa Centre to buy toiletries, checked into a love hotel near Desker Road, took a shower and went to work early.

Five a.m. early.

He wanted to get a head start on the day ahead, but also to drown himself in work to avoid feeling like unwanted, discarded cardboard that was used to clean ass.

4.

---

"**S**o *irregardless* of the outcome, we need to revert *back* to our clients within three days and repeat again to them the importance of the product. Also, remind them to *lock into* their account before they *undergo* any transaction with the company. Okay? Alright, that's all for today's meeting, lunch is served in the *whore* downstairs, and all are *encourage* to attend," Justin said, ending his speech. His bad English and pronunciation often gave Carol Ebola, and how he became senior manager, she didn't understand.

*He cannot be that good of a dick sucker, right?* She often thought. *I bet I give a much better blow job than he does.*

Carol decided to give the catered lunch a miss. She was not a fan of the cheap fried noodles, spring rolls swimming in oil, chicken nuggets that tasted like they were made from chemicals in a lab, cold chicken wings and sushi as tiny as a worn-down eraser. She wanted a quick ninety-minute getaway from the office, to be in her thoughts and to defrag her brain from the near-marathon four-hour department meeting. As much as she enjoyed the view on the forty-fifth floor office at the spanking new Guoco Tower in Tanjong Pagar, she wanted some fresh air and to go for a walk in the blazing afternoon sun.

Downstairs the nearby Tanjong Pagar MRT was abuzz with activity. Office workers in their power suits going for lunch, gym rats scurrying with their bags to squeeze in a lunchtime workout and assistants buying bags full of takeaway for their bosses and other minions only slightly more senior than themselves. With a plethora of lunch choices around Guoco Tower, she took her time to find one that did not have a long snaking queue of office workers. The sun was high and in its full glory. It had rained in the morning, and the ground was still wet, heated by the sun, the air heavy as a thin layer of hot steam began to rise from the heated pavements. She felt like she was drowning as she breathed and continued to fix her hair that didn't react well with high humidity. She finally had enough of the heavy afternoon air and the hustle and bustle of the area and decided to retreat into a restaurant nearby.

Called The Tiger's Milk, it wasn't a place frequented by the regular office crowd with its overpriced lunch deals, artisanal teas and coffees, and single malt whiskies. Decorated with an industrial-style theme with exposed wires crawling around the bare cement walls and exposed light bulbs hanging off blackened and worn wires off what was made to look like a disused factory ceiling. With heavy wooden tables aged and weathered to make them look rustic and mismatched dining chairs, the place was a hotbed of irony, contrast and disparity. And because she was one of four people there, the staff paid very good attention to her and served her well. Once she was done with her order of a quarter chicken with spinach, she paid her bill and slowly made her way back to the office.

*Shall I stop for my after-meal cigarette?*

*Do I have time?*

*Yeah, I do, let's do this.*

She made her way to the smoking area near the building. She lit her Winston Lights, took a deep drag, exhaled all of Justin's bad English out of her system, and felt at ease. The high humidity and the smell of ash didn't bother her as they usually did. She always found it weird that as a smoker, she couldn't stand the smell of other smokers' smoke or the smell of cigarette ash. Savouring each puff and lost in her own thoughts, a deep, male voice snapped her out of her post-lunch cigarette.

"Hi, Miss, can I borrow a light?"

Carol looked up and saw a tall, slightly pudgy man in a crisp white shirt and grey pants hovering over her with an unlit cigarette in hand.

"Yeah, sure, here you go," she said as she handed over her lighter. In jest, she said, "You do know the lighters are very cheap and available in almost every store here, right? Why don't you go buy one?"

"Oh, I'm sorry, I'll go and get one for myself later. And thanks for the light," the man replied as he lit his cigarette and gave her back her lighter.

"It's okay, I'm just kidding, enjoy your cigarette," she said with a smile as she prepared to retreat back into her thoughts.

A few seconds lapsed before he asked, "So, do you work around here?"

*Oh no, do I have to make conversation with him?*

*Shall I just ignore him?*

*That's pretty rude, isn't it?*

*I should just smile and nod, but no, where's the fun in that?*

"No, I actually don't work at all, I just like dressing up in office wear and coming here for lunch and a cigarette and watch people go by," she answered, her words dripping with sarcasm.

"Oh, wow, that is the best job ever!" he said, feigning enthusiasm. "How many dicks did you have to suck to get that job?"

Carol couldn't tell if he was being sarcastic or a douche. But she liked not being able to place a man. Men who shook things up a bit and could take as much as they could give. So they had quite a scintillating conversation by the time their cigarette finished.

"So, I work in that tower over there on the twenty-seventh floor, and I'm guessing you're more of a forty-second, or forty-third floor kinda girl?" he asked.

"Forty-fifth, to be exact," she replied with another smile.

*I'm quite enjoying where this is going. I wouldn't mind hanging out with him some more actually.*

"Great. Hey, I go to the gym on the sixth floor, this Virgin Active gym, they're having an anniversary celebration or something there tonight. Why don't you swing by after work, and come by to say hello? I'm Gerard, just say my name at the reception and they'll buzz you in as my guest, okay? Come by around seven, I'll be there," he said.

She liked how he seemed nonchalant and confident in telling her what she should do. Especially the way he asked her out, very casual, not needy and very smooth.

"And I'm Joanne. Yeah, I'll stop by if I'm back in time after my client meeting," she said, still using her alter ego and maintaining the casual air about her.

"Great, so I'll see ya then. Have a good rest of the day, okay," he said as he flicked his cigarette butt into the waste bin and walked away.

Carol got up as well and made her way back to her office. She was nonplussed about it at first. But she found that for the rest of the day, she couldn't stop thinking about the 'anniversary celebration or something.' She was genuinely excited by the prospect of talking to Gerard for more than the eight minutes they had over the cigarette. There was something about him that seemed different, that she couldn't put a finger on. Or something about him that needed to be fixed, she didn't know, but was more than willing to find out. She liked it when the man wasn't too keen or too enthusiastic about getting to know her, or getting into her pants, it made the game more exciting and interesting. It also added an air of mystery to the whole endeavour, which often meant that there were secrets to uncover, untold stories to be told and things unheard of that could be done. But she didn't like to be termed a player. That was such a frat boy term, and the cultural connotations attached to that was something she would rather not have. Nevertheless, it was a game essentially, and all the women and men were players whether they liked it or not.

*Wait. So why do I even want to go to that thing in the first place?*

*This guy looks to be quite interesting, actually. Not the most handsome though.*

*He seems smooth enough, and he doesn't look like the kind of guy who has a lot to prove.*

*Confidence, yes, that's what he has. Or nonchalance.*

*I hope he's not a serial killer. Or a rapist. Or a serial rapist.*

*He goes to the gym, so he should be in good shape.*

*Maybe I'll fuck him soon enough, if he plays it right.*

*I hope he doesn't have a weird fetish I can't handle.*

So the time came for the 'anniversary or something,' and Carol played it cool as ice. Despite her excitement, she took her own sweet time. She finished her work first, hung out with some of her colleagues, and finished a snack slowly in the pantry as she admired the largely unobstructed view of the city from the forty-fifth floor of the office, before she slowly made her way down to the sixth floor. She breezed right through reception after saying she was Gerard's guest and spent some time checking out the gym equipment, the facilities and the dinner spread. Finger food, mostly, sushi, grilled meat on sticks, vegetables on sticks, with the bar serving green tea, oxygenated water, whatever the hell that meant, and coconut water. *Typical of gyms*, she thought. Turns out, the gym was celebrating its fifth year anniversary of operations in this country and they were giving out promotional prices and classes to guests who showed up.

Carol spotted Gerard by the stationary bikes. Their eyes met, he smiled, she nodded an acknowledgement and went along on her own tour of the place, now appearing cold instead of cool. She was expecting him to come over and say hi, but he continued talking to a trainer instead. *Interesting*, she thought. They continued to do their own things as they threw glances at each other and chatted with other members, guests and staff there. Carol was waiting to see who would blink first in this standoff; she could wait. But apparently, so could he. They spent more than an hour talking to everyone else but each other. They did everything else at the gym but each other. She sampled each type of food served at the gym, he tasted all the drinks the gym had to offer. She listened to every pitch the trainers and staff had for her to sign up, and he spoke to almost everyone at the gym. Both were resolute. Or this game could just be something she conjured up in her head, and that he was just being him, as opposed to playing chicken to see who would fold first.

Finally, the moment came. He blinked first.

She was sipping her green tea and spacing out as she lounged on the couch when he came by, plonked himself next to her and said, "Well, it's about time we spoke to each other, since you are my guest and all."

"It's alright, I'm having a good time checking out the scenery and the people here, very friendly," she replied.

"I should be asking you to sign up for the gym, but you look like you already go to another gym, right?" he said, as he, almost imperceptibly, glanced at her legs.

She noticed that, smiled and said to him, "Yeah, I already go to another gym near my flat."

"Yeah, it's more convenient that way because you can get a good workout in and go straight home to shower," he said.

"Well, I don't know what your idea of a good workout is here at this gym, but —"

"Well, if it was with me, you *will* get a good workout, regardless of whether it's at the gym or elsewhere," as Gerard flashed an almost creepy smile at her and winked.

She laughed at that.

Which surprised her.

She laughed at that entry-level attempt at flirting.

Remaining neutral, she said, "Well, I bet you could."

"Yes, very much so. And *no hands!*" he exclaimed with an almost childlike enthusiasm coupled with an adult's smouldering tease.

She enjoyed that. And there were plenty of that from whence it came, and she ended up having quite a smashing time with Gerard. There wasn't even alcohol to be a social lubricant between the two of them, and their chemistry was almost magical. She liked how he threaded the line that separated cockiness and confidence and how understated he smelled. She enjoyed how cheeky he could be with his words and irreverent he was. He wasn't the type to ask for a date, he would tell the woman that they were going on a date, and Carol found that attractive. As opposed to the ones she had been used to, the ones seeking validation, the ones seeking her to define them.

He continued to almost shamelessly flirt with her, and she enjoyed the show, but time passed and as soon as she was sure this was not going anywhere, she got off the couch and told him she had an early day tomorrow and needed her beauty sleep. But instead of begging and being whiny or being nonchalant to the point of disinterest, Gerard sat back, crossed his legs, stretched his arm out on the top of the backrest, smiled and said, "Well, I bet you get a lot of that beauty sleep because it's working, and you sure are beautiful, even when covered in the grime of the workday," his eyes narrowed for the smouldering look.

Carol was bemused at first, yet also saw the funny side of that. It took her a few seconds to process what had just happened.

*How does one look like that and still be so self-assured?*

*Maybe he has a big dick.*

*Is that why I've been thinking about and reacting to all his predictable moves since lunch time?*

*But if this were to go somewhere, he needs to change things up, move this along, or I am out of here.*

"Well, thank you, Gerard, and as fun as this has been, I have to go now, thanks for the invite, and I'm sure I'll see you around the office soon enough," she said, getting a little bit tired of Gerard's flirting.

"Yeah, you're right, let's blow this joint. Let's go for coffee at Joe & The Juice downstairs and talk some more," he said, in a veiled attempt at prolonging the 'date.'

Carol hated having caffeine after six in the evening; it left her wide awake and bouncing off the walls till early morning.

*But maybe I can be bouncing off his dick tonight if he plays it well.*

A cheeky grin planted across her face.

And on that note, Carol agreed to go with Gerard to Joe & The Juice café nearby in the hopes of finding common ground with him. Although the thought of his dick was in the back of her head, she thought of it being in the back of her throat, or her cervix. They left the gym and proceeded to the cafe. In the very casual setting, the air was light and easy. The harsh orange lighting irked her senses, but she found it easy to relax with him. The soothing sound of bossa nova cafe music also helped as she threw her head back in laughter several times, merriment flowing as freely as the coffee and Gerard's told entertaining stories about his childhood and his friends. They exchanged tall tales of mirth and melancholy and things were going well. Very well, in fact. And it was at that point that Carol decided that she would fuck him.

He asked to go for a walk as the cafe shut its doors, but she said she was too tired to walk. He suggested sitting down on the park bench, but she said it was uncomfortable.

*Get to the fucking point and tell me you wanna fuck me already, you cute little weirdo!*

"Alright, since it's late, let me send you home."

"I can send myself home, thanks."

"But how are you going to invite me into your place for a night cap?"

*Cheeky little fucker are you?*

A smile escaped her face.

"Who's to say that I will in the first place?"

"Because you want this scintillating conversation to evolve from a verbal joust to one that is more of a physical dance."

*Well, he does have some way with words.*

Carol rolled her eyes in feigned disgust. But she liked it. She liked the way he used his words, almost without thought, nor did they appear scripted from a well-worn playbook. He seemed confident, genuine and deliciously flirty.

When they got to her flat, Carol did not waste time before planting her tongue in his mouth. She tasted his dinner and the coffee he had earlier and relished it. He wanted to take a shower first, but Carol objected, because she preferred to have that manly, sweaty musk on him as she ravaged him with her mouth. He struggled to keep up with her ravenousness, and she could see that despite going along with the ride Carol was getting him on, he was uncomfortable.

Carol reached down and unzipped his pants as her smooth, warm hands slithered in to grab onto his penis. It wasn't as big as she thought it'd be, based on her preliminary judgment as well as the way he behaved. She felt the very rock hard and hot man flesh in her hand, and it drove her into a frenzy. She couldn't wait to gulp it down her throat and to look up at him being pleasured by her. His penis felt at home in her hand, like it belonged there, and she enjoyed the look he had on his face as she played with it. Her eyes recorded every look of pained pleasure as she twiddled her thumbs around the bottom of the head of the penis. She felt every twitch and tremor of the engorged man flesh in her hand and heard every sigh and groan as she gently stroked the underside of the head of his penis. She could feel his muscles tense and almost palpitate as she wrapped her fingers around him. Soon, his sighs and soft groans grew louder and escalated into frenzied moans. Carol was taken aback slightly, but kept at it as she kissed him to try to shut him up.

But it was too late.

Soon, she felt, the warm, wet and gooey fluids spurting that began swirling and oozing around her hands. What had been a ball of tense and convulsing flesh and muscle now had relaxed and transformed into a pile of mushy cookie dough. She stepped back, took her hands out of his pants and saw that it was caked in white, warm spunk, some of which was dripping off her hand and onto her floor. She looked at her cum-stained hand in disbelief as a chuckle squeezed out of her mouth.

*I'm that good, huh?*

But it hit her immediately.

*Oh my god! He came!*

*Already? After, what, two minutes?*

*I'm not even naked.*

*Oh shit, did I just laugh at it?*

*Doesn't matter, just say something!*

"Wow, you come quick! I guess that's very...efficient?" she said as she realised how bad that must have sounded to him.

*What the fuck did I say that for?*

*Oh no, how horrible it must be for him.*

*But it is very sad, though.*

*For him. I wonder if this happens to him regularly.*

*Getting laid, I mean. Oh, those poor other women.*

*Wait. Poor me!*

"I'm sorry, this has never happened before," he stammered as Carol snapped out of her thoughts.

She looked at him as she raised her sperm-stained hand to him, and she saw a shrivelled, shrinking and retreating wallflower in front of her, teetering on the edge of a tearful and painful death by embarrassment. His face was caked in tear-stained pain as the corners of his mouth trembled. There was nothing anyone could say in that moment to make him feel any better, and anything said would make it worse.

Yet the silence was deafening, punctuated by his breaths that had now become a series of broken gasps. Unknowingly, Carol waved her hand in front of her, still looking at it in disbelief, before realising that she was parading his embarrassment and inadequacy right in his face. She might as well have rubbed the cum on her hands all over his face.

Without saying a word, she went to the kitchen to wash her hands, gathered herself and prepared to ask him to leave. Gerard had crumbled into the couch and cowered in shame. "I think it is best that you go now," Carol said in as sympathetic a tone as she could muster without breaking into a fit of giggles. She gave him a wet tissue to wipe himself down as well. He managed to conjure a faint smile as he wiped his crotch, gathered his things and left the apartment. She offered a handshake, which he declined, maybe he just didn't want to shake the hand that was stained with his shame. She watched as Gerard walked the walk of shame out her front door and into the elevator, all the while it was all that she could do to not giggle in his presence. She saved that for when he was gone.

She broke out into a hysterical giggling fit as she washed up for bed and even as she lay in bed alone. She giggled till her sides hurt and tears rolled down her eyes. But soon the table flipped.

*Is this as good as it is going to get for me?*

*Do I have impossibly high standards for a partner?*

*I must have high standards, right? It's not just anyone off the street that I want to be with.*

*I'm a good person, right? Why do I keep finding the faults in others?*

*Am I unable to see the good in them?*

*Should I 'train' Gerard, because he seems like a nice enough guy?*

*But that will be me settling for just some guy, literally off the street, right?*

*If he can't or doesn't know how to fuck, then why should I be with him, or anyone like that, for that matter?*

*Is that all there is in me? Or for me? Just a good lay?*

As she rolled uncomfortably in her eight-thousand-dollar bed, mattress and Egyptian cotton sheets with these questions churning in her head, the tears of laughter she shed earlier could very well become tears of sadness because not for the first time in her life, she had to contemplate mortality as well as the fact that she could face that mortality all alone.

# 5.

Alex stormed out of the school's general office with fire in his eyes, stomping on the warpath. Still seething with rage at the irony-deficient civil servants and the overbearing mum, he gathered his thoughts and things, drove home, got into his pyjamas and took a walk along the train tracks nearby. He took a pack of cigarettes with him to help clear his mind before realising that there was to be no smoking in the park-connector, a rule just implemented months ago in his neighbourhood.

Lost in his thoughts with his fingers bereft of his calming cigarette, he trudged along the park connector in Tampines as the MRTs rumbled above him, almost shaking the ground beneath his feet. Hands in his pockets, eyes on the ground, he questioned his choices, he reflected on his actions as people avoided and walked around him. His mind drifted to Lyna, and he wondered if he would ever see her again, let alone fuck her again. He missed her terribly, and it was in challenging times like these when he needed Lyna the most, and how easily she would oblige and indulge him. He imagined having Lyna tightly in his arms in a post coital coil, feeling her warm pink skin on his, breathing in-sync with each other wordlessly. He walked on and didn't bother to look up until he saw a pair of feet with nicely pedicured flaming red nails dressed in a shining pair of Havaianas that stopped him right in his tracks.

He looked up and saw someone strangely familiar. A woman, in her early-mid-thirties, in a vintage and worn out Rancid band T-shirt. She had smooth, youthful sun-kissed skin, with a short, brownish bob framing her cherubic face. Her dark eyes looked like there was a storm brewing in them, stared intently at him, and a round nose that stood out as the only unattractive feature on her otherwise pretty face. Her full, crimson lips thinned out as she flashed a wide, electric smile, exposing a near-perfect row of pearly whites, and she looked petulant as she stood in front of him, unmoving, arms across her small bosoms. Maybe it was because she was shorter than him that made her look like a petulant child, or the black skinny jeans that were wrapped around her not so skinny legs. Alex tried to recall who she was but drew a blank.

"Can I help you?" he asked in what was the tonal version of rolling his eyes.

"You don't remember me, do you, Alexander Daniel?" she said in an almost menacing but sexy whisper.

She full-named him, and Alex was low-key freaking out.

"Well, why don't you help me remember who you are, and we can get on with reminiscing as opposed to playing twenty questions, okay?" he said in his teacher's voice, his go-to voice when he was fearful or annoyed.

"It's Tabitha, remember? From Tower Records? Back in 1998, I was the cashier you bought the *Hopelessly Devoted to You Too* album from? I said, I liked track number 2, the Dillinger Four song, the best, and you shat on that saying that they sound like a grated iron rod going through a dog's carcass, and that you preferred the Mustard Plug song 'Lolita,' and I called you a paedophile?"

Those were very specific memories, but it did help him remember who Tabitha was. He then remembered how they dated back in 1998 for about three months before she left to go to the UK to study. But what he remembered most, apart from the way they met, were the deliciously freakish things she liked to do in bed. At that age, Alex had already been accustomed to light spanking and some hair pulling with the partners he had at that time, but Tabitha took it to another level by biting, slapping, punching and kicking. She also loved to be choked till her face changed colour and her primal survival instinct kicked in. Best part was, she absolutely loved it when he did the same to her as she did to him. Another one of her favourites was to be bitten till it broke her skin, and Alex had had to explain, many a time, the scratches he sustained on his back as she dug into his flesh with her nails. A night with Tabitha was like fight night in Las Vegas, with both ending up covered in bruises, blood, sweat and tears.

He got a boner just thinking about it.

"Oh, shit! Yes! I remember you! My gosh!" he exclaimed as they embraced. She smelled fresh out of the shower with soap and shampoo, and she felt a lot softer than he remembered. Maybe she had put on some weight over the years. He hung on to the hug for a bit longer, and a little bit tighter than usual, because he loved the way a woman felt in his embrace, and that embrace, that human contact, was what he needed the most after the day he had.

They walked together, and they caught up on each other's events and reminisced about old times. Well, there wasn't much to reminisce about, actually, seeing that they only dated for three months, so their conversation inevitably went to their adventures in bed. She showed him the scar he gave her during one of the sessions, and he showed her the ones she gave him. They laughed and continued talking when they realised that the sun had set, they had skipped dinner and lost count of how many times they had walked up and down the park connector.

"Have you ever wondered what things would be like if we had stayed together?" she asked him.

"The thought never crossed my mind since we broke up, but it came rushing back since we met earlier," he said with a smile.

Tabitha laughed a coy laugh, looked down in what could be seen as a submissive gesture as she reached out to touch Alex's hand. Alex held her hands tight as they continued to walk, no words exchanged, just a couple of people enjoying each other's light touch, each other's company on a cool breezy evening in the suburbs.

"Well, I'm single now, so I would love to give it another try. But only if you are also single and want to give it a shot," she said.

"Wait, what? How are you still single?" he asked in disbelief.

"Well, not many like, let alone can keep up with me in my, you know, extracurricular activities," she said with a hint of sadness.

"Well, I do have more experience now, and you know I can match you blow for blow, so yeah, let's give this another try, shall we?" he said confidently, without so much as knowing what he had gotten himself into. It had to be his fragile emotional state he was in because of work troubles that made him say such things.

Or it could just be something much simpler than that: the boner that the memory of Tabitha gave him.

So over the next few weeks, Alex and Tabitha dated. It was very vanilla at first, as they went through the usual but safe routines of dating. A movie here, and dinner thereafter. Lunch meet-ups, as well as late night drinks. It was all very casual in the beginning and holding hands after several dates had gone by. It seemed somewhat unusual for him, and a little bit awkward to say the least, but he enjoyed it nonetheless. He enjoyed Tabitha's company most importantly, largely because she was the window he could look out of to a much simpler and carefree time. And he was her window to a much rosier picture of her future. Her ideal vision of the future, realised and manifested in the way Alex looked at her and behaved around her. They both enjoyed the long walks they took, holding hands along the beach as joggers and inline skaters dodged and ducked around them, and giggled like schoolgirls as they fed each other morsels of whatever it was they were having at the time. And soon, time came to take the honeymoon to the next level as Alex broached the topic of sex and they both agreed to make their "first time" now, to be special, so neither of them did any self-servicing during the time they were together as they were determined to enhance the experience. Well, it was more an idea suggested by Alex, which Tabitha just went along with because it wasn't like she had sperm that she needed to shed in order to derive pleasure. And after some discussion over sushi and beer, they both decided to consummate their relationship over a weekend staycation at the Robertson Quay Hotel in the city.

The thought of sex took his mind off Lyna for a while. But even as he was with Tabitha, Lyna was never far off. In his quiet moments, he still wondered what was she doing now, was she taking her multivitamins, who was she fucking now, was she thinking of him as she fucked some white Russian guy in St Petersburg? But now that sex with Tabitha was in the cards, he prepped as well as he could for the day.

Finally, the day came for the staycation, and Alex packed very lightly because he figured he was going to be naked most of the time anyway. So he packed his toiletries, a change of clothes, a pack of condoms, some lubricant and that was all. They met at the lobby, checked in, got to the room, before Tabitha said she wanted to make a quick stop at the Cold Storage across the street at UE Square.

"Oh, you wanted to get rubber? No need, because I already bought a pack," Alex said to her.

"No, I'm not going to get rubber, you have them, right? I'm just going to get a few grocery things," she said.

He thought it was a little bit weird that she thought of groceries right before getting it on together, but he went along with it. *No harm done getting a few things and killing a few birds with one stone*, he thought. Plus he liked going grocery shopping with Tabitha anyway, because it made him feel like they were more than just together; it made him feel like there was a much deeper bond between them whenever they went grocery shopping even if it was just for toothpaste. He felt domesticated, and it made him happy, settled and anchored. He enjoyed holding her hand, or locking arms together as they wandered up and down the supermarket aisles picking out pasta sauces, toothpaste or dairy. It was probably the most human thing he had ever done with another human, also the most homely and subdued thing.

There, Tabitha picked four large bottles of olive oil and went straight to the checkout counter to pay for them. Four bottles of olive doth not make grocery shopping in his mind, so a little bit confused and annoyed at having to snap out of his own domestic fantasy, he trailed behind her as she left the supermarket to walk back to their hotel. All this while, he noticed that Tabitha had been strangely quiet and subdued. Maybe she was nervous, but why would she be? It wasn't like it would be their first time anyway. He also acknowledged that he himself had been very quiet as he indulged in his own domestic fantasy as well as brooding over Lyna.

Or it could be because he felt eyes on him. At the hotel lobby, as the bottles of olive oil clinked noisily in the bags, Alex felt eyes on him, yes, but one that made him snap out of his daze and look around. He noticed a pair of vintage Ray-Ban sunglasses sitting atop a head that crowned a pale face looking at him. Alex didn't notice much of her aside from a prominent vein that popped out of her bicep, and he instinctively slowed his pace and began to carve his face into an appreciative smirk, eyes squinting, head tilted slightly and lips pursed. Alex tried to look deeper, but her white T-shirt masked the goods he would like to have checked out, when he snapped back to reality and realised that Tabitha was far ahead and waiting for him, foot tapping impatiently, at the lift lobby.

Nevertheless, he let all of this slide and focused on the upcoming romp in the sheets with Tabitha. He storyboarded each and every move he planned to make in his head and scripted everything he was going to do and say down to the nth degree. He wanted to appear to be in control and a well-oiled sex machine, where slow was smooth, and smooth was fast. They got to the hotel room, put down the grocery bags, and he began kissing her.

But she pushed him away.

He was stunned.

"Take off your clothes," she whispered, somehow in a commanding tone that made him follow what she said. "Now go lie down in the tub and wait for me." She whispered the commands with ease and with much authority.

And so he did.

There he was, cold and naked in the tub, nursing a semi-thunderous boner at the anticipation of a feast of womanly flesh, waiting. Fearing that the cold would affect his boner, he turned on the hot water when he heard Tabitha barking at him, "Do not turn on the water, and leave the tub dry!" He scrambled to turn off the water and got the towel to wipe dry the tub. Confused, he just lay there in the cold porcelain tub, playing with his penis in an attempt to maintain his boner. Then the door opened, and a naked, resplendent Tabitha walked in with an almost dazed look on her face. He thought something had to be wrong, and that this was something out of the ordinary, yet no fear or panic overtook him, just anticipation and excitement. The fact that Tabitha was naked in the same room as he was made it easier to shut down the voices in his head telling him to get out of there. Wordlessly, she seemed to float closer to the tub, and he noticed that she had something in her hand.

It was a bottle of the olive oil she had bought from earlier, and for a second, he was frozen in fear. She uncapped the bottle of olive oil, raised it high above his body, and Alex, like a deer in headlights, just lay there fearing for his life, thinking she was going to hit him on the head with it. He shut his eyes tight and braced for an impact of shards of glass on skin and flesh.

But instead of an impact followed by a searing pain from the bottle, he felt the warm, slippery embrace of liquid raining down onto his face, torso and crotch. He opened his eyes and saw Tabitha's face, expressionless, cold and stony, as she emptied the contents of the bottle onto him and into the tub. She then repeated the action with a second bottle of olive oil. "Close your eyes, it might sting," her cold monotone voice boomed in the bathroom. He obeyed her and tried hard to lay still in the slippery pool of extra virgin olive oil as he slipped further and further down into the tub. Tabitha slathered him in olive oil as she emptied the second bottle and left it on the bathroom counter together with the other empty bottle. Alex lay there, naked and shimmering from the oil, eyes widened in shock, fear and anticipation, mouth agape with no words springing forth. His body shivered slightly in the cold and in excitement as the goosebumps grew more visible on his skin. His penis lay slumped to the side like a dead seahorse washed ashore after a storm. The dull smell of olives hung heavily in the bathroom, which, with eyes closed, could easily be mistaken for a kitchen. Tabitha stood next to the tub, naked, her brown nipples stiff and now reddened as they engorged with blood, her skin smooth and flawless, just as he remembered, before the bruising began. She looked down on Alex, cold and expressionless like a statue in the winter, with her dark eyes, hair falling lazily across her forehead.

"What is this?" Alex whimpered.

"Quiet, and stay still!" she commanded.

She drank the sight of Alex laying there, squirming uncomfortably in the porcelain tub, drenched in oil. She stood there imposing, predatory, like a hunter hovering over her prey, waiting for the right moment to swoop in for the kill. She was like an immaculate dream, made of breath and skin, who had been waiting a lifetime for him. Silence engulfed the bathroom for what seemed almost an eternity for him before Tabitha bent over, leaned in towards him, planted a kiss on his forehead, and gingerly got into the tub to lie next to him.

To say that it was weird – what happened next – would be an understatement of epic proportions. Alex had no mental frame of reference to describe it, let alone generate emotions on what to feel about it. He felt paralysed in the invisible vice-like grip Tabitha had over him, and at that point, he wasn't Alex anymore. He felt like he was just a primordial cell, unthinking, unfeeling, powerless.

"Just relax and stay still, okay," she whispered in his ear. She wrapped herself around Alex, arms and legs like tentacles all over and around him, swishing and sloshing about in the tub, grinding her flesh with his, rolling on top and getting below him, stopped for a few seconds, and repeated the actions. He felt like he was salad being tossed about in a bowl of marinade, and all this needed was a sprinkle of salt, a clove of garlic, some chilli, and it'd be a delicious aglio olio dressing for the pasta dinner he had in mind for later. She paused intermittently to tighten her embrace around him before continuing to silently roll with him in the tub of olive oil. She would stop and get nervous whenever Alex got an erection but continued rolling in the oil with him as his boner died down. There was no kissing, no petting, no humping, no penetration and no words, just an almost chaotic sloshing and thuds of human flesh and bone in a shallow pool of oil. She buried her face in his neck, ran her oily fingers through his hair and all over his slippery and shimmering skin, taking care to stay away from his crotch. She played with his anus with her fingers, but stopped just shy of sodomizing him. He thought he should reciprocate and touch her all over, but Tabitha slapped his hands away and shook her head disapprovingly.

They were writhing about in the tub of oil for almost an hour. Alex flitted in and out of consciousness, awakened by her finger on his anus, or when his elbow hit the tub in the rolling. She slithered up and down his body like a masseuse in a weird attempt of body to body massage. He could feel her breath, deep and slow, warm on his skin, and as he closed his eyes, her breath was all that he could feel. Apart from the sudden sharp and ticklish tinge of her pubic hair rubbing on his thighs and hip, she seemed to have melted into a dehumanised single cell organism, mindlessly squirming all around his body in what seemed like a prehistoric bowl of primordial soup. He couldn't tell where she ended and where he began, he couldn't feel her hands, nails, hair, as all her humanely textures melted away. He strangely felt calm and tranquil amidst the chaotic flailing and floundering of flesh and bone and felt at one with Tabitha. She pulled him in like the moon pulling the tide, and he felt that she had merged herself, her entire being with his, and it was a profound oneness that he couldn't put into words. It was as if their physical beings ceased to exist and dissolved in a primal chaos and all that was left was a single conscious existence drifting aimlessly through the ages.

It seemed to be an eternity and in an instant simultaneously before the gurgling rumble of a tub being emptied roared through the air followed by a sudden splash of cold water jolted Alex out of his existential trance. He opened his eyes, squinted at the bright orange fluorescent lights of the bathroom and saw Tabitha squatting over him and slathering herself with soap. She reached out for an orange loofah, slathered it with liquid soap and began scrubbing his body.

"Stand up," she said, and he did. She then proceeded to scrub every inch of his body with the loofah and soon the room was filled with the scent of vanilla and lime. He winced periodically as Tabitha roughly scoured his skin with the loofah, especially when she got to his nether regions. It was as if she was trying to rub off any traces of her that would have been left on him. But it strangely felt good to him. It reminded him of when he was a child and his nenek would rub him down almost the same way during bath time, and he felt at home.

"Stay there," she commanded as she fished out another sponge and began scrubbing every inch of the tub with soap, herself still covered in soap. With the deftness of a chambermaid and the efficiency of German engineering, she washed and scrubbed the tub to a perfect shine. She finished off by scrubbing his feet clean of oil, and he felt complete. She took his hand and led him out of the bathroom and locked the door. He stood there, naked and fresh as the morning, as confused as he was getting into the bathroom earlier. He put on the hotel robe, got on the bed and reflected on what happened. And the more he thought of it, the more his boner became thunderous. Intellectually, he was unable to process what happened, but the erection he was nursing now told him that it was something good. He gave himself a short tug to keep it warmed up in anticipation of a luscious and exquisite romp in the bed after the protracted foreplay in the tub.

Tabitha got out of the bathroom soon enough, but she put her clothes on and left the room without a word. Shocked but too spent to be going after her, he spaced out in bed and surfed the television in the room. He must have dozed off because he was awoken by Tabitha's heavy yet quiet breathing. Still nursing a raging boner, he reached out to touch her in the hope of getting something hot going, but she slapped his hands away and turned the cold shoulder to him. Still too dazed and confused to be upset, he just turned away and drifted off to a dreamless slumber.

He awoke the next morning to Tabitha sitting in the corner staring at him. There was a strange, faraway look in her eyes that also hinted at something almost sinister. At any point, he felt that she could jump on him and make sweet, mad, dirty love to him, or come at him with a knife and tear his torso to shreds. She smiled as she noticed his majestic morning glory peeking through the robe he fell asleep in. However, as it happened last night, she beckoned him out of bed, dressed him, and walked out of the room holding his hand as they went to the restaurant for breakfast. Over breakfast, he tried to broach the subject of last night, but she kept deflecting and sidestepping the topic. It was clear as day that she was avoiding the subject entirely, which left Alex even more confused. He let it go, careful not to offend her because the possibility of sex was still in the cards, and he was very hungry for it.

But that was not to be.

The heavy breakfast Alex always had in the morning usually fired up his digestive system to an overdrive, and his bowels were soon stimulated into action. A quick sip of hot, black coffee, and he was running back to the room toilet to take his usually massive morning dump. What he didn't realise was Tabitha following closely behind. He got to the room with an urgency of a man whose ass was about to explode, literally. He pulled his pants down and was about to close the door when a hand stopped him.

"I want to watch you," Tabitha said.

With the heavy knocking on his anus' door, he had no time to protest, because it was all he could do to keep it all in. He sat on the throne, and with an almighty groan and sigh, his bowels exploded into a fury of brown. All this time with her watching intently. He lit a cigarette, as he did during or after his morning dump and sat there, bewildered and spent, as she stood in the toilet opposite him slathering her eyes over every inch of his body. The cigarette smoke covered up the smell of his dump, and soon the toilet was awash with a white haze of cigarette smoke. He finished his cigarette and prepared to wash himself when she asked, "Are you done?" And he nodded.

She then got him to stand, bent over the bathroom counter. She then got to her knees, spread his butt cheeks and began licking his anus to clean it! He was shocked and jolted his body forward as a reflex, but she held fast to his hips with tongue and lips forming airtight suction on his dirty ass. He was afraid to look in case he would catch a glimpse of her shit-encrusted face and mouth. The thought of it was enough to make him nauseous. She then took the attached ass washer and began spraying his ass, and he could hear her gargling to wash her mouth as well before standing up, soaping her hands to properly wash his ass as well as her mouth and face.

That was the last straw for him.

After he was washed and felt as clean as he could being in the same room as someone who was just moments ago his toilet paper, he pulled her up to her feet and wanted to speak. But before he could get a word in, she leaned into him and wanted to kiss him. On the mouth. With her mouth. The same tongue and lips that had, moments ago, cleaned his ass. He could almost smell his own shit on her. He drew his face away in disgust and exclaimed, "Okay, okay, stop. Stop! What the fuck was that? What the fuck was last night about?"

"I like it. It's something I picked up in Utrecht when I was there on a uni exchange program," she said with a cheeky smile, a smile that seemed so strange and distant now to him.

"You went on exchange to Europe to learn how to eat ass and shit?" he cried out, his tone of voice reaching a high-pitched shriek.

"Well, yes. I like it though, don't you find it hot? To have a slave clean your ass like that? To make someone your personal toilet and toilet paper?" she said with that now unfamiliar glint of cheekiness on the curled corners of her lips.

"*No!* It's fucking gross!" he shrieked. "And what the fuck was that olive oil thing last night? I thought we came here to have sex!"

"Don't you find last night's session to be one that is deeper than just sex? There was a profound feeling of being together as one, right? Of being lost in each other's bodies, minds in space and time?" she explained to him.

"It was, yes. But it's our first time together, and you led with that?" an increasingly frustrated Alex exclaimed.

"Well, I wanted it to be special for us," she said.

"Well, I can deal with the olive oil and the existential space and time thingamajig, but you crossed the line when you cleaned my ass, my dirty ass, with your mouth! My gosh, how the fuck am I going to kiss that same mouth again? You know what, I'm leaving. I like getting my ass eaten anytime, but never like that. So if that's your thing, and you love it, I'm sorry, I cannot be a part of that," he said, putting his foot down as he stormed out of the bathroom.

She stayed in the bathroom and whimpered, "But I thought you'd like it because I like it."

"Well, I don't, and you are going to have to choose between me and that weird ass fetish of yours," he said, as he had had enough of arguing. He had never been good with arguing because with the slightest show of emotion, like what he heard from Tabitha, he would fold and fall like a sack of bricks. A weakness that Lyna often exploited.

Lyna. Ewalyna. How he missed her now more than ever. It had been such a simple time where things were much simpler. As dysfunctional as the relationship had been with Lyna, it was always easy and normal, as much as people, friends and some family frowned on their arrangement.

Because it was their normal.

And it was people like Tabitha who made Alex and Lyna appear as normal as vanilla as what people had them out to be. Alex stood by the bed in silence, and he looked out the window in longing for Lyna, with picture perfect memories of her scattered and swirling in his head. Of her always wearing his old T-shirt, riddled with holes, to sleep because it was the most comfortable shirt ever. Her deep, throaty morning voice as she said, 'Morning' regardless of how early it would have been for her. He turned to light another cigarette, took a deep drag and stared at the hotel room door, wishing she would come storming in and swallow him in her embrace. He also wondered if he ever crossed her mind as often as she did his.

A loud crash of a door being slammed interrupted his thoughts. So lost was he in the imaginary grip of Lyna, he hadn't noticed that Tabitha had come into the room, got dressed, collected her things and stormed out of the room. So there he was again, alone in a hotel room, wondering what the fuck went wrong. At least this time it was clear what did go wrong.

She made her choice, and it wasn't him.

# 6.

"Five more reps!" Eve the trainer bellowed in a voice that even drowned out Iron Maiden's 'The Trooper' blasting through the speakers as a class of forty adults groaned and whelped in despair. Limbs were shaking, muscles convulsing and straining under the weight of the barbells, sweat rolled into eyes, stinging them. On the floor, a small puddle of sweat formed underneath each participant as each and every one of them bathed in perspiration. And amidst the chaos of the clanging weights, the booming heavy metal music and the trainer's barking instructions and motivation, Carol cursed, "*What the fuck! Why of all days, did I decide today to push myself!*" She was at her thrice-a-week body sculpt sessions at the Fitness First outlet, and she had decided to lift heavier and challenge herself for this session considering what had happened in her personal life over the past few days. Nothing like sweating it out at the gym to take her mind off things and focus on form and intensity. As she doubled over, her hands on her knees, catching her breath and saliva dripping from her mouth, she noticed Khairul, another regular at the body sculpting class looking at her. He gave a bashful smile and nod of acknowledgement and continued with stacking his weights.

*Oh fuck, why does he have to look at me when I am in this state? So unglamorous!* she thought.

*Why, Carol, why? Why do you care if he sees you like that?* She immediately reproached herself mentally. She hated it whenever she lapsed into a state where she had to look good for a man when she believed that she was the only one who set her standard for looking and feeling good.

*No man should be the reason why I look or feel a certain way, good or bad*, she always thought. She believed wholeheartedly in the internet memes and positive out-of-context quotes like, "Don't ever let anyone dull your sparkle" or "A woman is unstoppable when she realises she deserves better." But deep inside, there was a bubbling pool of insecurity and diffidence that often threatened to overflow and break the internal levees that she had built to contain them. It was something she struggled with on a daily basis, this conflict between this dreamy idealism of what a woman believed and the harsh, unforgiving pragmatism of what a woman needed to get things done.

Soon, the lights dimmed in the exercise studio, usually a good sign as it signals the start of the cool-down exercises. She finally got to take a proper break to catch her breath, to relieve the lactic acid build-up in her muscles, stretch and relieve her tight and aching muscles.

*Hey, I actually smell nice, this post-workout musk.*

*I wonder what that Khairul smells like after a workout, especially this death camp of a workout today.*

*Should I have a protein shake and dinner after this?*

Lying on her back stretching her hamstrings, she glanced to the side and saw that Khairul was doing the same thing, and their eyes met. He smiled, and she gave a painful smirk. Nevertheless, she liked the way his skin glistened in the light with sweat rolling off his manly arms. Even in the dimly lit room, she could see every sinew as he lay on his back and stretched his smooth, hairless legs. On any other day, he appeared as a normal, run-of-the-mill gym rat with a future as bright as the room she was in, but tonight, he seemed radiant. Maybe it was the post-workout endorphins making their way around her body that made him appear attractive to her eyes, or it could just be the fact that she hadn't been with anyone for a while, and she was tired of rolling in her expensively assembled bed alone.

The class was instructed to get on their feet and stretch their trunk muscles, and Carol enjoyed the sight of his gym-sculpted glutes. He had an almost perfect inverted triangle-shaped torso, with wide shoulders and a thick neck holding up a rather small head of brown hair. Khairul turned to look back and caught Carol looking at him, and he smiled again. This time, she just nodded in acknowledgement. She just wanted to enjoy the sight of his butt and half hoped that he'd start flexing those cheeks in time with Seether's version of 'Careless Whisper.' The cooling down session was over, and applause and high-fives were exchanged all round for a job well done in surviving the class. Khairul came over with a towel draped across his shoulders, offered a handshake and said, "That was a tough one, right?"

"Yeah, it's alright," she said nonchalantly, distracted by his flawless chocolate velvety complexion with 'Fire' by Des'ree and Babyface oozing sticky sexy sludge out of the speakers. She tried hard to hear what he was saying.

"I've seen you around here a while but never got to say hi…"

"Well, now you have," she interrupted him, loudly, and almost rudely, but the act softened as she smiled at him.

"Haha, okay. Well, see you around here, then," he said as went about to clear his weights and bars.

"Okay," she said, still trying to be nonchalant.

As she discreetly bathed her eyes with the sight of every striation of his muscles, she inhaled and thought, *Ah that musk. Nice mix of sweat, shower gel, perfume and cigarettes, and no dirty laundry smell is always good.*

*Ah yes, squat, clean your area properly like a good boy. Show me that tight little bum.*

His bony ankles and bulging Achilles tendon somehow caught her eye, and she loved the way his smooth calves tapered at his ankles.

*Oh my. What cute ankles you have there. Ankles. Really, Carol? Ankles?*

*Okay, I should stop perving on him like this. Okay, Carol. Stop!*

She found his boyish, almost childish, charm irresistible and with the workout endorphins working its way through her body, it caused a riot of emotions running wild and lighting fires of desire in her loins.

*But he is oh so cute, I just want to bite him all over now.*

*Okay, I really have to stop. I have to shower, get dressed, get dinner and get home.*

*But look at that nice, round bum. I both pity and envy those tight shorts. Struggling to hold that bum, but yet gets to hold that bum!*

She squinted her eyes in pleasure looking at the way his shorts tried very hard to contain his round, chiselled bum and imagined herself biting that fleshy morsel of man flesh.

*Okay, he's standing up. Stop looking, Carol! You have shit to do!*

But like a fat man at a buffet table, her eyes were drawn to him. He stood up to do some final upper body stretching on his own, and she revelled in the sight of his rock hard pecs and his stiff nipples poking through his workout top.

*Hmmmm... Nice pecs. Those would make nice pillows for me.*

*He looks hairless, nice and smooth though. I could live with that.*

Aside from the hair on his head and eyebrows, he appeared hairless with no stray follicles peeking out from his under-arms. Not usually her preferred state for the man to be in but she could make exceptions. She had made exceptions.

*Stop it, Carol. Go shower and get dressed now!*

But like a thirsty vampire, she enjoyed the sight of his neck with his sharp Adam's apple bulging out from under the skin and sensuously moving up and down as he swallowed. She imagined sucking on that delicious Biblical forbidden fruit as he squirmed in her grip. She enjoyed the thought of being in total control of that muscly mound of man flesh and with just a flick of her tongue, a hot, controlled breath into his ear, be able to subdue years of strength and conditioning training.

Carol snapped out of it not a moment too soon, gathering herself to pick up after herself before scurrying to the shower. She resisted the urge to touch herself in the gym shower only because the anti-slip mat that the gym provided in the shower cubicles were hurting her feet. Also because she didn't want to lean on the poorly cleaned glass partitions of the shower cubicle. Dousing herself under the cold, pow-erful jet of water, she felt herself coming together, and soon she was in control of herself once again. She wiped herself down, dried her hair, put her clothes on and walked out of the change room and the gym.

"See you tomorrow, Carol," the pretty gym receptionist cried out. She managed to squeeze out a tired smile as she felt the sludge and slosh of her muscles becoming heavier. She could almost see the fatigue and pain creeping up with glee from under her skin and taking hold of her muscles in a vice-like grip. And every step, every breath and every blink of her eyes felt harder and more torturous. She could barely lift her arms to press the lift button to get out of this modern day dungeon into the welcoming arms of her bed.

Or Khairul's.

*Either are fine, but both is best*, she thought.

"Going down?" a whiny, almost squeaky, nasally and effeminate voice said as she wallowed in her increasing agony and discomfort. She turned her head and saw Khairul, resplendent in his skinny cut track pants and an Under Armour shirt that was bursting at the seams trying to keep all his muscles in.

*What the hell voice was that??* She thought.

*That's what his voice sounds like in real life when there is no music to distract?*

"Yes," she replied. "Going down."

She smirked as a naughty thought came barging into her head as she uttered those words. But his tone of voice still bothered her.

*Damn, I hope he didn't see that!*

"Good workout today?" he asked.

That voice still annoyed her.

She sighed, winced, tilted her head and managed to squeeze out a pained smile that stained the walls of the elevator. "It was okay," she said, using every ounce of whatever was left of her strength.

"Hahaha! It was *that* good, huh?" He laughed as Carol noted that nothing on his body jiggled. But the voice still grated her senses like metal claws on marble slabs. "Are you going to the Boost Juice bar downstairs to get your post-workout smoothie? I can redeem a free one for you tonight, being a loyal customer and all."

"How do you know I go there? Have you been stalking me, Mr Khai?" she joked as she stemmed the tide of fatigue that was threatening to overwhelm her.

He gave a bashful smile and said, "Yeah, you could say that. I've been noticing you here at the gym for a while now, just that I haven't found the right time to have a proper conversation with you."

"Oh, so now is the right time, ah? When I am all tired and melting into a bucket of pain swimming in lactic acid?" she retorted in jest, but it seemed to throw him off badly, and all his muscles seemed to be shrinking and retreating into a shell of insecurity.

*Oh no, I think I shut him down and maybe even shattered his fragile ego.*

"I'm joking," she said. "Actually, the best time to approach any woman is, honestly, any time. As long as you are sincere, confident and not creepy or threatening."

He seemed to gain confidence, like a soldier after listening to a rousing speech from a fiery general before war, and Carol could almost see the blood and life force returning to his loins, puffing them up as a smile slowly etched across his face.

*So he's easy to manipulate. This is too easy.*

"So, was I creepy and threatening?" he asked, looking for validation from her.

"No, you're alright," she assured him.

*Needs assurance and validation. All that muscle and man and he still needs that.*

They walked to the juice bar in the basement as they continued to make small talk with each other. She discovered that he was an IT specialist with a company across the street from the gym, and that he worked out almost obsessively. He joked that he suffered from reverse anorexia and he wanted to be big. "Like freak show big," he said. He seemed to know a lot, almost way too much, about working out and anything gym-related, from proper form to what he described as optimal muscle firing sequence. Things to do with exercise and things that got the heart racing at two hundred twenty minus age, multiplied by eighty percent beats per minute. Not exactly a problem for Carol.

*At least he is passionate about something.*

But the narcissism was something that bothered her. You couldn't work out that many times a week and not be obsessed with yourself.

*Maybe he is constantly improving himself and learning his hobby. That's always a good thing.*

By now she was trying hard to justify to herself why she was attracted to him and that there was more to him than just muscles, smooth skin and pretty ankles. She'd like to see herself as someone who was not shallow in her choice of men, going for emotional depth and intellect, but there were times, like this one, where she just wanted some eye, arm and pussy candy for herself.

*But not tonight, I am too tired to be exerting myself in bed.*

They sat on a bench outside Raffles Place MRT, along the grey walkways that cut the corporate landscape into smaller pieces that housed the tall, cold and brightly lit office towers that peppered the city skyline. Most of the shops were already closed, with most of them seeing their business peak at two in the afternoon. The hustle and bustle of the business district was winding down, and the alleyways were almost empty, except for the odd office worker going home late, and the occasional gym-goer trudging away from the gym on weary feet. They sat sipping on their protein smoothies as Khairul regaled her with stories of gnarly workouts, funny gym accidents, from its share of interesting personalities that showed up in the gym to the horrible injuries he witnessed. Carol tried hard to show some semblance of interest in the conversation, but she didn't even have the strength to lift a finger, let alone keep her eyes open. He noticed her fatigue and suggested they call it a night. Carol felt bad, so she took the initiative to ask him out for an after-work coffee at a nearby hole-in-the-wall cafe the next evening. They agreed to meet at 7 p.m. the next day, said their goodbyes and went their separate ways. Carol was spacing out throughout the ride home, and crashed noiselessly into her bed as her exertions at the gym consumed her and, like a switch, she turned off and was dragged into a restful and dreamless slumber.

The next day, Carol realised that she wasn't too excited about meeting Khairul. Maybe her sore, aching muscles had a part in that, or the fact that the endorphins had worn off. Nevertheless, she kept to her appointment and showed up at the cafe called Percolate five minutes early, finding that Khairul was already waiting, a fresh iced black coffee and a smoked salmon salad on the table.

"Oh, you're here early," she remarked.

"Yeah I did what I needed to do at work and decided to get off early," he replied.

Carol ordered her dinner as she chugged the last of her Casein and avocado recovery smoothie, which impressed Khairul. They chatted as they waited for her food to arrive, and the casual ambience coupled with the low yet audible hum of the Pet Shop Boys, made Carol feel at ease. Khairul opened up a little bit more that evening and told stories of his career choice, random bits about his family and friends from school. Carol didn't really mind his squeaky and nasally voice this time and was drawn into his world, as vanilla and kosher as she thought it was. He laughed, she giggled at how funny his laugh was. And it was clear to passers-by that they were having a great time together. She even forgot about her aching muscles that burned a hole in her body every time she moved.

*Once I get over the voice, I think I quite like this fella.*

*He has a bit of a funny bone too, doesn't he?*

*Yeah, he's alright. An alright that is attached to a hot body to boot.*

After dinner was done, they took a walk under the stars and the city lights along the river at Boat Quay that ran through the city. The distant thumping of house music coming from the bars nearby working hand in hand with the disembodied voices of the faceless crowd of office workers and tourists were the sounds of the sprawling urban landscape that both had gotten used to, so they were able to give each other their undivided attention. As they strolled through the crass commercial enclaves, she took every opportunity and made any excuse to touch him. His taut forearm, his smooth but calloused hands, and even ran her fingers playfully down his tight work pants from his thigh to his knee that felt like rocks perched at the edge of a cliff. He enjoyed the attention she gave him and reciprocated by running his fingers through her hair and down her cheeks. They both smiled brighter than the city lights that lit the night sky, and Carol felt something special brewing between them.

Soon, one dinner and one walk became two, then three and five. And it was more than just dinner – they watched movies together, they went shopping together, most importantly, they went on dates together. They met in the gym, they met before work, during lunch and after work and enjoyed each other's company each time. She loved his childlike enthusiasm about the life he had chosen to lead, and he loved the way she was when around him. She loved the way his bodily scent mixed well with his Paco Rabane perfume and loved running her fingers up and down his smooth, flawless skin, sometimes sending visible and pleasurable shivers down his spine. Carol couldn't wait to explore the uncharted territories of his chiselled body as her mouth watered thinking about how her body would react to his. After about a month into the budding relationship, they were soon on the same page physically and were ready to explore more than just the city together and decided on a staycation.

Carol had checked into at the Robertson Quay Hotel and was waiting for him in the lobby. Her vintage Ray-Bans perched on top of her head, she lounged lazily on the armchair and chuckled by herself as she saw a couple walking into the lobby carrying what looked like bags of groceries. The bag clinked noisily as the sound reverberated all across the lobby, but the bemused look of the man carrying the grocery bags amused her more than the groceries itself.

*Pretty couple though, I bet they'll make pretty babies.*

The man stopped to look, as if he heard her, turned and looked. Carol saw how painfully normal he looked with his naturally bronzed skin and almond-shaped eyes. He seemed to squint his eyes to get a better look at Carol, and gave a quick, playful smirk before turning to walk away with his partner. Not sure whether that was a friendly smile or a bashful cry for help, Carol just nodded her head in acknowledgement as they walked away into the lift lobby.

*The nerve the fella has. He's with his partner and still he has roving eyes.*

*Well, not to say I would blame him. My eyes would be roving too if it were me they were looking at.*

Khairul was late, so she went up to the room herself to rest up for the upcoming exertions she was expecting to be indulging in. He showed up, flustered but happy to be seeing her. She greeted him in her bathrobe that hung lazily off her shoulders, barely covering her heaving breasts. She kissed him deeply and explored his cavernous mouth with her snaking tongue. She ran her fingers and nails down his taut, V-shaped back as she pushed him away, and got him to turn around so she could admire his body. He flexed as if reading her mind, and she gasped at how alive it was. It looked like a flattened cobra's hood ready to strike its prey, and it drove her wild with passion. She clung onto him tight as she kissed and licked his back through his shirt and he moaned in pleasure. She reached down into his track pants, pleasantly surprised to find that he went commando, and felt the rock hard butt burning in her hands, which sent her into a delirious frenzy of sexual energy. Her hands circled around to his crotch as her lips clung onto his neck for dear life. She felt the tuft of pubic hair and rummaged around looking for an engorged, venous penis for her to pleasure.

But she could not locate it with her hands.

Perplexed but still lost in her passionate frenzy, she turned him around to face her. As she kissed him, she undid the drawstring of his track pants and pulled it down. She pulled her mouth from his, looked down and became very confused.

Baffled.

Because all she saw was a dark tuft of hair and what looked like dehydrated plums hanging down and out of the black forest of hair. Holding on tight to herself so that she would not be seen to react, she got to her knees to inspect his junk closer and realised that the dick was hiding underneath the thick undergrowth of hair. She took her time to fish it out and saw that his dick, erect, was roughly the size of her thumb. It looked like a shy mushroom with a fear of light and one that would retract at any moment should it feel threatened.

*Okay, maybe he's a grower.*

*I'm gonna see if I can make it bigger.*

She put his penis in her mouth, and it felt like putting an enlarged, genetically modified baby carrot in her mouth. Nevertheless, it was rock hard, yes, but it was definitely not something she would choke on.

*My puny hands are even too big for his dick!*

*My gosh, I can only hold it with my thumb and forefinger!*

*But it's erect and hard, so that's something good, right?*

She continued to suckle on his manhood and tried hard to repress her conflicting thoughts so that it wouldn't show in her face. She felt like a toddler again, sucking on her own thumb; the only difference was that the base of her thumb was tickling her lips, and she fought the urge to wipe it with the back of her hand.

*I gotta look like I am and will be enjoying this.*

She looked up and Khairul was in ecstasy. He had his eyes closed and was hanging on to the walls to steady himself, almost oblivious to the fact that he had the tiniest penis she had ever seen. She gave it a squeeze with her thumb and forefinger as she played with his testicles, and they felt rough and dry, like dehydrated figs in need of a shave, or moisturizer.

*I can do this, I am not that shallow.*

*After all, a penis is only as sexy as the man it is attached to.*

*And the woman pleasuring it.*

*I can do this.*

*You can do this, Carol!*

She continued to pleasure his dick and all the while, she felt like she was sucking on a brandy-filled chocolate, and soon, she felt the drops of brandy seeping out from the chocolate shell. She hadn't noticed that Khairul had tensed up and let out an almighty squeal of pleasure as he shed his three drops of bitter and salty semen in her mouth. With his clothes still on him, he climaxed in her mouth.

*I didn't even get to see his body.*

Khairul was fast melting into a pool of sludgy post-coital juice, and his penis had retreated back into the forest of pubes. He looked exactly like a living, breathing eighties Ken doll – chiselled, hard, smooth and with no man parts. They both crawled into bed as she stewed in her frustration. She got him to take his clothes off so that she could appreciate the living Adonis lying next to her. And he was a living Adonis, just not where it mattered most. And as she lay next to him, she caressed his Tic Tac of a penis with her finger and was careful not to scare it back into its cave. She tried to reignite the lascivious flames of desire as she kissed his thick neck and ran her tongue down his shoulder blades, leaving a trail of saliva on his dark brown nipples. He sighed in pleasure but soon, despite the intensely sensual work of her tongue, he drifted off into a slumber and was snoring. Carol lay in bed, rolling in resentment.

*Maybe I should just continue enjoying his body while he sleeps.*

But she didn't. She fixed her robe, turned away from him and tried in vain to relax.

*I'm not a size queen, I know I am not a size queen, but look at it!*
*He's a nice guy, he can make me laugh, but really? A cough drop?*
*I don't really need that much dick, to be honest.*
*But is this normal?*

*How is it that he seems to be unaware?*

*I need to take a walk.*

Carol got up, dressed, took her bag and quietly left the room to walk along what turned out to be a clubbing street in the inner city. It was almost six in the evening, so the shutters were about to open and the dinner crowd was slowly starting to pour in. Hands deep in her pockets, bag slung lazily on her shoulder, she walked past the people on the street without looking up, eyes fixed on the ground.

*After all, even a three-inch dick can get a woman pregnant. Well, that's what they say anyway.*

*And he does get very hard, so getting it up will not be an issue.*

*But really, a mint? A RICOLA MINT?*

*I am not a shallow size queen. I am not a shallow size queen.*

*What can I do?*

*How can he pleasure me?*

*Maybe he's good at eating me out.*

*But he doesn't look like one who likes eating a woman out. Look at how he collapsed in bed right after he blew his stupid load!*

For the first time in a long while, she didn't know what to think. She didn't know how to react. She didn't know what to feel. Carol contemplated giving him another chance and going back to the hotel room. But she kept walking along the Singapore Rover towards Alkaff Bridge with the hope of feeling something, or that an emotion would take root in her heart to guide her this time.

Something.

Anything.

Nothing.

So she kept walking and never looked back.

# 7.

Alex squinted his eyes in the blazing afternoon sun as he made his way to the school gate. Within minutes, he could feel sweat trickling down his back in the balmy tropical heat that burned through his school uniform onto his puny, twelve-year-old frame. There was a rising crescendo of children's voices happy to finally be able to get out of the clutches of school as the cars of waiting parents and school buses revved in anticipation of their charges barging into the vehicles to take them home. Alex felt proud that he never needed to have his parents, grandparents nor some strange Chinese driver waiting on him every day after school. It was a badge of honour for him to be able to take public transport on his own at twelve years old with his few friends from the school as well as other children from the neighbouring school.

Alex went to the all-boys St Stephen's School with a strong tradition of producing many a square peg to fit into the round holes of the country, but ultimately he had just been happy to be going to a school with the biggest football field he had ever seen. The size of five football fields, it offered his friends and him endless hours of football, rolling in the mud, playing catch and Police and Thief. The field was always muddy, having not dried properly from the overnight dew, and always gave off a faint, yet pungent stench of bog and wet grass. A scent that he had come to find comfort in after years of playing in the field, rolling in the mud, and getting spanked by his teachers because he would walk into class with muddy shoes and shorts. Huge flame of the forest trees lined the perimeter of the field, and they offered cool shade from the tropical heat, and a nice spot for rest, and even a nap, save for the occasional centipede threatening to crawl into one's uniform or into one's ear. Alex shuddered at that thought as he waited for Rahman, his going-home-from-school friend, also his best friend. Rahman was a strong, fat kid who could outrun most of the kids in school despite his tubby frame. His dark skin made him appear more imposing to his peers and even his teachers, who were often afraid of the way he breathed. That heavy, almost guttural gurgle he had that sounded menacing. His sheer size and physical prowess made him one of the most popular and feared kids in an all-boys school, so Alex, with his skinny, puny bully-able size, rode on his best friend's coattails all throughout primary school.

Rahman came running out of his classroom, pushing past the other, much smaller kids like a bowling ball smashing through the pins, leaving behind him a trail of kids on the ground wincing in pain. Rahman grabbed him by the collar, pulled him along and said, "Hurry hurry, let's go, I heard from Wayne that Zubaidah will be at the bus stop today!"

"Zubai-who?" Alex asked as he was dragged out of the school gate past the pedestrian crossing toward the church and the bus stop beyond.

"Zubaidah! The pretty girl from Siglap Primary. I heard she is so pretty!" Rahman said with such excitement. "So come, come quick!"

Alex ran breathlessly behind Rahman as he tried to keep up through the church near their school. He had no time to stay and hang out by an aviary that housed exotic birds, and one that could speak, which amused Alex each time he stopped by on the way home from school. Being skinny and slight in frame, he was often the baby of the group,  and Alex had no desire for the opposite sex yet, so he had no idea who nor why this Zubaidah person aroused such excitement among the older boys in school. In the time he had hanging out with them, he had heard her name mentioned more than several times and often accompanied with an "Oooooooohhhhh" and a love song. He often laughed with them even though he wasn't really aware of what was going on, just because they were much bigger than him and everyone else for that matter. Like a lot of people, the big boys just loved having Alex around, that puny, introverted boy with an easy smile and an infectious laugh, who could quote lines from popular movies and television series in his conversations. Maybe he was their entertainment, a court jester, but he didn't mind being just under the upper hand in the social circles they travelled in. As long as that hand protected him from bullies and did not beat him up, it was all good.

Rahman and Alex jay-ran across the road in a show of boyish machismo to the other kids and settled at one end of the bus stop as Rahman kept his eyes peeled for Zubaidah, his eyes trained on the pedestrian crossing about twenty meters away from the bus stop. Alex perched on the railings with a happy smile painted across his face at the thought of going home and spending time with his nenek and aunt, women who raised him in place of his working parents. Even the heat and the clangour of the playing kids did not bother him one bit, and he imagined his nenek's gentle voice and her pudgy frame as he hugged her. He loved the way she smelled of old lady and talcum powder and how her weathered hands felt comforting as she gently caressed his face every time she saw him. He also enjoyed his aunt's shrill voice and even found comfort in her daily, often volatile mood swings, which often resulted in physical violence, one that he had gotten used to.

It was like he had been Stockholm-ed by her to the point where if she was in a good mood and was nice to everyone, he would feel something was amiss. Most of all, he looked forward to spending time with his baby sister, who even as an infant, would look for and reach out to him whenever he was around. His favourite thing to do with her was to carry her in his arms when no one was looking and look into her face and playfully ask her, "What?" It provided him with endless entertainment as he loved making her smile.

Lost in his own world, he didn't realise that the boys around him were suddenly jumping, shouting and singing, like monkeys in heat, nursing raging boners in the jungle. He looked up and saw that the boys had their attention focused on a girl with smooth, almost shimmering, caramel skin, big innocent eyes, hair tied in a ponytail at the back as neat, almost painfully measured, bangs fell across her forehead. She walked with her entourage of other similar-looking girls, all with dread written across their faces, as prominently as their eyeliner, a dread of the moment they had to be at the bus stop amidst the howling monkeys in heat. He rolled his eyes as he laughed at the spectacle unfolding in front of him.

As the girls gingerly approached the bus stop, the boys' passion were whipped up into a frenzy of cat calling, singing, dancing, high fives and exaggerated laughter and struts. It was like watching a pantomime circus approaching its climax, accompanied by the music of the blaring traffic whizzing past. Alex looked far into the horizon at the clear blue afternoon sky dotted with HDB blocks and the occasional speck of green, and as the pre-teen mating ritual in full display before him, he retreated back into his world, occasionally reacting and laughing to the jabs Rahman and the other boys made just to appear as part of the group. He couldn't understand why the boys acted that way and even felt embarrassed by it. His eyes caught Zubaidah's and he noticed the anger and resignation in her eyes as he shrugged, rolled his eyes hard, and gave her a sympathetic and reassuring smile that said, "Hang in there, this will be over soon." She smiled back, almost pitifully, like she was hoping that he would save her from this most uncomfortable theatrics.

But she soon decided that she should save herself.

Alex, still lost in his own world, suddenly felt a smooth, sweaty hand grabbing his arm that jolted him out of his daze and realised Zubaidah was there next to him, hanging off his arm. He raised his eyebrows, perplexed, because it was the first time he came into physical contact with a girl. He felt a surge of emotion in his chest that almost overwhelmed him but he swallowed it hard. Soon, that same surge barrelled down south to between his legs, and he felt a stirring in his loins, the same feeling he felt when he saw an undead Amy Peterson in a sheer white dress, nipples clearly seen underneath the dress. The clangour of the boys became more tumultuous as they saw what was happening between Zubaidah and him. She buried her face in his shoulders in embarrassment while Alex sat frozen and wide-eyed in fear as his nonchalance evaporated in the afternoon heat from Zubaidah's touch. Unbeknownst to him, the look he gave, that wide-eyed, confused, quizzical look, was interpreted as anger, with the piercing eyes of an alpha dog telling the rest of the monkeys to keep quiet and leave them alone. Soon enough, the din melted away as the boys soon lost interest in Zubaidah and retreated to the other corner of the bus stop, far from the two of them. They soon found a new toy to play with, a skateboard another boy brought along to school. Alex looked around and saw Wayne and Rahman looking at him with mouths curled up at the corners as they slowly nodded in approval. Rahman especially, seemed to be beaming with pride, at how his best friend, the tiniest fucker in the whole world, seemed to have possession of the prettiest girl in their known world.

Bus number 25 arrived soon after and Alex and Zubaidah went on board. She sat next to him, and he enjoyed the pungent but feminine musk of girl he smelled on her. It smelled like damp, old parchment paper mixed with a musk of sweat, shampoo and baby powder. The smell somehow reminded him of the time when the family took him to visit the library at the university his cousin went to in Australia. Alex sat there in silence, not knowing what to say to her as he bashfully rubbed his bony shoulders on the cool and smooth skin on her arm. She didn't seem to mind and even went further to stretch out her pinky finger to touch his. His fingers retreated bashfully at first, but soon, with bare shoulders rubbing and pinky fingers touching, she said, "Thank you for helping me out back there."

"How did I help you? And why did you come to me?" Alex asked naively, still too shy to look into her eyes.

"Because you were the only one at the bus stop who didn't seem to care that I was there, and the one who those damn boys would listen to. So I thought you could tell them to keep quiet and not to be so noisy," she said.

"Oh. Okay," Alex said, unsure what she meant by that with his mind still on the pleasurable sensation he felt of his skin on hers.

"Next time, can we just hang out together at the bus stop, just so that the boys won't embarrass me like that? They do that all the time, to the point where I would stay late in school just to avoid them. And my friends are useless because they keep telling me it's a good thing, but it's not!" she said, exasperated.

"Okay, sure!" Alex said, with no idea what he was agreeing to, but one thing he knew was that it meant that he could see her every day, and it became something he would look forward to.

Every day.

And he did.

Every afternoon, he would wait excitedly for her outside the church of Our Lady Of Perpetual Succour by the aviary. Some afternoons, they would take some time to play on the swings and the slides at the playground as Wayne and the other older boys walked past, stealing envious glances at them. Other afternoons, they would be seated by the aviary where Alex would regale her with stories and facts about the birds in the cage, facts that he would have read in the encyclopaedias provided in the school. They exchanged numbers one day, and soon, met up on weekends, where they would meet at Bedok Library. She would read her *Nancy Drew* and *Famous Five* novels while he would be tearing through five to six series of his favourite *Asterix* and *Obelix* comics. Both nestled comfortably at the corner of the sofa, dangerously close to each other, with Alex feeling this was the closest to heaven as he would ever be. After they were done with the library, they would go to the nearby A&W fast food restaurant and share a plate of hot waffles with ice cream and chocolate sauce.

"How come you have so much money to spend?" Zubaidah asked one day.

"What? What do you mean?" Alex answered, as he hurriedly scooped ice-cream into his mouth.

"Like, how come you can have money to eat at A&W every time and pay for me? It's not cheap, you know. Your parents rich?"

"I don't know. But they give me pocket money every morning before they go to work, or before they go out and leave me at home," Alex replied nonchalantly.

"I wish my parents are as good as yours. My mum is always scolding us, and Dad never talks to us. They don't even give us money to eat sometimes," she said, with a slight tinge of sadness in her voice.

"Same! My mum scolds me a lot too, but she always tell me that it is not scolding, it's called 'nagging.' And she does it because she loves me. My dad also scolds me a lot, especially when I make mistakes on my homework and tests," Alex responded with his mouth half-full of waffles and vanilla ice cream.

"I think my parents don't care about my school, because they never ask me or help me. Mum keeps telling me to work hard, but I don't know how to. And my dad just watches TV, and he never play with us anymore now. Once in a while, he would shout at us and Mum tells us to keep quiet," she said as her face fell.

"Mum and Dad always take us out to the beach, to dinner on Saturday, or Sunday breakfast. So annoying, because we have to wake up early," Alex complained.

"You're so lucky! I wish my parents could do that with me. Your parents spend time with you and give you money. My parents only know how to scold and scold. The last time they took us out was five years ago, where we went to have dinner at Burger King. I want your parents to be my parents!" she exclaimed.

"Ewwww, no. That means you will be my sister, and I don't like to hang out with my sister. She is so grumpy now that she is in high school," Alex said, referring to his elder sister.

Zubaidah laughed a hearty laugh and Alex enjoyed the sight of her perfectly aligned, white teeth sitting in a perfect row behind her smooth, reddish brown lips. He would also notice how pink and red the insides of her mouth were and sometimes wished he could touch it out of sheer curiosity. She usually had her hair up on school days but on weekends, she would have it down, and her long, dark brown hair flowed like a river of dreams down her shoulders and always smelling of apples. Alex enjoyed the way she touched, played with, and adjusted her hair once in a while and resisted the urge to touch her hair. He wondered if it was alright to take some time to sniff her hair. Soon, he felt the warm and smooth touch of her hand on his, and a tide of emotion that he was unable to recognise flooded him again. He swallowed it hard and that sensation began swelling up in his pants, and he felt his first pangs of the pleasurable discomfort that was a boner. It was a touch that he would give up everything to have, and the kind of touch he would spend the rest of his years looking for.

Just one touch that would stop his world from spinning out of control. The one touch that would calm his soul. The one touch that would be a harbour in the tempest raging in his soul, and the one touch to fill the rest of his days with vivid colour.

"I like you, Alex. You're very smart, and you are not like the other boys," she gushed.

"And you are also not like the other girls," he said as he remembered a line from a late night romance movie he watched some time ago. It was the first ever pick-up line he used on a girl. His world soon became more colourful, and all he could taste right now was this moment and no one else mattered; as far as he was concerned, the world was just Zubaidah and him.

It was a taste that he would be searching for the rest of his life. The taste that would extinguish the brightest of flames, kill the dry desert in his mouth with a gush of sweet water. Also a taste that would eclipse his heart forever.

She blushed and squeezed his hand as they tucked into the shared waffle with ice cream, sometimes playfully feeding each other spoonfuls of hot fudge and melted vanilla ice cream. They found every excuse to be touching each other, on the shoulder, hand to hand, they helped wipe each other's lips, and it was a picture perfect scene of young, budding love. A few weeks down the road, she kissed him on the cheek before she got on the bus, triggering rapturous shouts of victory and admiration from his monkey friends as he basked in the glory of being the only boy to have Zubaidah's heart.

But as the months went by, they found that they were seeing each other less and less. He didn't know how to communicate to her that he wanted to see her every day if he could. He wished he could say to her that he wanted to hug her and never let her go. But soon, she stopped coming to the bus stop, and most likely, to school. Sometimes, Alex would wait for her in vain at the playground, or by the aviary, for her to not show up. The church groundsman soon became accustomed to the lonely, forlorn figure and would sometimes stop by to keep him company and give him cold Yeo's packet drinks from the church pantry. He would wait till the late afternoon on some days, just hanging on desperately to the most tenuous string of hope that she would come walking around the corner, lighting his world up again with her smile. On weekends, he would try calling her home, but there was no answer when he dialled her phone number. He would also go to the library, hanging on to the faint hope that she would be sitting on the sofa reading her novels, looking up at him as he entered the door to the reference section and smiling.

That beautiful smile that would colour his world in bright hues of happiness and joy.

He wanted to think of her and keep her alive in his mind. Her smile, the way she smelled, the touch of her hand on his, her lips on his cheeks, and sometimes, he would imagine how her lips would feel on his. But with the PSLE just around the corner, he was unable to do so as he had to focus on his studies. Soon the exams came and went and, as the year wound down to a close, the memories he had of Zubaidah and of their time together became a faint, fleeting shadow on the wall where the paint was peeling. It was a matter of weeks before he had forgotten to remember her, and this lay the foundation of Alex's idea of women and relationships.

As easily as they came to him, they went away just as easily as well.

# 8.

---

*You need cooling, baby I'm not fooling. I'm gonna send ya, back to schooling...* The lyrics oozed out of Carol's earphones from the maniacally sensuous voice of Robert Plant accompanied by the dirty and gritty blues of Jimmy Page. Complemented by the fat and sticky bass of John Paul Jones and the thumping, banging drums of John Bonham, Carol weaved and bopped her head alone in her bedroom. Her musical trance was soon interrupted by a loud, shrill voice of her mum saying, "Hurry up, Carol! We are leaving soon!"

Carol and her mum were on their monthly retail therapy binge. Well, the therapy was more for her mum, who would usually dump her at a barbershop owned by one of her friends as she tore through the aging shopping mall. She barely had time to grab her walkman and the one cassette tape she had in her possession before her mum whisked her out of the house and into the sweltering heat of the midday sun. The sun was high in its full glory, casting blazing hot rays of light, and Carol could feel it burn right into her bones. The air was heavy with stifling heat and hot gusts of wind almost burning her skin and blinded her eyes. With the nauseating smell of exhaust fumes from the snaking cars and public buses that lined the streets, the blaring traffic jarred her senses, and she longed to be away from the sickly city bustle and into the cool, air-conditioned arms of the soulless suburban shopping complex.

Throughout the journey, all that was swirling in her head was the deliciously soulful voice of Robert Plant, even as her mum tried to make conversation with her. "Carol, you are fourteen years old now, and in secondary school already, so you better study hard, okay, girl? You need to start preparing for and do well for your post-secondary school education so you can go to better schools and get a good, well-paying job when you grow up, okay?"

Carol had allowed herself to drift away with Plant's voice lifting her up, but her mum's jabbing her shoulders brought her crashing back into reality as she nodded her head furiously to show that she got it.

"Listen to me! This is the real start of your education, Carol, and it is best that you get the best start possible and go to a good junior college so you can do well in the future, okay?" her mum continued.

Carol looked at her, a woman in her forties, and realised that the lines on her face seemed clearer as days went by, no matter how hard she tried to cover them with the pink and brown powder she always carried around with her. Looking at the soft and frail face, as the smell of Chanel's Mademoiselle filled the air, Carol almost forgot how tough and frightening her mum could be when she made a mistake in school, or when it was deemed that Carol "has not given her best effort."

It could be overwhelming for a fourteen-year-old girl sometimes to be under increasing academic pressure mainly from her mum, so her escape came in the form of the music her father often encouraged her to listen to. Her dad had always been more relaxed about her studies and school. "She doesn't need to be pressured only for her to be like every other kid in this country; let her develop her own sense of identity," he once said to her mum. Unfortunately, the words stuck only for a few weeks before the pressure on her came back. On her birthday, her father gave her a cassette tape of Led Zeppelin's *Led Zeppelin II* album, a cassette which had been in his possession for years now. It could be a case of him forgetting to buy her a proper gift and giving her anything that he could get his hands on in his bedroom, but she didn't care because she fell crazy in love with it. Also it was because anything her dad did or touched became something cool in her mind. So she would listen to the songs every day after school, before bed, while she showered, pretty much all the time. Largely because it was the only cassette tape she owned at that time. She loved the bold and defiant guitar licks heard in 'Heartbreaker', and every time she listened to 'A Whole Lotta Love,' she felt a surge of physical emotion rising in her as Plant's almost orgasmic moaning and shrieking stirred her into a frenzy she couldn't understand then.

Still lost in her world, Carol and her mum ducked and weaved through the shopping centre amidst the cacophony of noises coming from the textile salesmen that filled the mall. But soon, they arrived at the back of the mall where, over the years, it had become a spot where she would be babysat by her mum's friends. "Keep an eye on her for me, okay, Sam? Don't give her any candy, but she's allowed some peanuts or sunflower seeds if she gets hungry. Here's some money for you to get those if she asks for it." Her mum's voice pierced the air around the sleepy and laid-back salon. It was a quiet day at the R&S Salon, with lead stylist Sam basically falling asleep on the couch, her messy yet luscious black hair falling lazily over her face. Rachel was sweeping the floor with her thick, wavy, Bon-Jovi-esque hair flowing freely over her shoulders, curly bangs falling over her eyes. Tattoos crawling down their arms were proudly displayed by these rock and roll women. They were both scoundrel-looking, rough on the edges but good-hearted women ultimately, which was why her mum didn't hesitate to dump Carol in their care as she went on to do her shopping. Also, Mum had spent a king's ransom at the salon getting her hair done over the years, so it was alright to ask them to watch Carol for a while, and these two women were the cool aunties that Carol liked to have around.

Sam beckoned her to sit on the well-worn armchair, giving her an old comic to read while she stretched. Carol quite enjoyed spending time at the salon. She loved the smell of talcum powder and the strong scent of chemicals that lingered about like a house guest who never wanted to leave. Even without air conditioning, it was always comfortable there. Maybe it was the laid-back vibe of chilling out at the worn out leather sofas and armchairs. The black and white posters of models from the sixties with hair from the fifties that hung on the walls like shadows or windows into a time where brooding men wore suits, looked straight at the camera and struck a pose instead of just standing still, and women were always bright and happy, always looking off-camera, faraway into the distance. Carol also found comfort in the buzzing sound of the electric razor, the cold, clinical snips of the scissors and the faint rustling of the broom sweeping hair off the floor.

Carol got bored of the comic soon enough, fished out her walkman, slid in the cassette tape and pressed play. She had wanted to be lost in the Led Zeppelin world to raise her spirits and find tender soul-searching moments in their tunes, when Sam stopped to ask, "Girl, what song are you listening to?"

Carol fished out the cassette cover and showed it to Sam and said, "My daddy bought this for me for my birthday."

Sam squinted her eyes for a closer look and said, "Ah, your daddy has good musical taste, but I think mine are better," as a cheeky smile came crawling across her face. In the back, Carol could hear Rachel chuckling; she turned to look and saw how much Rachel's face lit up as the conversation seemed to have taken a musical turn.

"Yeah, this is the only cassette I have," Carol said with a tinge of sadness in her voice.

"You like the songs in that one?" Rachel asked, pointing to the Led Zeppelin cassette she clutched in her hand.

"Yes, I do," she replied with a smile.

"Why do you like them?" Rachel probed further.

"I like how they make me feel. Like very strong. Some songs like the first one 'Whole Lotta Love' is weird, and I feel weird when I listen to it, but I like it," Carol replied with an air of authority. "I also like the guy's voice, it's very wild and the drums also, it's very loud and booming," she continued. Sam and Rachel looked at each other and gave nods of approval as they were amused but ultimately impressed by Carol's budding musical preference. At least that was what Carol thought at that moment in time, as she discovered in her later years that the 'weird feeling' she felt was actually stirrings in her loins.

"Well, your daddy has given you a good start on your musical education," Rachel said, "but now, Auntie Rachel is going to teach you some more about not just good music, but *very good* music, okay?" Rachel ruffled Carol's hair. Carol could not imagine at that time that there could be any other music better than Led Zeppelin because no other music she had she heard was, be it from the radio that Mum was always listening to or the television that her friends loved watching when she visited them. But she was curious indeed at how it could get any better than what she had been listening to all this time.

Carol looked around and saw Rachel and Sam whispering to each other, in the throes of discussing what to play for their young rock and roll disciple. And soon, Carol heard the opening, the sound of a bunch of men shouting, "Step inside, walk this way, you and me babe, hey hey!" She was unimpressed by it at first, but it was a matter of moments before thumping electronic drums burst forth and was soon accompanied by jangly and wild opening guitar riffs that began to bleed out of the speakers in the salon. It was the opening to Def Leppard's 'Pour Some Sugar On Me.' Carol didn't like it in the beginning because she found the song to be sluggish, and all she could imagine was the sloshing of mud from the time she went on a school trip to the mangrove swamp. It was dirty, sticky and sweaty as the song reminded her of clumsy, sweaty boys who tried to talk to her by making fun of her. And the lyrics were weird too, because all she heard was a mix of video, radio, shaking a bottle, breaking a bubble, and then, *pour some sugar on me.* The song did not make any sense!

She forced a smile in between clenched teeth in a vain attempt to be polite to the aunties and not offending them, but something caught her eye. It was the way Auntie Sam and Auntie Rachel danced, eyes closed, hands in the air, hips swaying sensually, their heads bobbing hypnotically and with looks on their faces that mesmerised her to no end. It was an expression that burned itself into her memory somehow, and from then on, every time she listened to a song that moved her, the expressions these ladies wore on their faces were ones that Carol would have on as well. She could not take her eyes off the two ladies who were deep in the throes of the song, lost in the sluggish and almost slobbery rhythms, revealing bits of their bodies and skin that made her blush. She felt embarrassed by the unfolding spectacle in front of her, but she also realised this had to be what she looked like as she listened to Led Zeppelin. Carol closed her eyes and hitched a musical ride along with the aunties to the song, and soon she felt the beats and the melody embracing her in an easy, comforting and warm light. Carol felt comforted, and most importantly, powerful. The giggling of the aunties broke her trance and she felt compelled to join in the giggling.

"You like that, huh?" Rachel asked.

"I don't know. I don't really like the song, but I like how it makes me feel, like, very nice," Carol said as she struggled to find words to describe what the song made her feel.

Sam nodded approvingly and said, "Yeah, that's normal. Soon, when you're older, you'll find that songs do that to you, and it will stay with you forever. So, now, your life will never be the same again, you know, girl?"

"Now, let's try listening to this one," Sam said as she slid another cassette tape into the player. A very dramatic and atmospheric sound bled out of the speakers as plucked notes from the guitar floated just above the atmosphere, and soon, the high-pitched voice of Tom Keifer wailed with the utmost melancholy about counting the tears falling before his eyes. What Carol noted was how similar his voice was to Robert Plant's but with a much more calming and soothing tone to it. She loved the way the song built up to a climax of maniacal wailing of longing and sadness, Keifer claiming to be 'Nobody's Fool.' Again, Carol found herself eyes closed and head bobbing to the tune.

Soon Carol could see from the corner of her eyes, her mum approaching the salon from a distance, and she straightened herself up to leave with Mum.

"Before you go, here are some more tapes to add to your collection," Rachel said as she winked. Carol took a brief look and saw Whitesnake, Bon Jovi, Poison and Scorpions. They seemed new, and she felt that she shouldn't be taking them, but Rachel and Sam insisted that she did, gave her a plastic bag to store them, and as she hugged both Rachel and Sam, Rachel whispered in her ear, "Music is life, Carol. Remember that, okay?" Carol nodded and went home with her mum.

Carol spent the next few months with her head plugged into her earphones as she pored over each note, singing each melody from the music that Sam and Rachel had her listening to. Her mum didn't mind as long as she kept to her four-hours-a-day studying regime, she was all good. She found the bombastic sound of Whitesnake and the hyper-masculine voice of David Coverdale to be strangely comforting and soothed her soul. She found very powerful moments in 'Here I Go Again' where the music lifted her spirits to soar higher than she could ever dream of. She felt the tender, emotional and soul-searching moments deep in her soul in 'Is This Love,' and thought that it would be nice if someone said those things about her. At times, she even felt that David Coverdale wrote that song about her.

In Bon Jovi, she threw her fists in the air and let loose cathartic screams in 'You Give Love A Bad Name,' and in 'Living On A Prayer' she found Tommy, the kind of boy she would love to hang out with, a boy who would whisper to her in rough times, "Baby it's okay, someday," and she found an ideal alter ego in 'Wanted Dead or Alive' in the shape of a lone cowboy, a rebellious outlaw, raising her fists in the air in the land of control and repression where her mum was queen. 'Never Say Goodbye' painted a picture for her, one of an ideal partner who would "dance so close, and dance so slow," one who "swore to never let you go, together, forever."

She found out how danger and ambiguity could be very seductive in the image portrayed by Poison. Somehow, the androgynous manner with which CC DeVille and Brett Michaels were depicted on the album sleeves appealed to her. As weird as she felt about men in bright coloured tights, big hair, feminine makeup, she also felt excited by them and loved how she felt connected to the way they sang their songs. Mostly, she was wildly curious as to what it meant to be 'talkin dirty' and why would anyone want someone to 'Talk Dirty To Me.' But she strangely found something else in that song. In the lyrics where Brett Michaels sang, "You know I call you, I call you on the telephone. I'm only hoping that you're home so I can hear you. When you say those words to me and whisper so softly, I gotta hear you," she found in those lines what she wanted Tommy to say to her when things got better.

She tore through Scorpion's *Love At First Sting* album and danced wildly to 'Rock You Like A Hurricane.' She absolutely loved the catchy guitar riffs complemented by the simple singalong lyrics and chewed on them and spat out the lyrics like the mental bubblegum they could be. Sometimes she didn't even sing the words but just imitated the guitar sounds, eyes closed, lips pursed and pouted, using her badminton racquet as a guitar and jumping about on her bed. Sometimes, when she was in the car with her family, she would hum the tune 'Big City Nights' to herself as her dad drove through the city. But the song that tugged at her heartstrings the most was 'Still Loving You.' The heart wrenching lyrics, coupled with the smooth wailing tone of Klaus Meine sang and touched the depths of her soul and conjured up within her a wild melancholy and yearning she never knew existed. She felt like crying out in pain and emotional anguish every time Klaus hit the high note in the climax of the song. Fists clenched, face scrunched up, on her knees, she would lip-sync the song in her room and in the shower. She often pictured Tommy, or a Tommy, singing those songs to her to court her, to express his deep yearning for her as she ran toward him and melted into his arms.

So it was through these songs that shaped Carol's idea and vision of what and how a boy, and soon, a man should be like for her. Not in the way they looked, because she found the androgynous men with makeup sporting four brightly coloured animal print scarves around their neck and wearing shiny, tight pants to be rather disturbing actually, more so as she grew up. Rather, more in the way of articulation and courtship. She fantasized about a boy named Tommy wooing and flirting with her using the lyrics from those songs, singing to her, "I don't need to be the king of the world, as long as I'm a hero of this little girl…" And when they fought, he would win her back by singing to her, "I can still feel so much pain. Like a knife that cuts you the wound heals but the scar, that scar remains."

As she grew up and got older, she still clung on to these ideals in her search for an ideal partner. Largely because it was a romance that she yearned for, the thrill of courtship, being made to feel special, like how these rockers made her feel special, in an age of instant hook-ups that had suffered a terrible loss of the language of love and romance.

An ideal she was hanging on to and she was paying the price for.

# 9.

"**S**awadikaaaa." A melodious wail in Thai reached Alex's ears as he walked out of the claustrophobic confines of the plane and into the cold, grey and spartan Suvarnabhumi Airport in Bangkok, Thailand. He enjoyed the garish and loud traditional costumes the Thai ladies wore as they welcomed him. He loved the way they had their hair up in a high bun as his eyes feasted on the sight of their slender necks and imagined running his wet tongue over their supple necks. But he snapped out of it because he was a man on a mission. A mission that only he knew about. A personal threefold mission where he needed to get over people. He wanted to wash off the bizarre experience with Tabitha and was hoping that Bangkok would have him in her loving arms and make him forget about Tabitha. Most importantly, he wanted to get over Lyna in a way that only he could think of: by suckling on the teat of fleshly pleasure till he was fat and could suckle no more. To fill the emptiness and void that Lyna left in his life. Lastly, he had been going through a fetishistic phase of sexualizing Caucasian backpackers in Asia and wanted to satisfy that fetish. What better place than to stay in the backpacking hub of Bangkok, a place made famous in the movie *The Beach*: Khaosan Road. Something about the carefree, rough and tumble nature of female backpackers appealed to his loins, and he badly wanted to explore this phase he was going through.

Getting out of the airport, the city heat and humidity smacked him in the face and again as he alighted the cab at the dingy, run-down Hostel Overstay. It was a four-storey shophouse on the main Charan Sanit Wong Road that was predictably bustling with traffic and the *tuk-tuks*, the motorised rickshaw, ubiquitous on Bangkok's roads, weaving dangerously in and out of traffic. The hostel itself stood out amidst the greying walls and the rust of urban decay in inner city Bangkok with its brightly coloured walls and its DIY signage. Stepping through the door and into the dark reception, he scanned the area for Yuval, his contact person for the hostel. He rang the bell at reception, which doubled as a bar with a plethora of liquor bottles displayed proudly on the back and a tall, skinny and dreadlocked man stepped out from the back, shirtless and looking like he just woke up, and probably still drunk or high from last night's partying. His pale and pasty skin belied the fact that he was living in a city with one of the highest temperatures in the region, where the scorching sun seared into skin on a normal day. Alex introduced himself, and Yuval grunted and beckoned Alex to follow him up the stairs.

"You room is on the fourth floor; you are going to have to walk up plenty of steps to get there. You okay with that?" Yuval muttered, slightly slurring in his speech.

"Yes, sure, no problem," Alex said, the thought of getting some backpacker pussy still pounding strong in his mind.

They got up the stairs to the second floor where Yuval shared with him that this was the shared dorms, the cheapest accommodation in the joint. Alex realised why it was so because he noticed that it was just an open space with a few bunk beds stacked against windowless walls. The floor was littered with slippers and clothes from the occupants and scattered over worn mattresses. There was a faint odour of sweat and other bodily fluids, which bothered him a little bit. He was glad he didn't go through with his original plan of getting a shared dorm room looking at the nuclear wasteland of a dorm, and he didn't hang around there for long. Yuval and Alex climbed up to the third floor of the hostel, where Yuval told him this was the individual cubicles, and that they were slightly more expensive at two dollars fifty per night.

"Yours is what we call the suite, because it is the biggest room we have, but, seriously, don't expect much at four dollars a night, okay?" Yuval said. "This is your own toilet." Yuval pointed to the closed door, half eaten by moisture. "And this, good sir, is your room," Yuval exclaimed proudly.

Alex walked in and was horrified at what he saw. Yes, the room was large, but only had a single mattress on the floor, which was littered with cigarette butts and ash around it, was bare, and had no sheets to it, and Alex could still see the sweat stains left behind by its former occupant, shuddering at the thought of the kinds of ecosystem that mattress was supporting. The air reeked of sweat and the musk of body odour, mixed with the sharp, dusty smell of cigarette ash, and Alex could feel a coughing fit creeping up and his sinuses acting up. Or was it lung cancer? He wasn't sure. The somewhat nice and avant-grade artwork on the walls brightened the room a little bit but did nothing to ease the worries he started to have about his health and hygiene, and he was starting to have second thoughts about staying there.

Yuval ran out of the room, started screaming at someone next door, and in came a dark and stocky Portuguese man, Arman, with a broom and dustpan. It appeared to be that Arman worked for Yuval and was tasked to clean the room before Alex's arrival but failed to do so. A very apologetic Arman went about to swept the room without a fuss. There was a thin cloud of dust and ash being kicked up in the room as

Arman swept and soon, the room went from being *very* dirty, to just dirty. Alex took the keys from Yuval, closed the door, and sat on the edge of the mattress thinking about what the hell he had gotten himself into.

*For the pussy. Sweet, sweet backpacker pussy.*

He thought to himself and that strengthened his resolve. He put his bag down, remembered that there was a 7-Eleven nearby, went there and got himself several face towels which he used as a bedsheet. *This is going to be a long five days and four nights,* he thought as he wandered around the now deserted fourth floor. He soon stumbled upon a door, ajar, with voices that could be heard behind it. He gingerly pushed the door open and discovered a rooftop balcony. It was dirty, grungy and in a state of disrepair, save for the four plastic chairs and a weather-worn table in the middle of it. The open area was somewhat sheltered, with what looked like fishing nets spread across wooden beams decorated with fairy lights in preparation for a party there tonight. Yuval sat sprawled across the chair, skinny legs like a pair of chopsticks strewn across the table, a rolled-up cigarette resting lazily between his lips and dreadlocks crawling out of his head and hanging menacingly off his shoulders. He peeked out from behind his sunglasses, smiled and said, "Come, friend, sit. Welcome to Overstay."

Alex sat across the table from him, lit a cigarette, and they began talking about Bangkok, the glitz and glamour, the warts and scars. Deep in their conversation, Alex noticed a young blonde woman who came into the balcony and sat with them at the table. She introduced herself as Sara from Newcastle, lit a cigarette and slid seamlessly into the conversation. Alex looked at her and had identified his fetish target. Sara was exactly the kind of woman he was looking for. Fleshy yet sinuous, wearing old, slightly dirty clothes, she strutted around the place in blue rubber slippers. Her wavy blonde locks rested untidily in a bun with a chopstick to hold it in place. She had dusty green eyes that shimmered in the heat, and it appeared to be the only clean and hygienic part about her. There was a thin film of sweat on her skin that was mixed in with the dust hanging in the air, which gave an ominous glow about her. She appeared to be restless and twitchy and was almost constantly swatting away imaginary flies and scratching mosquito bites. That was when Alex noticed how dark residue would be scratched off her skin, and sometimes she would play with and roll it about in between her fingers.

Yuval suddenly got up and excused himself to attend to some matters, leaving Sara and Alex alone together under the barely there shade of the nets. They continued their conversation together and shared travel tips and regaled each other with funny travel stories. Suddenly, Sara stood up and whined, "Man, it is hot out here! I feel so sticky, I'm going to take a bath!"

"Ah okay, right. Well, enjoy!" Alex said, stubbing out his cigarette in the makeshift ashtray made out of a disused carton of milk. He too stood up and wanted to make his way to the bar to get himself a cold beer.

"Where are you going? Stay here, I'm not going anywhere," Sara said.

He shot a quizzical look at her as she pointed to a pail several paces away from the seating area. Alex went over to have a look at it and saw that it was filled with brackish water, and a white towel, blackened by grime and dust, hung off the side of it. Sara picked up the towel, dipped it into the brackish water, gave it a wring and began wiping herself down with the towel that must have been used to wipe the slopes of Mount Doom clean.

"Yeah, this is how I have been bathing myself since I got here two months ago. It saves water and cleans you up real nice," she said happy at the fact she shared a useful pearl of wisdom to a fellow traveller.

Alex smiled through gritted teeth as he felt his skin crawl. He winced at the sight of the brackish trails of water that rolled off her skin and internally cringed when he saw Sara wiping her armpits and inner thighs with the towel from Hell.

"Excuse me, I am going to the bar and get myself a cold one, can I get you anything? A clean wet wipe maybe," he said.

"Haha, no thanks, I'm alright. I'm leaving to go have vegan porridge nearby, you wanna come with us?" she asked.

"No thanks, I'm alright for now," he said, knowing that any food he consumed at that point would be churning in his belly and come right back out. "I have a massage appointment soon anyway. But, I'll see you at the party downstairs tonight?"

"Yes! I'll be there. Cool! I'll see you at the dance floor and we will tear it up good," she said with a twinkle in her eyes.

"Excellent," he said as he went indoors, itching for a long, cold, cleansing shower. He went back to his room, fished out his towel and went to his "private" bathroom. It was like stepping into a seedy red light district after a monsoon – there were puddles on the blackened floor that felt like pudding on his bare feet. And he swore he saw something furry scurry away as he opened the door. There wasn't proper lighting, and the only source of light came from an exposed red light bulb hanging off a wire. His eyes adjusted to the dimly lit bathroom and saw what he thought was a bathtub. But it looked like a swamp with unearthly creatures threatening to pull you in and kill you slowly with their awful stench and a blood infection. The shower head was in the form of a rubber hose hanging off a hole in the wall, attached to a pipe in the wall.

For the second time that day, he found himself questioning his choices on this trip. But he repeated his mantra, *backpacker pussy, sweet backpacker pussy*, several times and pushed through. No, he could not take a full on shower, but he washed his face and body. But soon he had to leave the place to explore more of Bangkok that he liked. He reminded himself that the party started at 9 p.m., so he needed to be back at Hostel Hell by then and to prepare for some party loving. Alex walked out of the hole, took a thirty-minute cab ride through the heavy Bangkok traffic and went to the gym for a long, cleansing shower. He felt like a weight had been lifted off his shoulders and his hair as he left lighter and raring to reap what the sprawling urban mass had to offer him. He took in the sights and sounds of the city, but Sara was always at the back of his head as he rehearsed what to say, when to say it and how to say the things that would take him on a glorious odyssey into her dirty pants. He took a walk down the street to the main tourist strip and went in a bar for a drink to escape the heat and humidity. He tried to get in touch with Olivia, a woman he fucked some time ago who lived in the city, but he got her voicemail instead. He sat back, enjoyed his cold pint of Heineken beer and went through his game plan.

However, his mind distracted itself with an encounter he had at the airport before he checked into his flight. He had been passing some time at Starbucks when a couple sat at the next table, obviously on a date. He had noticed the woman: beautiful, confident, self-assured to the point of being intimidating, and cool as ice. He had loved the way she smelled as he unsubtly walked by her and sniffed the air around her. Alex hung around a lot longer than he should around the couple of strangers. He had been in love with the perfume she wore, and it got him to spend more time than usual at the duty-free shops looking for the scent. He found out that it was Chanel's Mademoiselle. She had long wavy hair tied tight in a ponytail, but what he had noticed most were the veins that popped up on her hands and arms that crawled over her limbs. He had also noticed her slightly deep voice, and her articulation that hinted at a certain class she possessed. Another thing he noticed about the woman was how he had managed to catch her humming what sounded to him was a Scorpions song, a very familiar song he grew up listening to, which he thought was interesting. She had been with some forgettable guy, and he thought briefly that he would be a better companion to her than that loser could ever imagine. He couldn't understand why he was thinking about the stranger, maybe it was the perfume, or could be the song. But he enjoyed the distraction nevertheless.

Alex finished his beer and resumed his trek around the city, went into shopping malls, took more cab and *tuk-tuk* rides, stopped by temples and shrines, spoke to tattoo artists about the different ideas of tattoos he had been thinking of getting done, bought souvenirs for some of his closer colleagues, went to the tailors and got himself measured and picked out fabrics for a suit he been planning to get and ended his day walking around looking for a massage parlour his friend Ian recommended him to try out. He found the place, but his choice of masseuse wasn't working that day, so he decided to come again the next day. He had his mind on the party at Hostel Hellhole all day and it was all that he could think of. *Backpacker pussy, sweet backpacker pussy.* With a handful of shopping bags in tow, and a fitting date to be had in two days' time, he sauntered around the shopping district alone, occasionally fending off a transsexual street walker who wanted to spend time with him for a price, before deciding to go back to the gym for a shower to wash off the city grime for the party later that night.

Soon enough, it was half past eight at night, and Alex was too tired of hanging around the city not doing much. He took a cab and made his way back to Hostel Mordor buzzing with anticipation for the party. With the city traffic, he made it back to the hostel in an hour and the party was just starting, with several backpackers sitting amongst themselves in the dark. Yuval enthusiastically welcomed him back and bought him beer, drank straight from the bottle and insisted he "have lots of fun tonight."

And Alex did! He met the other occupants of the hostel, shared beers with them, took happy party photos, danced to sludgy and grimy trip-hop beats, before noticing Sara cutting a lonely figure by the bar. She was wearing a different top from earlier that day, and he could see that she wasn't wearing a bra. Her breasts, held up by her tight, canary-yellow top seemed to be nestled comfortably together, nipples poking out from underneath her clothes. She was drinking beer straight from the large one and a half litre bottle, which he thought was very sexy. He loved the way her lips pursed and pouted as she swallowed the beer. And the way she drank from the bottle, how she would put the entire opening of the bottle into her mouth, Alex wished that he was that bottle. Time to get his move on, and he sidled up to her, said hello, bought her a beer and clinked bottles together. Soon, after what seemed to be a lifetime, he invited her to the dance floor, and they were soon dancing together, getting dangerously close to each other, and made flirty advances to each other. Alex had his arms around her waist and took a whiff of her backpacker musk. It was not as pleasant as he thought it would be, but the thought of pussy overwhelmed everything. One flirty thing led to another, and soon it got physical and they were making out on the dance floor, being bumped about by the dancing crowd that was forming that night. It was starting to get a little bit uncomfortable and claustrophobic for the lovebirds, so Sara invited him to a quieter place to enjoy each other.

Both scurried up the stairs past the shared dorms and up to her cubicle. She locked the padlock behind her as Alex lay down on the grimy mattress on the floor and waited. "Well, here we are, Mister. What would you like me to do?" Sara purred.

Alex stood up, pulled her in close, kissed her deeply, with hands roughly caressing her body and whispered in her ear as he gently bit into it, "Take off your clothes. Slowly. Sexily. Tease me." Sara pushed him back to sit on the mattress and began to slowly peel off her clothes. She danced like a cobra under the spell of a charmer, the sinews of skin and flesh glistening in the orange light. She turned away from Alex as she pulled off her top, painfully slow, in time to the beats in her head. Alex noticed and counted the moles on her back like a connect-the-dots game and planned to trace them with his mouth and tongue. She threw her top at him, and he held it up close to his nose and took a long whiff. It smelled like fresh laundry. *That's a good sign.* Alex drank the sight of a topless Sara in front of him, flesh writhing in pleasure in a room heated by lust. His erection visible through his shorts, he began to touch himself, but had his hand smacked away by Sara.

"No no no," she moaned. "Tonight, that will be my job to do," she said with a cheeky smile. He wanted to get naked, but Sara stopped him and said, "That, too, is my job for tonight." Swirling in excitement and lust, Alex could barely keep his boner in his pants but held on to his horses.

Sara peeled off her shorts and threw it in his face, and again, he took a whiff, but something about it made him nauseous and gag. It was a smell that did not belong on a pair of shorts worn by a sexy little minx like Sara. But maybe it was not laundered properly, so he let it slide. He playfully bit into her shorts and held it in his mouth so that it prompted a playful giggle from Sara. Now in just her white panties, she teased him even more by giving him quick glimpses of her womanhood and her chocolate starfish. Time seemed to have frozen in its tracks as he felt the excruciating longing to ravage her in many an indecent way he could think of. He was grabbing the edges of the mattress as Sara teased him mercilessly, touching him with her dirty feet, running her breath along his ears and neck, and putting her breasts up close to his face. That familiar body odour came rushing into his nostrils and again he had to suppress his gag reflex. Sara then took a step back, turned around, and slowly pulled off her panties, exposing her perky butt to him. She turned around and threw her underwear into his face. It was such a hot thing for him to be at the end of; he caught the underwear with his mouth and playfully wiped his face with it. He took a whiff of the underwear, and that was where his gag reflex could hold no more. As much as he tried to suppress it, he could feel that he vomited a little bit in his mouth because the smell of stale sweat, urine and faeces combined to give out a strong, smoky odour. Smoky. Like the smell of burnt flesh being left out in the tropical humidity for days. He pulled the underwear off his face and took a close look at it, and what he saw killed his erection immediately.

He saw skid marks. Not just one skid mark, but several. There was one big one, as well as several other small ones that combined into another large, brownish skid mark. It was as if the purity of white had been horribly defiled by her lackadaisical approach to genital hygiene that was later involved in a horrible car crash that left a human stain on the road that could never be washed off. He didn't know what could have caused it at the time but soon realised that it was largely due to her suspicious hygiene habits as he took it to his nose and sniffed it. She obviously didn't wash nor wipe herself properly after going to pee or take a dump. Nor did she clean herself of her menses as well as she should. So, it was a combination of faeces, menstrual blood and urine, all of which came together like a meaty stain. He forced a smile to disguise the sheer horror and disgust he felt. And to think he wiped his face with that underwear and had it in his mouth to boot!

Alex looked up at her and saw nothing but a thick, wild tuft of pubic hair coming menacingly close to his face, and he imagined the habitat that the forest could be supporting with the amount of moisture and waste accumulating there. Sara grabbed the back of his head and pushed his face into her pussy and began to grind hard on his nose. He could not decide whether he couldn't breathe or that he was holding his breath for fear of vomiting right then and there into her womanhood. She then turned so that her ass was facing him and again, grabbed the back of his head and began to grind her anus on his face.

*This is it. This is how I am going to die. With a dirty anus in my mouth and the infectious disease that will come from it.*

But Tabitha came into mind, and he figured if she could do it, why not him? He willed his tongue to slide out of his mouth to lick her ass, and she gasped in pleasure as he did so. But he just could not continue doing it for fear of diarrhoea as images of Ebola, cholera, shingles, salmonella and hepatitis began playing on a loop in his mind. He pulled his face away from her ass and lay on his back in a state of shock. Sara stopped, turned to look at him and asked, "What's wrong? Is everything okay?"

"Yeah, everything's fine, just that I have been taking some antibiotics for a viral infection I had last week, and it is not reacting well with the beers I had all day," he said, half impressed with the excuse he came up with.

"Well then, you just sit back and let me fire up this bad boy," she said as she kissed his mouth, that by now, smelled like ass.

Her ass.

He sat back and let Sara start work at getting his shorts off and gave him a nice, long, slow blow job. She worked her mouth and tongue well, and it was a matter of minutes before his rock hard boner came back, and all was good in his world. But another thought came rushing into his head. The thought of having his dick not just up close to, but inside her pussy, reverberated through his body like a lightning bolt from the god of lightning himself. So in order to kill his erection, Alex began distracting himself by sniffing her underwear, thinking about his friend Ian, thinking about the slobbering mess that was his boss and the heat he had been giving him the past few weeks, and true to form, his erection softened to a halfie. Sara however, like a true sex trooper that she was, kept going at his dick like it was a lollipop. It was hard work to not get aroused by her soft, wet mouth on his testicles, her tongue and lips going up and down his shaft, but the prospect of fucking that filthy pussy was enough to make him work that hard too. Alex pulled her off his penis and said, "I don't think this is happening. The beer is churning in my stomach and I can feel it coming up. I am so sorry, I don't feel too good," he said as he got up to put his pants back on.

Sara's face was now a mask of disappointment, and she refused to even look at him, getting up to put her clothes back on. Alex ran out of her cubicle, up to his "suite" and with no care nor dignity left in his world, crashed into the filthy mattress he had in his room and wished to be swallowed by a hole in the ground. It had been clear that this was an ill-advised trip, but he let his penis dictate his entire itinerary and he swore he could feel the universe and its minions laughing maniacally at him. All he wanted right now was to be in Lyna's arms and be comforted by her. In tough times, or in times of doubt, Lyna always popped into his head, and the image always comforted him, and in foul weather times like these, he needed his foul-weather friend to be with him. And it was as if the universe heard his anguished cry for help – his phone rang, leaving him no time to wallow in his poor choices, and it was Olivia who wanted to come see him for the night. Alex was beside himself in joy as he listened to the sound of her voice, and her sing-song twang of Thai-accented English. He called her over to get him from Hostel Shithole, and she came waltzing in within half an hour.

She showed up in a white shirt, denim skirt, heels and a Prada bag slung over her shoulder. It was as if an angel came to life from the centrefold of a fashion magazine, and in a place filled with filthy, broke, drug-fuelled backpackers, she stood out and everyone seem to be frozen in awe of her presence. Her bright brown hair lit up the entire room as she looked and judged each and every person in there for the poor choices they made in coming to and staying at this part of the neighbourhood.

"So fast?" Alex exclaimed.

"Because I live very near na," she said as she hugged him.

Alex brought her up to his room and immediately, Olivia took a step back, looked around the wasteland that was the "suite," cringed, and began to yell at him.

"Darling, why you live like this? I know you are not poor, you have money, you have good job. So why you like this? Me, I am not rich, yes, but I cannot live like this, because I respect myself. Why do you choose to live like this? You no respect yourself, ah?"

Alex felt like he was in primary school once again, being yelled at by Miss Janet D'Silva for walking into the classrooms with filthy shoes from playing catch in the school field. Embarrassed by this, Alex looked down at the sordid floor, now littered with cigarette butts and ash mixed with pieces of his self-worth and self-respect.

"Pack your things, come, you stay with me for a while, okay, darling?" Olivia said as she began to pick his things up off the floor and placing it into his bag.

Olivia was an older woman who worked as a Thai amulet saleswoman. She travelled all over the region hawking her company's wares, which she claimed were blessed by celebrity monks and forged through fire in India and Tibet. In a region still steeped in superstition and mysticism, despite its enormous economic successes over the decades, amulets filled with corpse oils, when properly marketed, could still sell like iced water deep in the Sahara Desert. Alex had met her in a bar some time ago and hit it off, because she was a lonely business traveller on the road for three to six months on end, while he still missed Lyna and was convinced he had found a clone of her in Olivia. She possessed the same headstrong badassery and drive coupled with a deep sarcasm and wit that could slice her victim to unrecognisable strips of flesh and bone. She just did it in a different accent and language than Lyna. Even her orgasms were similar to Lyna, with the deep, guttural growl and gasps followed by visible muscle spasms as she exploded into a glorious mound of quivering flesh.

But fucking her was the last thing on Alex's mind right now as all he wanted to do was to take a long, hot shower in a clean bathroom, wash himself down with an exfoliating body scrub, shampoo and condition his hair with something that smelled like fruit, take a dump on a pristine, alabaster toilet with angels washing and wiping his ass for him with moist towelettes made of silk.

Better still if there was someone to do it for him.

He communicated that to Olivia, who frowned and said, "Darling, I'd love to, but my boyfriend will be back in Bangkok day after tomorrow, so you cannot stay for long. And I have work tomorrow, so you are going to have to find another place by tomorrow, okay? Don't worry, I know a good, clean place for you, cheap cheap."

They soon arrived at her studio apartment, which was as big as his "suite" at Hostel Shithole. But it was clean, very clean. The plain white walls made it look like it was a sterile field with no contagions, and Alex couldn't even feel the tiniest layer of dust on her cement screed floor. Olivia took pains to be obsessively clean with her living space and as a result, he could eat anything off the floor at her place.

"Wait, what? You have a boyfriend? Since when?" Alex queried her as he sat on her couch.

Olivia, who had been pouring for Alex a glass of whiskey and cracking open a bottle of Chang beer for herself, replied as she served the drink and sat next to him, "After we make love that time, you say you no looking for serious girlfriend. I like you, darling, very much, and it hurts me when you say that. But I have to respect what you said because that's how you are, what you feel. I tell you now that I was looking for serious partner and thought you could be one. And then you say that, so I cannot wait you for so long. You very nice man, you good man with good heart. But I think your heart is not here. Your heart is not with you. I think your heart is with someone else, someone very close to you, but also very far away from you."

Alex stared into his whiskey, dumbfounded at Olivia's astute observation and instincts about his state. He sat on the couch in silence, swirling the whiskey in the glass, swimming in his own thoughts, his boner and lust long dissipated, and he was in a daze. In his head, he had the vision of Lyna rolling around in a field wearing her favourite maxi dress, the one he liked to have reaching her ankles. She turned to look at him with her flaming red lips in a smile brighter than a thousand suns, her blonde locks flipping nonchalantly in the breeze. She sat back, propping her body up with her hands on the ground behind her, and continued to smile without saying a word. He tried to crack a smile but found nothing to make him do so. There were no words, with nary a grunt nor a sigh that could help alleviate this shit stain of a situation to one that he could chew on, swallow and digest. The truck that crashed into his emotional state kept rolling on, dragging his mangled body with it along the road. And the saddest part of it for him was that the truck driver didn't care and that there was no one that was horrified by it. There was no one running after the truck screaming for it to stop and no one to be inflamed with rage and swearing vengeance at the truck driver. He had died, horribly, alone in a strange place along a lonesome road where no one would find his body and throw a funeral for him, and most depressingly, where no one would miss him.

Olivia patted his head and ruffled his hair sympathetically, knowing that she had dealt him a sledgehammer blow that might take him a while to recover from. A blow that he needed, but ultimately not one that she wanted to clean up after. She chugged her beer, got to her feet, changed into her pyjamas and got ready for bed. She rubbed moisturizer all over her skin, an act that would normally induce an erection in Alex, coupled with seeing a naked Olivia, but there was nothing. Not a stir in his loins, no flames ignited.

"Tonight, you sleep here, okay, but tomorrow you have to go. I start work at ten a.m., so I can help you in the morning to look for a new, better place. We eat first, then we go out, so you no need unpack your things. You can use some of my boyfriend's things just for the night," she said with a very clinical tone. Cold, if you were not aware of the subtle nuances of Alex and Olivia. He got up and went into the bathroom and took a long shower, cleaning every corner and crevice of his body. As the warm water ran over his body, Alex was looking for the feeling of being cleansed, but there could never be enough water in Thailand nor the world that could clean the way he was feeling about himself. He crouched in the corner of the shower with the water from the shower head pounding on his head and skin and went to his happy place, the rolling field basking in the sun with Lyna.

But even that had no longer become his happy place.

# 10.

---

**S**wipe left. Swipe, swipe left. Oh hell no, I will swipe the shit out of that to the left.

*Oh, he's cute. Okay, swipe right.*

"You got a match. You matched with Norman, have no fear, Tinder is here." The message splashed across her mobile phone screen.

*Meh, I'll wait. Keep swiping.*

*Urgh, left. No way, swipe left. Fuck! Left! Left. Left! Why are there so many losers on this app?*

*Oh, he's alright. Swipe right.*

"You matched with Andy, you'll never meet 100% of the matches you don't message," the app screamed at her.

"Hi, Carol, sorry I'm late!" a very flustered Charmaine said. "Traffic was so bad and it is so damn hot outside! The three minutes it took for me to walk from the carpark, I can already feel sweat rolling down my ass crack!"

"It's okay, I've been entertaining myself with this Tinder app my colleagues have been telling me to get," Carol said as she logged out of the app and put her phone away.

"Well, let me see!" Charmaine squealed.

They spent the next forty minutes talking about, laughing at and ogling the men on offer in the app on the tiny screen of her smartphone. As weird as Carol found that to be, she was also wildly entertained by this. As they debated the merits of the male prospects' photo filter, camera angles and sartorial choices, her phone kept beeping, sending notifications of messages she received from the matches she made on the app.

With Charmaine's help, she navigated to her inbox messages and discovered that she had received over ten messages from the matches she had ignored for the past hour or so. Nine of which said, "Hi," which turned her off mightily.

*You want to get my attention, you so have to do better than just say hi.*

*I am not expecting you to message me like Sartre writing to Simone, nor the Peter Cetera or Jani Lane level of message, but put some effort in it, for fuck's sakes!*

So Charmaine taught her how to 'unmatch' with them. And she went on to read the last match of the day's message, and he appeared to be quite interesting. It was written by a Lawrence, who appeared to be a sun-kissed fisherman in his display picture. The message read, "Well hello there, match number 25454654. Yes, that is the amount of matches I have had, all of whom never replied to me. So this is what caution to the wind sounds like. I am a short defence analyst riding on my noble steed into your mailbox to say hello, and I hope to hear from you soon, even if it's to tell me to bite someone else's ankles. Have a good one."

Carol chuckled at the message and quite liked the self-deprecating tone of the message and replied to Lawrence. He seemed to be quick on the draw, as Lawrence replied to her message almost instantly, and Carol felt bad burying her face in her phone with Charmaine taking pains to make plans to catch up with her at their favourite cafe in the city. So she put her phone in her bag, dating out of her mind, and began to be present for her dear friend Charmaine. But try as she might, the app was scratching and constantly gnawing at the back of her head, and she felt an almost insatiable need to check her smartphone. Thankfully, she was able to resist all temptation emanating from the smartphone buried deep in her bag, and their lunch meeting went by swimmingly. After Charmaine left, Carol hung around the cafe for a while longer to read and reply to Lawrence's message.

With her phone connected to a fully-charged power bank, she sat there, alone, face buried deep in her smartphone, exchanging small talk with Lawrence. She had wanted to come across to him surrounded by an air of enigmatic mystery, but Lawrence seemed to be one who liked to cut to the chase and ask her probing questions, even in their initial exchange of messages.

"So, are you close with your parents?"

"Do you like a guy who is organised, systematic and plans for everything, or a guy who lives off the cuff?"

"Do you prefer morning wake-up sex or night time got-to-sleep sex?"

"Do you have plans to get married, have kids and settle down?"

*What the hell is this, an interrogation?*

'Do you prefer a beach holiday destination or a big city holiday destination?"

"Are you good at talking and communicating with old people?"

*Oh my god, why is he asking so many questions?*

He even answered Carol's question about him with a question! Nevertheless, Carol managed to stay engaged in this weird twenty-first century digital flirting to the point that, when she finally got her face out of her phone, she discovered that the sun was setting and her coffee was cold with a thin layer of dried, brown, milky gunk having formed on the surface. She was surprised that the staff left her be instead of kicking her out. But as she looked around the cafe, she saw how almost everyone, even those in the company of friends sitting at the same table, had their faces buried in their smartphones and randomly smiling or giggling, so it must not have been out of the ordinary for the staff. The irony of this was how she used to laugh and judge those who did that, and now she had become one of the zombie horde walking around plugged into their devices, oblivious to the glory that was life unfolding around them. Carol gestured for the bill, which she discovered was already taken care of by Charmaine, so she straightened herself up to leave the cafe. As she walked out, she fished out her mobile phone and saw that Lawrence had replied to her earlier message, and she excitedly logged on to the app to read the message. Face in her phone, with both hands holding it up, she almost walked into a pillar and in the wrong direction. She laughed at herself and came to her senses as she put her phone back into her bag, corrected her posture and began to strut toward the taxi stand. She took her time to have a look around,; with the water up ahead, the area was a hub of entertainment and merriment with pubs, restaurants and cafes lining the waterfront. The bright city lights danced against the backdrop of the darkness of the night sky. It was like a battle between good and evil, of darkness and light, played out on the city skyline as Carol battled her own desire to withdraw from the life around her and to slip back into the confines of the smartphone apps and her budding conversation with Lawrence.

*Okay, I'll just find myself a place to sit for a bit and answer his ONE message.*

She sat on a stone bench on the banks of Singapore River, oblivious to the revelry of life that passed her by, as she gave her undivided attention to her smartphone and in sending and replying messages to Lawrence.

*Damn, he is a nosy fucker. What is with all the questions?*

*Are all defence analysts this inquisitive?*

*Maybe it's a job hazard; he needs to know lots of information before he can, you know, analyse shit.*

"Where would be your next, ideal holiday destination?"

"Are you a cat person or a dog person?"

"What are your views about the current political climate?"

"Do you believe that our country is a democracy or a guided democracy?"

The questions came in thick and fast, and Carol felt like she was being interrogated by her phone. After almost an hour sitting on the cold, stone bench, her bum began to ache and she could feel her left leg falling asleep on her.

So she quickly typed out a reply to Lawrence: "Look, I am not good in this messaging thing, for I prefer to communicate in person, so how about this, we meet for coffee tomorrow at the airport terminal three, Starbucks 3 p.m., and you can ask all the questions you want, and I, too, can batter you with questions on my own about you. Okay? So I'll see you tomorrow then."

Lawrence replied in two minutes with a, "Kay *smiley face* *thumbs up* *beating heart*."

Carol rolled her eyes at his attempt to be cute but ultimately let it go because she was excited to dip her feet into smartphone dating and hooking up.

*Technically, this is a blind date, right?*

*I haven't had a blind date since I was 17! Maybe he will turn out okay. Or at least has a big dick.*

She cringed as she was reminded of the horrible time he had with Khairul's Tic Tac dick.

*Okay, let's not have a repeat of that.*

*Stop thinking about it, otherwise the universe will make him appear!*

*And I have no strength to deal with THAT fallout.*

In haste, Carol got up and made a beeline for the taxi stand, boarded the cab and went home, for fear of bumping into Khairul. When she arrived home, she drew a bath, poured herself a glass of wine, and chilled the rest of the evening, semi-excited about her date tomorrow.

The next day, a casually dressed Carol rocked up to Changi Airport Terminal 2 Starbucks ten minutes early for her date. She was wearing a loose fitted, slightly sheer, burgundy chiffon V-neck blouse with short, ruffled batwing sleeves, and seasoned denim jeans. She liberally spritzed herself with Chanel's Mademoiselle, put on minimal war paint, lipstick matching her blouse, and slipped into her matching leather flats, grabbed her handbag and went to the airport. She might have turned a few heads on the way there, and the taxi driver audibly gulped every time she "tsk-ed" in annoyance at her phone or gave him directions. She arrived at Starbucks, ordered her black coffee and found a table right by the entrance where she could see Lawrence coming up as well as gaze at the human traffic going by the cafe. Leaning forward, an elbow on the table as she rested her chin on her fists, she waited. Drumming her fingers, with a slight scowl on her face as the bitterness of the coffee hit her, she looked like someone with a score to settle.

*He's late. Five minutes. But still late.*

*What the hell am I thinking?*

*Why did I even bother to dress up?*

*Well, this is not technically dressing up, actually.*

*But still, effort was put in to look nonchalant.*

*Not like he will notice it. Not at first anyway.*

*And he is still not here.*

*Alright, I give him ten minutes before I walk.*

Just as she said that, a man with a bright, cheery face, and an easy smile gingerly approached her and said, "Hi, I am Lawrence, you must be Carol?"

"Yes, I am Carol, and you, Lawrence, are late," she said, almost dripping with venom.

"Sorry sorry, I couldn't find a slot in the carpark," he said apologetically.

*Why does he speak like my teenage cousins?*

*What is he, nineteen?*

"Come, I buy you drink, to say sorry."

"You already said sorry, Lawrence, and no thanks, I already have my own drink. So quickly, get yourself a drink," she said, this time making a concerted effort to sound less snarky.

Lawrence looked much older than he did in his display picture. There was a sliver of white hair parting his head, which made him look like an awkward Pepé Le Pew. He appeared skinny, but with a slight paunch, which he tried his very best to minimise by sucking it in. With brown, sun-kissed skin that glistened in the bright light, Carol caught a whiff of sunblock as he came near. The clincher was that he wore a red sports jersey, which she abhorred on men, with black denim pants and running shoes. Carol was already dreading the meet-up. No longer was it a date for her.

*Damn, what have I gotten myself into now?*

*Why is he dressed like he's going to the shops to get groceries?*

*Maybe he thinks this is how men should be dressing up on a date?*

*At least put in SOME effort, for fuck's sake!*

Lawrence soon came scurrying back with a plastic cup of coffee with whipped cream.

*Can't even get a proper man drink, huh?*

Carol was already judging him to hell for his language, sartorial decisions and choice of beverage. But she didn't want to get all dressed up for nothing, so Carol entertained Lawrence and his Socratic approach to dating – asking her questions – while she spaced out and didn't even bother to try to conceal her disdain for the date. Resting her cheeks in the palm of her hand, she sat back and tried to be as evasive as she could when it came to answering his questions. But, in the corner of her eye, she noticed someone looking at her. Not a glance, but someone drinking in the sight of her. She glanced briefly to see a man in a maroon short-sleeved shirt, sleeves folded up to reveal the taut biceps almost screaming to be released from the grip. He wore brown khaki pants, with a matching belt and Doc Marten boots. He looked normal, and he did not stand out in the crowd, but there was something about him that invoked in her a familiar sensation. A sensation she recalled from years ago when she listened to and hummed the tune of Scorpions' 'Still Loving You' repeatedly.

*He's cute as a button. And built like a brickshit house. Carol like.*

Their eyes met. Briefly, before Carol, being uncharacteristically demure, broke eye contact and looked down.

*What was that, Carol? Did you just submit?*

*Well, at least he is much better dressed than this Lawrence man-child.*

*I like that look too, all matchy but not too much of an effeminate clothes horse.*

*Haha, he looks like he's making love to that cup as he looks my way. Kinda hot, to be honest.*

Lawrence had excused himself to go to the men's room as she snapped out of her own headspace with that mysterious but plainfully beautiful stranger. Her eyes searched for him when Lawrence was gone, strangely drawn to that man like a shark, drawn to a drop of blood in the vast ocean, as she began to hum Scorpions' tune.

*Oh, he's coming over.*

*Wait, is he?*

The man sauntered toward and then past Carol and appeared to take a strong whiff of the air, eyes half closed and let out a soft but audible sigh.

*Did he just sniff me?*

*Hahaha, what a loser!*

Carol then noticed him hanging around, a lot closer to where she was seated, and a lot longer than any stranger should in the situation. She smiled at herself and continued to hum the song in a concerted effort to project an image of nonchalance. That stranger, obviously pretending to be uninterested in her, leaned against the rails that separated the Starbucks from the main public area for what appeared to be an eternity in a second. Their eyes met again, he smiled, she smiled as well, and looked away. It was a moment in time that froze, yet fleeting, because it appeared that he was beginning to realise how creepy that could be and soon rushed off to the departure gates.

*Wait, why did you run, you idiot!*

*You stupid matchy-matchy idiot.*

Lawrence came back as Carol lost sight of that mysterious loser. "Hungry, let's go to eat, okay?

*Go to eat. Urgh.*

"Yeah, sure, let's just go to the bar upstairs near the lounge, okay?"

They got to the bar in a jiffy, ordered their food, and ate together, almost in silence. Carol no longer was in the mood to entertain this road accident of a date and was drifting in and out of her thoughts. She wolfed down her food in record time, just so she would spend less time with Lawrence. Meal was done, and Lawrence asked, "How was the meal?"

"It was alright," a very nonplussed Carol replied.

Lawrence then took out a laptop from his bag, and said, "Okay, I am going to book air tickets for us to go on holiday to New Zealand, okay? I have set aside the month of November for us to travel together. You okay with premium economy seats, ah?"

"Wait, what?" Carol protested as she choked through her thinly veiled disbelief.

Lawrence turned the laptop to show her a PowerPoint presentation with forty-seven slides of a very detailed itinerary involving the two of them in New Zealand, right down to what time they had to be up in the morning, and what time they would have to sleep, and even when would be the window in which they could have sex together! There were images attached, an Excel sheet to track both their expenses, and web references to sites for car rentals, train tickets as well as five choices for accommodation, ranked by user reviews and price per night. It felt like sitting through a sales presentation with Lawrence rambling on about the facts of the vacation, as well as the pros and cons of travelling together, and how the pros outweigh the cons in this case. Carol was just too shocked for words and was left there, incredulous, mouth agape, hands shaking in anger with a touch of fear.

Before Lawrence could finish, Carol finally found her tongue and almost hysterically screamed at him in disbelief, "You planned an entire holiday for the two of us even before we met? What the fuck did you think, I was going to say yes, I'll go on a holiday with a total stranger? And you are asking me on that holiday on *our first meeting together*, after just a couple of hours barely talking to each other? Bloody hell! We haven't even had dessert yet!"

"Ah, I see," he said, and without much expression, proceeded to order a slice of tiramisu cake for her and a slice of apple strudel for himself. Carol was still beyond outrage, eyes widened in anger and disbelief, seething with white hot rage to the point of speechlessness as the waiter placed the morsels of dessert on their table. He went on and on still, oblivious to her rage, about how New Zealand was the perfect holiday getaway for the two of them because it allowed them to spend quality time getting to know each other as he inhaled his apple strudel and asked if she wanted to eat her tiramisu. It took every ounce of her strength, patience and humanity to not fling herself over the table and rain punches on his stupid, smug face, right after poking her thumbs into his eyes. With an almighty scowl on her face, she shook her head, and Lawrence took her plate and inhaled the cake as well.

And then he said, "Alright, we already ate dessert. *Now*, can we talk about the holiday?"

Carol punched the table, drawing the attention of the other customers at the restaurant and yelled, "Are you fucking kidding me?"

"Yeah, first you said we haven't even had dessert, now we eat already, so now we can talk about the holiday," he protested.

"Hell fucking *no!* I am at a loss for words at how you can think this is a good idea, really. Who the fuck does this?" she said.

"Because you are a modern woman, right? All you modern women are the same, right? Because all they want are long holidays, more money and all want sex, right? Well, okay. Okay. If no holiday trip, then how about sex? After this, okay? I have to settle a few things first at work, but let's make another date for eight p.m. tonight, Fragrance Hotel down Sims Street. You know the place, right? Of course you know, you must've been there many times with your toy boys and your party boys. You get the room first, text me the room number, then I go see you. Okay?" he brazenly suggested, as if this was a very normal thing to ask a woman who had just rejected his advances.

Carol laughed in sheer and utter disbelief at his vile and offensive drivel about the modern woman. Somehow, she just did not have the strength to combat this kind of madness, so she stood up, flipped the table, and walked away from that abortion of a first date. She did not even bother looking back to answer Lawrence's yelping of her name. As far as she was concerned, she was never seeing him again, not even in Hell. She was never going to that restaurant ever again, nor was she ever going back to that damned dating app. She felt like the universe just poured pig's blood on her and got all its gods and angels to point and laugh at her in a bizarre, celestial, Carrie-like scene and wished that she actually had Carrie's telekinesis, and with the mood she was in, she would will the entire world to spontaneously combust, killing every living soul in hell fire as hot as her rage. She whipped out her smartphone, deleted her app, blocked and deleted Lawrence's contact and stuffed it back into her bag. Consumed by wrath, any normal human being would either be overwhelmed by emotions or vengeance like a snake coiling up in the body, constricting their souls till all they could see and breathe was vengeance.

But she was not any normal human being.

She was Carol.

She maintained her ice cool demeanour as she strutted around the airport, hoping to walk off that stench of a bad date, to kill that sinking feeling in her chest that threatened to pull her into depths unknown to her. She needed to wash off that sour taste in her mouth that occurred every time something bad happened to her. However, whenever a cataclysm such as this happened, Carol refused to take it tragically and live among the ruins and build new habitats. The sky might have fallen on her, but that just meant she got another chance to live in the clouds.

Nevertheless, at this point, all the world seemed to merge into a blur of out-of-focus photographs flapping in the wind, almost at random, yet in tandem to some silent symphony of the universe. Sometimes in moments of loss, that was when you found your true self, and in moments of chaos was where you found true peace and serenity. In moments of obscurity, that was when one found clarity. And it was at this point where she received some clarity of thought.

She knew something needed to be done.

She was also looking for something.

*A cigarette maybe, or a shot of whiskey.*

But it was more like someone, a *who*, that she was looking for.

And as strange as she found it, it was inexplicable that she was looking for someone who was but a speck of dust accidentally blown onto the thread of her universe.

That stranger with the biceps.

The man who looked painfully normal.

That man who surreptitiously sniffed her as he walked past her at Starbucks.

The man with the matching belt and shoes.

The man who made her hum the song 'Still Loving You.'

# 11.

"Take about half an inch off the shoulders, please. And another half an inch off the thighs as well, I want this suit to look sleek and sharp and not like as if I am wearing armour. And can I change the fabric for the shirt as well? I look like a cow wearing that," Alex barked at the tailors taking his second fitting. He always got suited up when he was in Bangkok because it was much cheaper to get a good one there, and they could get it done in three days to boot.

"You must have lost weight since we last measured you," Paul the tailor said in jest.

"Yeah, I must have. It's either that or you have slacked off in your craftsmanship this time round," Alex said bluntly.

Paul laughed it off and went about his duty as a self-professed world class tailor in Bangkok, made markings on the fabric, and muttered instructions in Thai to his bevy of assistants. He could be cursing him for all he cared, but Alex didn't care. He enjoyed the attention paid to him by these craftsmen. And mostly, he enjoyed the end product of a unique and very sharp suit that he would show off in school. As self-effacing as he tried to be, he was prone to bouts of brash inhibition that either got him laid, or, more often than not, in trouble. But there, at the tailors, his phone kept making notification sounds, a sound he had never heard before, but he ignored it and went about his affairs.

Once he was done at the tailors at the Amari Watergate Hotel, Alex went downstairs to the lobby to take advantage of the free hotel Wi-Fi to send out a few messages and to plan his next route. He was reminded of the notifications he apparently received while getting suited and went on his smartphone to figure out who or what had been sending him those messages. Sitting on a very comfy sofa, leaning back and legs crossed to look like a customer of the hotel, he soon figured out that they were WeChat notifications. WeChat, the Chinese version of WhatsApp, Facebook and Instagram. He had downloaded the app because he had heard that it could be a Tinder of sorts where he could meet and hook-up with like-minded women, and he did love his women. So he opened the app and saw that he had received thirteen messages, all from gorgeous looking women. Excited at the thought of him being a WeChat stud, he replied to all of them and spent the next ten minutes hunkered down in the corner of the sofa replying to the messages he received. He wouldn't mind a date with a local girl there, especially a gorgeous one, to take his mind off his most recent, very disgusting backpacker girl experience at Hostel Shithole. So he ended up making a date with a gorgeous lady called Rieki on WeChat to have dinner at a mall near the hotel he stayed at.

Walking to the Chit Lom train station, he felt like he was walking on clouds as the swing in his step and the smile on his face returned. In the land of smiles, it was a good thing to have because everyone on the street acknowledged him and smiled at him, making him feel confident and raring to face the rest of the day. Back at the hotel, he enjoyed the creature comforts that Hostel Hellhole hadn't provided for him, like a clean bathroom, a large, clean comfortable bed, a wall-mounted flat-screen TV and fresh towels. There was a pleasant silence in his room, a welcome solace from the hustle and bustle of the Bangkok metropolis. With still some time on his hands, he decided to get naked and roll in bed, yet resisting the urge to shake one out before the date. As he mindlessly flipped the cable TV channels, he thought of Lyna and wondered what she was up to these days. His messages to her on social media had been left unread and him unsatisfied, and he often imagined what it would be like if she were to come waltzing into the room out of the shower, smelling as fresh as the morning dew and giving him a nice, long and slow blow job. Slowly, he began to have an erection, which he killed just by thinking about the amount of work he had to get done once he got back from Bangkok. He lazed in bed on clean white sheets under a nice warm blanket and drifted off to a dreamless nap with a movie playing in the background, and the dialogue soon became a collection of disembodied voices saying random words that didn't have meaning nor context, where each individual voice, thought and moment came right after one another but disconnected from and unrelated to each other.

He jolted out of his nap – after what felt like three hours for him – about twenty minutes late and made a beeline for the shower. He washed and scrubbed himself from head to toe as he so often did before a date. Not like he needed a date to wash himself as thoroughly as he did, coming in from the harsh heat of the city. He took his time to get dressed, did some last-minute manscaping, put some manly perfume on and was ready to sweep any woman off her feet. A cigarette to calm his nerves, and he was really good to go.

Yes, he did get nervous, no matter how many times he went on first dates and got laid.

The mall where he was supposed to meet his date Rieki was about a five-minute walk from his hotel, or a one-hour cab ride, so he took a slow, languid stroll amidst the peak-hour traffic. Hands in his pockets, looking nowhere but down, he wanted to go through his game-plan for the night, but a random memory popped into his head. For the first time in months, a different woman occupied the space in his head where Lyna was.

It was the Mademoiselle at the airport.

The Mademoiselle with the strong arms, veins popping up from underneath her skin.

The Mademoiselle with the ponytail and wearing the deep red dress.

The Mademoiselle who locked eyes with him, like a meeting of souls that he did not want to break nor end.

The Mademoiselle whom he heard singing 'Still Loving You' as he creeped by to sniff the air around her and eventually walked past.

He smiled to himself as he thought of her as he wondered what it was about her that made him remember those details about her, a random stranger.

Maybe it was her perfume, he loved Chanel's Mademoiselle to an almost unhealthy degree.

Or it could be her poise and posture because he adored statuesque women who seemed carved in alabaster by God's divine hands.

Perhaps it was how she looked like she could verbally joust him to submission and drink him under the table all at the same time.

His smile attracted a streetwalker who approached him, mouth still full and chewing her snack, and asked him if he wanted to party with her tonight. Alex politely shook his head as he carried on walking toward the mall, weaving in and out of touts, beggars and prostitutes plying Main Street. It was half past six in the evening, smack in the middle of rush hour, so the streets were packed with office workers going home in buses packed to the brim with humanity like sardines in a very flimsy moving can, *tuk-tuk* riders honking for business, and chock-a-block traffic at a standstill. To the uninitiated, it was total chaos, but there was a method in Bangkok's anarchy, a sort of mechanical anarchy. Like looking at an abstract piece of art, one had to find order within the seemingly indecipherable chaos, like how the vehicles gave way to each other. There seemed to be a hierarchy on the road the vehicles adhered to: public transport vehicles were often given the highest priority by the road users, followed by taxis, then *tuk-tuks*, especially if they were seen transporting a Buddhist monk, and private cars seemed to be the lowest in the pecking order. Regardless of how big, shiny and expensive they were, they often gave respectful ways to those higher up. Motorcycles were kings of the road, weaving in and out of traffic in between cars and buses, often at relatively high speeds. They appeared reckless, but it was a recklessness that came from years of experience, enabled by a certain grace in road behaviour, in spite of the chaos swirling about on the roads.

Because of the heavy traffic, the only way to get across to the mall was via an overhead bridge that seemed to have been built in the seventies, with rusted railings, its tiles coated with dust and grime. Alex climbed the steps, careful not to touch the walls, keeping his hands in his pockets, and up top, he got a bird's eye view of the snaking queues of cars that were occasionally interrupted by the seeming lawlessness of the motorcycles moving in between the vehicles. It was like a snake actually, with small moving parts under the bright shiny scales that moved the big body bit by bit. He would stay longer to admire the one thing that Bangkok was known for, but the fumes from the traffic below coupled with the noise was making him dizzy. He hurriedly crossed the bridge, skipped down the steps and into the cool, welcoming arms of the Terminal 21 Shopping Mall.

He was ten minutes early for his date, so he settled in a corner of the Chu Chocolate Cafe to collect himself, sign in with the free Wi-Fi provided by the mall and checked his messages. Nothing much to take note of, aside from the eight new messages from gorgeous heavily made-up women in excessively filtered display pictures saying hi to him. He gave a very brief, standard reply, copied and pasted it to all, and sat waiting for Rieki. Leaning back, legs crossed and his foot swaying playfully to a beat in his head, he spied with his bright brown eyes one of the prettiest women he had ever seen on WeChat.

Rieki sashayed into the mall with a confident swagger, leading with her hips, swaying hypnotically, utterly mesmerising. She recognised Alex, waved and strutted toward him, and he could feel all eyes in Bangkok were on her and that there was a collective boner being induced in all the men at the mall. It was as if danger herself had just walked in. She was wearing a tight, olive-green dress, her hourglass silhouette undulating seductively, and the mall was fast becoming a land where time stood still. Alex got on his feet to welcome her, and was becoming very self-conscious of the erection that was stirring below. Rieki was soon upon him, all of her one-point-seventy-five meters tall, towering over him. She smelled like she doused herself with a sweet, flowery, feminine musk and it was all Alex could do to stop himself from burying his face in her chest and start sniffing. She had broad shoulders, much like a swimmer he dated before, their shoulders both bony and taut, both perched at opposite ends of an inverted triangle that was her torso. They hugged, and he felt like he had a lean and mean machine in his arms, almost without an ounce of fat or loose skin on her. Her fair skin was radiant, further enhanced by her makeup, her full, pouty lips shimmering in the bright fluorescent light. Her brown eyes were bright and full of life and happiness and emanated an infectious energy that took control of him.

"Hello na! So happy to see you!" she said to him, and he felt a flutter in his stomach as he heard her voice. Or did that flutter come from somewhere lower?

Alex was beaming with happiness as he smiled, kissed her cheeks and said, "Me too, so happy to finally meet you!" However, he did note something interesting, albeit strange about her voice. It was almost boy-ish, like a pre-teen whose voice was about to break, but not yet. But he didn't mind, because he soon caught sight of her glorious cleavage, decorated with a sprinkle of glitter.

"Come, darling, we go eat upstairs," she said. He walked next to her and felt like a toady hobbit, utterly dwarfed by her aura and beauty. But never one to entertain such thoughts, he made himself feel one-point-eight meters tall, and he was soon walking as if Rieki and the rest of the city was his. Walking through the narrow aisles and getting on the escalator, he took every opportunity to check the rest of her out. From the brief glances he took of her, she seemed to be a perfect specimen of womanhood and femininity. Aside from her feet, which he thought were so big that it would take three men to tip her over off her feet. But he didn't give it much thought as he drank the sight of the smooth, supple skin of her legs and the sinews of her thighs that peeked and pulsed from underneath her dress. They didn't talk much while walking as she allowed Alex to drink in each and every sight of her he could as they walked, and they finally settled on having dinner at a Japanese restaurant. They sat opposite each other, and Alex felt that finally, the date was under way.

Rieki had a small tattoo on her ring finger, and he used that as an excuse to touch her fingers and hand, in the guise of asking her to tell him the story behind the tattoo. He grabbed her hand, playfully caressed her tattooed finger and asked what it meant. She regaled him with a story of a monk who changed her life, but all Alex could think about was how soft her hand was, and how they were bigger than his. But as usual, he got distracted by her sparkling cleavage. And he could feel her foot rubbing on his calf as she played footsie with him. *This is going very well,* he thought, and he was very excited at the prospect of Thai pussy after dinner. They spoke about superficial topics as she smiled coyly each time she spoke, while he seemed to have grown in size and stature, not just below the waist. Dinner was done, the bill was called and paid for, and they decided to grab a takeaway coffee and go for a walk around the mall. Alex, reluctant to delay the inevitable anymore, invited her instead back to his hotel room where they could drink coffee together without having to deal with the crowd and prying, envious eyes.

She seemed shy at first but eventually agreed after he said it was very nearby. So they walked the noisy streets of Bangkok, her arms linked together with his like a pair of budding lovebirds enjoying the spring of their love. As they walked, they both turned heads and Alex enjoyed the attention that almost the entire city was giving them. He was transported back to the time when all the boys were envious of his relationship with Zubaidah at the bus stop from long ago, and his ego swelled. They reached the hotel, and in the lift, they just couldn't keep their hands off each other, yet resisting the urge to kiss each other. They just looked deeply into each other's eyes as they caressed each other. They rubbed their noses together with the slightest, faintest touches of their lips, and Alex made up for the lack of a kiss by wildly grabbing her firm butt. He took her hand as they walked out of the lift and toward his room. Some of the other hotel guests were there and gave a wry smile as the lovebirds flitted past them, and that pleased Alex even more.

"Sit there," Alex commanded her as they entered the hotel room. Rieki obeyed the command like a puppy waiting to be given a treat. He made two cups of coffee from the pantry and served it to his resplendent guest, now laid out suggestively on the couch with a megawatt smile. They both took a sip of the coffee when the irresistible urge overwhelmed the both of them and they started kissing each other hungrily. It was less kissing but more sucking each other's lips and faces as they fumbled about to rip each other's items of clothing off.

Alex pulled her off the couch, and they were standing there face to cleavage as he knelt down, caught the hem of her dress with his teeth, and began to slowly peel off her dress using only his mouth. As sexy as that was, Rieki had to help him take her dress off, and he was greeted by a pair of perfectly round, firm and gravity-defying globes of lady flesh, with the highlight being her light brown areola engorged with blood, and firm till it was almost deep red. Alex cupped her breasts, and they felt like rocks as he buried his face in her cleavage and explored every inch of her ample bosoms with his tongue and lips. She moaned and sighed deeply, which threw Alex into a near frenzy of pleasure as his erection became much harder than how her enhanced breasts felt. He hurriedly tore his shirt off as Rieki ripped off his pants, pushed him to sit on the edge of the bed and gave him an almighty blow job.

He leaned back to lie down on the bed and realised that he was being blown within an inch of his life. He had to grab the sheets as his body twitched and twisted in pleasure at Rieki's warm tongue and lips working his member. He convulsed so hard, he felt a cramp developing on his glutes and his inner thighs. After what seemed to be an eternity and at the same time a second, Rieki stood up and Alex looked at her in all her glory and saw that she was wearing a pair of tiny boy shorts. She turned around seductively, and Alex noticed her taut back and drank in each and every sinew. He grabbed her breasts from behind and began kissing her back and traced his tongue down her spine, her ribs right to where her boy shorts began, and buried his face in her butt. Using her butt to push his face back, she began to peel off her shorts, painfully slow for him, and by this time, Alex was beside himself with pleasure and lust. Nothing was going to stop this pleasure train from stopping. Her small, boyish yet undoubtedly firm bum was now right in his face as Rieki spread it open for him. Instinctively, he stuck his tongue out to give her a quick rim, to which she squealed with delight. She pushed his face deeper into her ass as he licked and ate her delightfully cute butthole, and he enjoyed looking at it as it pulsed and winked at him.

Unable to hold it anymore, he stood up with his thunderous erection raging between his thighs, spinning her around to kiss her lips once more. That was when he felt his raging boner meet another hard and raging lump of flesh.

Surprised, yet intrigued, he looked down and saw that his rock hard erection was facing another rock hard, erect penis. It was like an erection-lite, an erection junior, but the size had nothing on how thunderous and raging it was. Alex looked up and saw Rieki smiling coyly at him as she grabbed his penis and began to tug at it. With his presence of mind all focused on pleasure, they continued kissing each other with a passion of the ages as their cocks pressed and rubbed against each other's, in a bizarre fleshly swordplay.

She then shimmied her way up his body until she straddled his chest and leaned over so that he was presented with an engorged pink penis right in his face. This was a moment of indecision for Alex, but again, deep in the throes of pleasure, his tidal urge to have some lovely, lustful flesh won out and he thought, *I can do this, it isn't that weird, and it's probably only fair to return the favour.* So, he wrapped his lips around her cock and started to give the first, and only, blow job of his life. He was nervous and timid about having a dick in his mouth and had to admit that he most likely gave a really lousy blow job. All he did was have the head in his mouth and sucked hard. And he could tell she wasn't really enjoying herself too much, so he changed it up and moved his mouth to her balls and started licking the smooth hairless skin.

She gasped in pleasure.

Alex then stuck out his tongue to lick from the base to the tip of her cock, then sucked on the head and taking her until he gagged. The intensity increased to an almost fever pitch as she thrust her hips harder into his face, fucking his mouth with her glistening pink cock. Gaining confidence, he took a page from all the porno movies he watched in the past and began to use his other hand to coat her dick in saliva and started stroking it as he sucked hard. He listened to her little moans as he blew her cock, massaging her balls and using his tongue to circle her cock head as she tried to get her dick deeper in his throat.

She did this for maybe a minute before she pulled out, pushed his face off and grunted.

"Darling, I almost cum," she said coyly.

Alex smiled as he felt a surge of confidence washing over him. With a cheeky twinkle in his eye, he licked the tip of her dick and asked, "You want to cum, darling?"

She bit her lip and pushed her dick forward to his tongue, jerking it a little. "Yes, but I feel bad," she said sheepishly. "Too fast na."

Alex laughed and just started bobbing his head on her dick again before taking it out and saying, "Do you want to cum in my mouth?"

"Mhmmm," she purred.

"Or do you want to cum on my face?"

Her eyes lit up, and she pulled her cock out. "Oh my god, darling! Yes, I do!" She started jerking it slowly, staring down at him while he looked up, tongue out of his wide open mouth, licking her cock head.

"Cum on my face, baby, give me your cum," Alex moaned, encouraging her, remembering how hot it was when women purred and moaned as they encouraged him to pop his load all over them.

She started jerking harder, looking down at Alex. "Close your eyes," she said breathlessly, smiling a little as her orgasm approached, "I'm about to cum, darling, close your eyes."

Alex closed his eyes, feeling her cock at the tip of his tongue. She let out a cute little high-pitched, falsetto moan as she came. Alex soon felt her warm cum shoot on his face and cheeks, a little bit getting in his hair and dripping back to his tongue.

"Oooh yesss, baby, that's so good. So good. So beautiful."

She kept shooting her cum on his face, finally finishing and sitting back on the bed. He kept his eyes closed to avoid getting semen in his eyes and started licking it off her dick, trying to swallow it. She gently pushed him back and left, coming back with a wet towel, and cleaned his face off.

"Oh my god, I came in your hair." She laughed.

He smiled and shrugged, kissing her lips as she finished cleaning him up.

"I think it's your turn."

She pulled him up and started sucking his penis again, thrusting his cock all the way down her throat over and over again, getting his cock to full mast in under a minute. Alex let her tight mouth suck and slide on his raging boner as waves upon waves of pleasure washed over him. Soon enough, the urge to cum built back up in him. Her hands ran over his ball sack, massaging his nuts and two of her wet fingers went to his anus, rubbing his hole while she sucked.

"Lick me there, darling," Alex implored, and Rieki obeyed with no questions asked. She rimmed him to heaven and beyond as his eyes widened in disbelief, toes curling at the pleasure he was feeling. Rieki cupped her mouth over his anus and suckled on it as her tongue playfully teased his now wet asshole. That almost caused a cramp in his feet as he curled his toes hard. Alex couldn't contain himself and the pleasure that he was feeling to the point where he doubled over as his knees gave way. He felt like her warm and wet mouth enveloped his entire pubic region, holding him captive and enslaved by the swathes of pleasure that crashed into his body over and over again.

"I want to cum. I want to cum in your mouth," was all Alex could grunt out.

She moved back to his now throbbing man flesh and swallowed it whole down her throat. She moaned, "mhmmmmmm," which sent him over the edge, and he wasted no time in exploding deep in her throat while she kept sucking. He shoved his balls to her chin as she milked his pulsating penis with her mouth, one hand playing with his anus, the other pulling him hard inside her.

"Sssshiittt... Fuck!" Alex squealed as he came really hard in her throat. She didn't gag or make any noises at all. She just swallowed it, and when it was done, she pulled away and licked the tip of his penis, squeezing out the last bit of semen with her little hand.

The orgasm took everything out of him as he collapsed back in bed naked, catching his breath. She stayed on her knees sucking his cock until it got sensitive. Then she got up, and she kissed him again, spanking his butt and going to the bathroom to fix her hair.

"I have to go to working na, I give you my number okay, tomorrow we go eating again together, okay mai?" she said as Alex grunted a yes. He would have agreed to anything at this point. Reiki got dressed in haste, kissed him deeply on the lips and walked out of the hotel room, but her scent still lingered as if watching him slowly pass out in bliss before its victorious march out of the room.

He lay in bed amidst the crumpled sheets for a few minutes, barely catching in his breath. He fell asleep soon after with the last thought in his mind was how she drained everything out of him.

Alex woke up the next morning confused. His body ached the good ache, the just-had-wild-sex-last-night kind of ache. His glutes were burning, and his thighs were swimming in a pool of burning lactic acid, and he had trouble walking to the toilet to wash up. After getting dressed, he hobbled down to the cafe next to his hotel, ordered his usual breakfast and began reflecting over what transpired last night. As the waiter set down a piping hot plate of Pad Thai noodles topped with a sunny side up and a glass of sweet Thai milk tea, he fished out his phone and began typing a message to his best friend Ian.

"Dude dude dude dude!"

"Oh God, what did you do now?" Ian's reply came, almost instantaneously.

They had been friends for over nine years, and now best friends because neither judged each other for their often questionable life choices. They confided in each other whenever one of them needed a non-judgmental shoulder to cry, spit and lean on, and it was only with each other that they were comfortable revealing their quirks and the social missteps taken. They were always game and open-minded to seek and try out new experiences, although Ian, being older than Alex, had begun to settle into his perceived role as the village elder. Being an older gay man, Ian had a unique perspective on the things Alex got up to, and Alex often tried to hook him up with random men in misplaced and often mistimed acts of gratitude. It was Alex's way of showing Ian how much he appreciated his advice and how Alex saw him as a cool older brother, especially after Rahman died years ago.

"Dude, I just had sex," Alex typed, well aware that his breakfast was getting cold, but this was just something he needed to get off his chest.

"Yeah, so? What's new for you, slut?" Ian replied dryly. Well, it was interpreted as dryly in any case.

"I just had sex with a tranny. She had a dick!" he typed furiously, and by now, his face was buried in the screen of his smartphone.

"Wait, what? You had dick last night?" Ian quizzed him. "How come YOU can get dick and here I am still just watching porn on Tumblr? Did you take it up the ass like a good boy?"

"No no no. I bum sex. I just blew him her. Then she blew me, and it was the best blow job I ever had!" Alex mused.

"Of course it's the best blow job, she HAS a dick. She KNOWS what it would take to make it feel good!" Ian said.

"Yah, but it was weird! Like when I was sucking her dick, it was like sucking on an inflated balloon that smells like soap and sweat," Alex typed as he sniggered to himself. He glanced at his breakfast that was not warm, his iced tea now forming a layer of melted ice on top, with beads of condensation dripping furiously down the sides of the glass.

"What did you expect it to be?"

"Well, I thought it would be fleshier and not so rubbery."

"Well, now you know what the women you're with go through, dude!"

"So what does this make me? Gay? Bi-curious?"

"In your case, it's not an easy question to answer, because what you did with her last night does not fit into any gendered stereotype, nor any clear classification. So I can't say for certain, but I know for sure that you are experimenting and are sexually adventurous, so just be careful, okay?"

"Be careful of what?"

"Be careful that you might enjoy dick too much and then you would be encroaching on MY dating pool!!"

# 12.

---

Carol hugged her knees closer to her body as the studio appeared to get bigger and much colder. It was the year 2001, and her first day in the new semester at The University of Western Australia, there for her first module, Theatre Studies 205, a module she decided to study for in order to indulge her exhibitionist streak and give her inner narcissist a good workout. She didn't know what to expect as she looked around the studio, a vast open space with cold grey walls bathed in an off-white light, a light that seemed to be holy and pure once but now tainted with the grime of sin and debauch.

*This IS the Bradley Studio, right? The place the class was supposed to be meeting?*

*What a shitty place. It's like God woke up one morning, scratched his armpit and this studio fell out.*

There were random items scattered in the studio all up against the walls, grime encrusted, formerly white plastic chairs stacked haphazardly that reminded her of an aftermath of a very rowdy but cheap wedding. A dusty piano stood in the corner, its surface wood cracked and broken, with what looked like a weather worn maroon velvet throw draped over the top, its frayed edges hanging lazily off the piano. It looked like an over-the-hill prostitute at the street corner quietly hustling in a business that had broken, beaten and scarred her mind, body and soul.

*Man, that piano looks like it could suddenly start playing on its own!*

*I bet it would play the theme song from* Tales from the Crypt.

*Or at the very least, the main song from* Phantom of the Opera.

She shuddered as she noticed a lonely flight of stairs that led up to a mezzanine level into what looked like an office space or a storage room, with its windows covered with what appeared to be black cardboard paper or trash bags. It gave the studio a dark and foreboding atmosphere made worse by the creaks and squeaks that seemed to come from the walls. She felt like she was in a bad Halloween haunted house adventure at a cheap amusement park and wasn't sure if the goosebumps she felt were from the cold winter squalls outside that bled into the studio or from the overall seemingly macabre and disturbing atmosphere in the studio.

*Gosh, I can so imagine this place being a soundproof dungeon of sorts complete with instruments of torture, bodily fluids in a puddle on the floor, and all looked after by some old hunchback Eastern European guy with a name like Igorov or Nikolai.*

*Why is it so cold in here? It's fucking twenty-two degrees outside.*

*What, is it the spirits of dead thespians and crew living here — that's why it's cold?*

She was getting very close to walking out of the studio when the heavy double doors creaked open and in walked several familiar, friendly faces.

Carol smiled as she saw Miyuki Sasamori walking in. The pint-sized Japanese girl with the brightest, most cheerful face Carol had ever seen, rushed to give Carol a hug, genuinely excited that Carol was in the module with her. She was eighteen, a year younger than Carol, but she looked like she was twelve because of her size. Miyuki always smelled like mothballs and shampoo regardless of what day or time of day it was. It was a very unique smell that hung around like a harmless stalker and a smell that she looked forward to sometimes as it was one that was comfortable and something familiar. Miyuki had long unruly hair that she tried desperately to tame with well-placed pins and hair bands, often tying her hair back, exposing her clean sun-kissed face that had only two expressions most of the time: an intense scowl or a bright and cheery smile. They met and bonded over their love for karaoke on Thursday nights at the local bar near the uni and had done many a drunken Spice Girls and S-Club 7 duet together.

Behind her, Tracy Sharpe, Carol's classmate in Reading Theory 201, with whom she had had many a lively discussion about postmodern cultural theory during seminars and tutorials. Tracy was a tall and lanky girl with big, smoky and intense eyes. She was Carol's age, but she looked twenty-nine because of her height and her smouldering intensity. She struck Carol as someone who had just started making her journey out of the awkward teen phase and taking her first timorous steps into young adulthood and had an air of uncertain feminism about her. She buried that uncertainty by being stoic, but ultimately she was someone who wasn't sure of herself as a human. Like Miyuki, she had long unruly hair that she never bothered to tame, so she had bits of fine hair sticking out of the sides of her head like a frizzy halo. Tracy had sharp facial features and an intensity painted on her face even as she smiled the unsure smile she often tried to have on.

Carol felt relief washing over her as warmth began to creep back into her, and the Bradley Studio now seemed smaller and less imposing as a smile came crawling across her face.

"I thought I was in the wrong place! This place is a hole!" Carol complained.

"Well, get used to it, you're gonna be spending a lot of time here this semester because the rehearsals and production will all be done here," Miyuki said, referring to the end of semester play that the students would have to stage.

Tracy adjusted her hair and took off her sweater, and time seemed to slow down to almost a standstill for Carol as she caught sight of Tracy's flat and sinuous belly. In those few seconds, she could already memorise the number and pattern of the moles Tracy had on her belly and imagined herself tracing out those moles with her tongue. Carol could not understand the hold Tracy seemed to have over her. For all of her nineteen years, she had always been attracted to boys, the skinny, the stinky, the sweaty and the clumsy boys. She had been taught by her friends in secondary school and junior college about boys and how cute their boy flesh could be when you held it in your hands. Auntie Sam and Auntie Rachel also gave her their piece about boys and what she could do to them and most importantly, what they would do for her. Maybe it was because Tracy was built like a teenage boy, or maybe Carol was at an age of experimentation in a foreign country with all the privileges of an adult but none of the responsibilities yet.

"Yeah, when I spoke to some of the seniors from last semester's Theatre Studies modules, they said the same thing, the Bradley Studio became their second home. Good thing there's a toilet and a shower room there," Tracy chimed in with her lazy, jangly accent. She always spoke like she had that little bit of beer collected in the corner of her mouth, making her accent sound like a sexy, lazy drawl that seemed to pleasure her ears.

"Yes, and if you don't mind, you can chill and fall asleep on the old, skanky sofa in there as well, been there for years," Miyuki said. "But you would probably get an STD just by breathing near that sofa, because you never know the kinda gunk it has accumulated and the sin that has happened on it!"

"Ewwwww," both Tracy and Carol exclaimed, followed by a fit of giggles that reminded them of when they were in secondary school.

"What? What are you guys laughing at?" a male voice with a slightly high-pitched, nasal but soothing and heavily accented drawl interrupted their laughter from out of nowhere. They turned around and saw Zac Gilliam, an impossibly pasty Irish boy with ginger hair that seemed to be prematurely thinning. Zac was doing a double degree in law and arts, and theatre was his creative outlet for his writing. He looked like he was covered with freckles and bits and patches of ginger hair in random spots on his face and neck. He would look barbaric if it weren't for the glasses he wore and his buzz cut. Zac must've had a presentation done earlier because he was dressed in his crisp white shirt, sleeves folded neatly up his arms and black pants pressed to make him look sharp. Carol enjoyed looking at Zac, who for her had the right mix of clumsy idiot boy and smooth velvet steel of a man. The right mix of pragmatism in him doing law and romantic idealism in his arts degree; one foot in making a comfortable living, the other foot in making waves in his creative pursuits, and with both his eyes on the future. Carol especially enjoyed looking at Zac in his outfit today because she had a thing for crisp white shirts with their sleeves folded, exposing good forearm action. She enjoyed visually going back and forth from Zac's forearm to Tracy's taut belly and found herself biting her lips as that familiar but subtle rumble in her loins began, and she found herself almost breathless.

As more of her new classmates showed up, Carol snapped out of her lazy mid-afternoon stupor and began to get into tutorial mode. She met the rest of the class, all of whom were the artsy theatre thespian types.

There was the wannabe theatre writer/director/producer.

The wannabe stand-up comic.

The here-to-earn-an-easy-credit-without-having-to-sit-for-exams type.

The just-happy-to-be-part-of-this type.

And then there was Carol, Tracy and Zac, the three who seemed inseparable from the first day of Theatre Studies, with their intellectually combative natures and their penchant for the drink. From that time onwards, the trio would be seen at every karaoke night, every birthday party and costume parties. And it was at these parties where alcohol flowed freely and inhibitions were non-existent, Tracy, dressed as Marilyn Monroe, kissed Zac, who was dressed as a G.I. Joe; Carol, in a French maid outfit, then kissed Tracy later in the night and made out with Zac at another party as a deliciously bizarre love triangle began to develop.

With the rehearsals for their annual theatre production heating up, their cast mates remarked how they hardly ever saw one without the other's face attached to their faces. And how it was painfully obvious that it was becoming an equilateral love triangle, one where all sides were equally slutty and hot for one another. But the passion had always been ignited when there were just two of them. It was Zac and Tracy in the laundry room of the theatre, Tracy and Carol in the green room, Zac and Carol backstage, often in view of other cast members. Despite knowing about being in a somewhat bizarre sexy triangle, the trio never really spoke about it to each other and were happy to give off the impression that they were sneaking around behind each other's backs. As much as it confounded Carol, she went along with it, as she too found it intriguing and exciting to be fooling around seemingly on the sly.

Carol felt both excited and confused by her bold experimentation.

*I love how Tracy is such a soft and tender person wrapped around a ball of ravenous muscle hungry for flesh. And she always smells so nice.*

*I wonder if her other lips taste and smell as good as the ones on her face.*

*But I also love what a bumbling idiot Zac is. His unkempt boy scent and his rough, almost sandpaper-like skin turns me on, and I love how he can overwhelm me with his arms and mouth. I wonder if his dick smells like he does, musky and sweaty.*

*Mostly, I love how they both make me smile whenever they come around. I love how they run their fingers through my hair and how much they want me when we kiss, when we make out, when we grope each other.*

*I wonder what it would be like if all three of us got together at the same time?*

*Would that be considered an orgy?*

*Is there a way back from there? Like once you try an orgy, do you always want to have one because it's that good?*

*Will we then be the kind of people that only have orgies?*

All her orgiastic contemplations were answered when they found themselves on a protracted night out that involved several house parties. As members of the theatre community, they were often invited to house parties, usually from the extras hired or the stagehands who wanted to be part of the cool thespian crowd. So it was one particular night when Tracy invited Carol out to a house party in what seemed to be a seedy part of town.

It was an unusually wet night, with the skies unleashing a deluge of almost biblical proportions on the city. Carol was wrapped in her heavy leather, ankle-length coat braving the rain with Tracy and walking briskly to the address written down on a black and white photocopied invite. It was a regular house that neither stood out nor was unique in its features, but it did have a foreboding, almost haunting aura about it. It was like it was ensconced in a force shield of negativity, the kind that would make babies cry and beasts stay away.

*This looks like that Amityville house.*

*Wonder which demon will be taking over whose body tonight.*

They walked into the front yard confidently, as neither of them knew anyone in the house, and they just walked in, took a beer from a tub that was filled with beer bottles and ice. They stood around, chugging their beer, and looked for a familiar face, straining their ears over the thumping house music for the sound of a chummy voice, anything that wouldn't make them look like total strangers in a house that was starting to look like an abandoned den of sin and debauchery.

*How the hell did we get here?*

*I'm sure I don't know anyone here.*

There was no furniture in the house save for a white plastic chair that was used to put empty beer bottles. The floors were wet and covered with a thin film of blackened dirt and dust as it seemed that the smokers flicked their ashes and cigarette butts on it without a care. If you had an open wound that came into contact with the floor, you were bound to get gangrene and within days would need to amputate that limb.

*My gosh, who lives here?*

*The rent better be dirt cheap!*

The walls were white, bare and with paint peeling in some parts, scratch marks on others. Carol looked up and saw that the ceiling had its layer of cement falling off, exposing the floorboards, and she could even see faint shadows of footsteps from the people upstairs.

*Are those rats in the ceiling or people walking about?*

*I am so close to regretting this.*

All around Carol and Tracy were unfamiliar but friendly faces milling about. They were all dressed in black for some reason, like the harlots of hell, making the more normally coloured duo feel even more out of place than they already were.

*If I hold my breath, it will minimise the chances of infection.*

Carol tried very hard to hide her disgust at the squalor that was the house and was certain that some insect was crawling up her leg or flying about into her ear. She tried to make a beeline for the back door to get some fresh air when a skinny, pasty, long-haired and thick-bearded goth appeared as if out of thin air. He stood in front of her, blocking her exit, swaying to an invisible beat. He had a large three-piece luggage hanging under his eyes and was shirtless, and Carol could see that he was so emaciated that his ribs poked out from underneath his pale skin. His hands were moving as if independent of his body in an almost comical way, and Carol was more amused than threatened. Carol put her hands on his waist to gently push him aside, when he suddenly fell, almost soundlessly onto the floor. Carol watched in sheer delight as this skinny, goth stranger writhed and rolled uncontrollably on the wet and slippery floor. Streaks of black dirt began to form all over his pale skeletal body, yet his face was a mask of serenity.

*Well, that was interesting.*

*Creepy as fuck, but definitely not something you see every day.*

Carol stepped over that piece of squirming goth man and finally stepped out of that filthy den. Outside, she took a long, deep breath of fresh air and savoured the fresh smell of grass and rain. Relieved, she shuddered and felt like she had broken out of prison. She unknowingly, and very visibly, wiped herself clean of the sin of being in that house.

"Aw, come on, it can't be that bad in there, can it?" a familiar voice boomed amidst the maniacal laughter and booming bass beats. Carol snapped her head around and saw that Zac was sitting on a lawn chair in the corner, nursing a now-lukewarm bottle of beer, smiling a smile that lit her heart and brought her joy to no end.

"Zac!" she screamed. "So fucking happy to see you here! What the fuck house is this? Who the fuck are these people even?" she asked as her voice raised in decibel and pitch, both signs of despair and excitement.

Zac was about to launch into an explanation when Tracy came out and flew into his arms in relief and begged the two of them to take her away from what was turning out to be the fourth level of Hell. Always wanting to ride things out, Carol was undecided, but the sound of breaking glass, inhuman screams and the sheer sonic chaos that emanated from inside the house made her decision for her.

"Quick, to my car, I drove here!" Zac shouted as he pointed to his banged up – or as he called it, near-vintage – Daihatsu Charade. The trio ran through the backyard toward the bucket of bolts and steel without looking back. And as the echoes of Hell faded in the distance, they felt that they had shaken off the demonic chains that had them spellbound by the den of sin and felt an almighty relief washing over them.

Maybe it was the pouring rain pelting their faces, but they were just happy to get past the gates of hell and back to reality. They all squeezed into the sedan, and pedal to the metal, they hightailed past the kerb crawlers and the streetwalkers back into more vanilla areas of the suburb. The trio broke out into fits of uncontrollable laughter at how the night turned out to be as Zac suggested, "Hey, there is another party tonight. You guys remember William and his girl Arwen? Yeah, the dance choreographers. They just bought a pad nearby, about twenty minutes from here, and they invited people over to-night. How about we make our way there, get there, get dry and get pissed?"

"YEAHHHHH!!" the ladies shouted, and what followed was thirty minutes of car-raoke with the three of them singing at the top of their lungs to songs they didn't even know about, making up lyrics as they went along, each song punctuated with fits of giggles and brief moments of silence as they all seemed to be catching their breaths in time with each other. It was a picture of three good friends having the time of their lives and with no care in the world, and it was good.

*Look at Tracy. I love how moist she looks.*

*I would drink each and every drop of rain that falls off her hair, especially the ones that roll off her skin.*

*My gosh, what is happening to me?*

*I never thought I would crush on a girl.*

*I wonder what pussy tastes like. Is it like kissing a toothless mouth? I should be good at it. I know how I would like to be eaten out.*

*But no, Carol, no. Let's look at Zac. How can someone who looks like such a vanilla, generic white boy be so appealing? It's like having and loving a bowl of plain oats soaked in warm water in the morning, every morning.*

*But look at that idiot, he is such a bumbling buffoon who would apologise for cumming on my face.*

*Look at these two sexy, schmexy plates of noms. I want them both, this wet, with this smell of sweat, perfume and rain. But I don't know how.*

*Maybe Zac knows.*

*Nah, he is too much of an idiot to know how to.*

*I'll drop the hint to Tracy later. I'm sure Zac would be on board, the horny little idiot that he is.*

They arrived in what looked like a rough neighbourhood with broken street lamps, walls covered in graffiti and smelling like urine. But William's place was a nice, much cleaner, classier loft. Party central was on the second floor, a sprawling open space with big cushions, oversized bean bags and artsy mattresses littering and scattered all over the varnished wood floors. The room was brightly lit with a large, gaudy chandelier installed for its irony, and the walls were shabbily but chicly decorated with framed vintage movie posters and pin-up girls from the fifties. The alcohol was arranged neatly around a floral centrepiece on a large wooden table in the centre of the room. Soft trance-ey beats hung around the air that created a very chilled out ambience, and the hushed chatter of the people there added to the mellow atmosphere and even gave it an air of class, of quasi-sophistication. Carol recognised some of the faces at the loft and immediately felt relaxed and at home.

"Ahhhhhh, *the thespians are here!*" a burly, rough looking, six-foot, built-like-a-brick-shit-house man announced to the nonchalant guests. "Ewww, you guys are moist," he said in jest. "I'll go and get you guys some towels so you can dry off," William, the host, graciously offered. Carol tried her hardest to stifle a despairing, protracted scream of protest at the thought of her two objects of desire being cleaned up and dried but smiled through gritted teeth and accepted the gracious offer. Warm and dry, they were ready to mingle, while Carol was ready for something much naughtier.

As the night wore on, the alcohol flowed, conversations became louder, laughter more raucous, and inhibitions lowered, Carol sidled up to Tracy, cocktail in hand, and ran her fingers through Tracy's hair. She wrapped her arms around Tracy's taut waist and bashfully planted her head on Tracy's shoulders as if to announce their arrival to make out city. Tracy, getting the idea, looked deep into Carol's eyes, smiled, and kissed her, interrupting what looked like a lively conversation about the theory of everything. Others, quite used to the randomness of these things at a party, just quietly faded out of the scene as Carol and Tracy stood there faces  and lips planted on each other. It didn't look like they were a couple of over-eager younguns going at it, because there was an elegance in their dance of lust, which was why they weren't out of place in William's loft. Carol soon pulled her lips back, playfully combed Tracy's hair back with her fingers, directed Tracy's gaze to Zac and said, "I'm feeling very naughty. Let's call him tonight." Carol had a naughty glint in her eye and a playful grin on her mouth that Tracy loved so much.

Tracy recognised that look and gasped in equal parts surprise and joy at the idea of a ménage a trois with two of her favourite mounds of walking flesh. Without much thought, Tracy furiously nodded her head and said okay, and the both of them wasted no time in pouncing on a clueless Zac as he was about to launch into one of his tirades about the creative process of writing. Amidst the surprised, incredulous giggles, the snooty tut-tuts and the gleeful cat-calling, Tracy grabbed him by the collar, almost like picking a fight, and furiously kissed his lips as Carol jumped in on his side and began to plant wet kisses on his neck. Double teaming him and pinning him against the wall, Tracy and Carol took turns to press their lips together in a series of ravenous kisses.

There was a palpable sense of relief, more than anything, resonating in the room because everyone knew about the love triangle that was developing and was afraid that it would result in a messy, three-way brawl. But ultimately happy that it ended in a three-way of love.

The hostess Arwen, aware of the potential awkward show of flesh and bone bumping uglies that could happen in party central, briefly interrupted the trio of lovers and like a love shepherd, directed them to a spare bedroom below, with a couch and a coffee table for company. "Here you guys go, enjoy, and don't make too much noise, please," Arwen begged as she shuddered at the thought of the sins the walls were about to bear witness to. Once the door closed behind Arwen, the three of them took some time to savour each other's company as well as the moment, a moment they never thought would happen, not even in their wildest of fantasies.

Carol had already plonked herself onto the sofa, leaned back, crossed her legs and shivered in anticipation at what was about to transpire. Tracy stood nearby, slowly got to her knees and slowly crawled toward Carol. Tracy then moved her body to hang tantalisingly above Carol before gently letting her weight settle down onto Carol as they playfully and lightly kissed each other. Their kisses deepened as the fire of their passion was stoked by the inevitable taste of flesh that was hurtling toward them. Tracy's fingers ran roughly through Carol's hair before her fingertips begin to dance lower, starting to explore the soft warm body stretched out underneath her. Tracy smiled as she pulled back slightly from their kiss, her eyes looking down to watch her fingers disappear underneath Carol's top, pushing it up as fingers explored her now exposed flesh. Tracy sat up just enough to slowly drag the shirt up and over Carol's head, small hands coming to rest, cupping Carol's now bare breasts, squeezing her hips as she ground gently down into Carol's.

Tracy flashed a grin as she gazed into Carol's eyes before she tugged her own top slowly up and over her head, dropping it next to the couch as her hips steadily and slowly rocked against Carol. She slipped further down Carol's body and slowly tugged her pants down her hips, taking the cute little panties down with them. She glanced up to meet Carol's eyes with a grin and a naughty glint in her eye as she licked her lips slowly before dipping her head down. Her hands gently gripped Carol's thighs and spread them apart, settling between them as her tongue darted out to drag along Carol's exposed and now quivering flesh. A throaty and guttural gasp slipped from Carol's lips as Tracy's tongue started to explore up and down her soft wet flesh. The tip of her tongue circled and flicked Carol's clitoris before dipping down to dart her tongue inside her hungry, quivering flesh. Tracy let out a moan that rumbled against Carol's bare flesh as she eagerly ate out the delicious bare pussy in front of her. One of her hands slid up Carol's body to squeeze a lightly heaving breast as her tongue darted in and out of her.

*Ah yes, she is so good at this.*

*Damn, I hope I look alright.*

*I hope my belly fat behaves tonight and looks at the very least decent.*

And in an instant, a shiver ran through Carol's body as Tracy's tongue devoured her wetness. She sunk one hand into Tracy's hair, holding her face against her own wet flesh. Carol's hips rocked up to press tighter against Tracy's warm mouth, moans of pleasure slipping from her lips as her breathing got heavier. Her eyes darted over to the door and she couldn't help but blush red along her cheeks as she saw Zac standing nearby, mouth agape, his erection visible through his pants at the sight and sounds of her pleasure.

*Oh my, look at that idiot boy who is such a man now.*

Tracy's back arched slightly, pushing her ass further up in the air as she settled on her hands and knees, licking and lapping at Carol's flesh. A wide, yet almost clueless grin crawled across Zac's face as he stepped closer to the pair on the couch, watching a woman on her knees with her face deep in between her friend's legs. He reached down to tug at his own shirt, pulling it up and over his head then dropping it to the floor. He ran one hand along the back of his head and down his neck as he moved closer, his gaze dragging along the two women stretched along the couch as his erection throbbed hard in his pants.

*Ah, such a sight, drop the pants down quickly, you idiot, and give me that.*

Tracy's eyes darted up as she saw movement beside the couch, a satisfied smiled crawling across her face, spreading along her lips as she buried her face back between Carol's thighs. She wiggled her hips as Zac moved closer, his hand instinctively drifting down to squeeze his hard manhood through his pants, leaning down to get a better view of Tracy lapping at Carol's now engorged flesh. His sunk his hand into Tracy's hair, still smelling of the rain and stale cigarettes, as he pulled her towards him and into a deep kiss, sharing Carol's taste before he grabbed her hair and pushed her face back down between Carol's thighs. Zac slipped his hand from her hair and slowly began to trace down her spine as she resumed licking and teasing Carol.

*Come here and kiss me, I want to taste myself in your mouth.*

Tracy arched her back as Zac's hand reached out to drag down her bare spine before slipping down to squeeze and

170

knead her ass. She moaned into Carol's pussy as he started to tug her shorts down, exposing her dripping wet pussy before she heard the sounds of his zipper going down. Tracy lifted her head to watch as Zac's hand wrapped around his penis, squirming slightly as she saw his pale sinuous arm flexing with his stroking. She dipped her head back down between Carol's thighs as she felt Zac start to move behind her, spreading her thighs as she let out a moan of anticipation. Shuddering as she felt the head of Zac's penis probing against her needy flesh, Tracy's tongue darted out to tease Carol's clit.

Carol's hand slipped up to squeeze her bare breast as the other kept Tracy firmly locked between her thighs. Zac's hand joined hers with a hard grip on Tracy's still-damp hair as he started to sink inside of Tracy. Zac was coated in more of Tracy's arousal and need as he buried his fleshly sword inside of her. He felt like he was swimming in warm oil, pushing her firmly forward against Carol before he started to thrust.

*Ah yes, fuck her well and good. Soon it will be my turn, you sexy ass idiot.*

Tracy moaned loudly against Carol's now hot and inflamed womanhood as Zac started to pound into her, wasting no time in filling Tracy up over and over again, mounting her from behind as his firm grip shoved her face into Carol's pulsating mound of woman flesh. Knowing with every lick that Carol was getting closer and closer to smothering Tracy's face with her thighs, Zac leaned over Tracy, growling into her ear the first words he had spoken since he got home and pounded into her relentlessly. Thrusting heavily between words to add emphasis, his heated breath against her neck, he growled, "Lick that pretty pussy so she can cover your face in cum, baby, I wanna see your face drenched while I own your needy little pussy. I know how badly you need to cum, baby, make

Carol cum so your man can lay claim on your sweet pussy, baby, and make you cum."

*Wait, what did he say? Is he going to fuck me?*

Carol's body shuddered and shook as Tracy moaned against her wet flesh, thighs spread wide on the couch to give her complete access to her body, in need of fleshly succour. Tracy's tongue pushed her closer to the edge of exploding with every dart of her tongue, plunging in and filling her as Zac railed into her from behind, forcing Tracy's face against Carol's bits with every thrust. Carol's hand dug harder into Tracy's hair as the pleasure built, rocking her hips against Tracy's tongue before Carol's head fell back, crying out in pleasure as she felt the distant rumble of a thunderous climax coming closer and braced herself to be pounded by waves of pleasure.

Carol let out a throaty, bestial growl as she felt like a rag doll tossed in the tempestuous ocean of pleasure. She could feel the strong pulsing originating from her crotch and reverberating through her whole body as it shook, shivered and flail about. Her muscles tensed to the point of cramping, her flesh, her body kneaded by invisible hands into mounds of pleasure so intense that every inch of her body and soul curled, every inch of her flesh rolled into a tight fist and punched the couch in pure savage and vulgar delectation.

Zac's hands slid down to grip onto Tracy's shoulders, holding her body steady to take his pounding as his hips moved harder and faster, filling the room with the sounds of pleasure and wet fucking. Tracy shuddered and cried out as he plunged so deeply inside of her. She squeezed around his manhood as she lapped at Carol, plunging over the edge as Tracy's fingers dug into her flesh.

Tracy exploded as waves of pleasure pounded her relentlessly, and she found it hard to catch her breath as she coated Zac's throbbing pink flesh in her fluids. His fingers left an angry purple mark on her shoulders. He thrusted a few more hard times before the pleasure overwhelmed him. Burying his throbbing manhood deep inside of Tracy, he started to fill her with thick, hot ejaculate. The room was now filled with the sounds of mutual pleasure, bodies shuddering and grinding into each other on the couch, gasping for breath as the trio started to come back down.

Tracy smiled as she stretched beneath Zac, reaching up to press a heated kiss to Carol's lips, sharing Carol's taste with her as she milked Zac of every drop of hot fluids. Tracy's fingers slipped into Carol's hair as they kissed, hips rocking slightly back against Zac as his heated body rested on top of her. A grin tugged at Tracy's lips as Zac growled into her ear, just loudly enough for both her and Carol to hear.

Carol lay back as her pleasure subsided and enjoyed Tracy's rolls of sweaty flesh against hers as Tracy planted soft kisses on places her lips could reach. Tracy was breathless, as was Zac, who lay on the couch like he'd been shot, his glistening, pink flesh slumped on its side like a dead seahorse along the shore with a drop of fluid still hanging on for dear life at the tip of his penis.

*Wait.*

Does this count as a threesome?

He fucked her, but not me. We all clearly had orgasms, but I wasn't fucked, that's the most glaring fact..

So, is that it?

Carol sidled and shuffled herself out from under Tracy and crawled over Zac and was ready to devour him and for him to pound on her as he did Tracy moments ago. But that was not to be because the effects of the alcohol consumed combined with the exertions moments earlier had caused Zac to be overcome by a slumber so deep, that despite her efforts, Carol could not rouse nor arouse Zac, as Tracy rolled about in her sleep, leaving Carol standing naked on the floor, still feeling Tracy's tongue on her, when she would rather feel Zac's dick in her.

# 13.

"Dude, dude, check out the new girl," Ammar said as he nudged Alex in the ribs. Alex looked up from writing his English composition about a boy's life in war-torn Nazi Germany and scanned the room. Ammar and Alex were at a community outreach after-school tuition program, where teens went to be mentored and tutored by seniors. Three times a week, a fifteen-year-old Alex dutifully went to the landed house in Eunos that had been converted to improvised learning spaces, where the students sat on the hard and uncomfortable ceramic floor and the tutors teaching off a tiny whiteboard. It wasn't the best nor the most conducive environment for fourteen to seventeen year olds to do some extra learning outside of school. The tutors weren't particularly good at their subject matter either, so there had been many a time when Alex asked too difficult questions for them to answer. But what it did was provide a safe space for these kids to hang out and socialise in after school. And Alex enjoyed having friends outside of school, especially – coming from an all-boys school – the girls he got to meet there.

The first girl he met there who he took a liking to was Nurain, a fair-skinned, brown-haired, aloof little minx who always seemed to be too good for everyone at the centre. Alex loved her big, innocent brown eyes and her naughty smile and often fantasized about tracing out the moles on her neck and chest with his tongue. Alex was never one to be afraid to talk to girls his age, so he became good friends with Nurain, which allowed him certain physical privileges that drove other boys wild. Like playing with her wavy brown hair, wiping off dirt from the corners of her lips when they ate and sitting so close together their arms would be touching. Nurain reminded Alex of Zubaidah, someone who was gorgeous in every way, but didn't think she was, nor needed to be gorgeous. For months on end, they were always seen together before and after the tuition sessions, but she soon drifted away from him after Aisha came into the picture as the alpha-female of their girl group. Aisha was an average-looking girl, with thick and luscious lips that were always painted red, as well as all the other colours of insecurity. And it was her who filled Nurain's head about how she needed to do better than Alex, and that she should be seen with someone older and more handsome, and that his crooked teeth and off-beat humour just wouldn't do.

There were other girls Alex enjoyed the attention of, so he didn't really mind drifting in and out of favour from the girls there. There were the identical Azizah and Norizan twins, both cute as buttons who could fit in your pocket. They had darker skin and were built like netball players, toned, muscled and like a battery that never ran out of power. It was Alex's first experience with girls who were built powerfully, and he enjoyed how they felt when he hugged them goodbye every night. The elder twin, Azizah, had a crush on Alex, so they would always find excuses to be sitting together, arms and shoulders touching, and would spend hours on the phone talking, both regaling each other with stories. Truth be told, Alex loved having Azizah around because she always made him feel good about himself and always empowered him to be better than he saw himself to be. She was the first girl to challenge him to be better, and he appreciated it.

Then there was Rina, an olive-skinned, sassy girl with tight curls who, like Azizah, always found excuses to touch him. She always smelled of musky baby powder as well as hair oil, which she used abundantly in her hair to straighten out her curls. She would randomly come around to sit next to him and hang her chin off his shoulder, or to lie down on the floor with his thighs cradling her neck. Alex had gotten away with many an inappropriate physical touch on Rina, but she seemed to be more than happy to accommodate Alex's roaming fingers. As a girl, Rina was taught by Alex's mother in primary school, and they had spent some time together at similar after-school programmes for children, so it was a commonality that she milked for all it was worth. Alex had friend-zoned her early on, but he did enjoy the attention Rina gave him, and they did have interesting conversations about Tolkien and Gilles de Rais once in a while as they indulged each other. Well, it was more a case of her indulging Alex, in every which way she could think of just to keep herself visible in his eyes. She always denied having a crush on Alex, but everyone knew she did, and that she was always ready to pick up all the broken pieces of Alex to put it back together for him in the hope that he would soon fall for her.

Aside from Rina, there was Siti, a tall, skinny, nerdy-looking girl with a voluminous helmet of hair. Alex quite liked the way she carried her hair with wild abandon, and Alex found that it always smelled like vanilla. Siti had a  high-pitched, whiny almost nasal voice which many boys found to be annoying, but Alex found it to be quite interesting and unique, and he made it known to her as well as the other boys that she had a unique voice everyone should be proud of. As a result of his openness toward her, Siti was always asking Alex what his plans were for the weekend and would make her plans around his, where she would "accidentally" bump into him at the cafe or the shopping mall, and regardless of who he was with, they would always end up spending time together. They were quite tight for a while, and they even had their own handshake, which was just another way for Siti to hold hands with him for a little while longer. And they would spend hours on end hanging out at the playground together after school, talking and laughing together. She would always joke about how she hated the way the school uniform made her body smell, but Alex loved the very feminine musk she produced and sometimes made a show of it by sniffing her neck and her armpits and complimenting the way she smelled.

Alex did appear to be one of the popular teenage boys at the centre, especially among girls. The older boys, especially those who were entrenched in their "bad boy" ways, as well as those who were much better looking and more stylish than he was, often looked upon him in envy at the amount of attention and affection that he got from the girls in the tuition centre. And for years, even he didn't know what it was about him that girls found to be so attractive, but it lay in the way he made them feel. He accepted them for all that they were, and all that they would be, warts, pimples and never made fun of their insecurities, making the girls feel very comfortable with and about themselves. To the untrained eye, he would be seen as friend-zoning, or bro-zoning them, and it did appear to be so. But his physical irreverence to playful touching, the impudent language and tone he used on the girls occupied the tiny breathing room between being rude and being playful yet only slightly inappropriately flirty, and it always kept them on their toes, as they were never allowed to be too comfortable nor feel too safe around him. Not that he was aware of all this scheming and plotting, which made him more attractive and more dangerous than any teenaged bad boy could ever be. At the same time, he was empowering them, but just enough for them to be under his magnetic influence, which allowed him to have most of his way with them.

Alex looked past his bevy of groupies hunched over on the floor writing their compositions and noticed a tall, fair-skinned Chinese girl with her hair tied untidily in a bun. The new girl Ammar was pointing out to him. She was easily the tallest girl in the room, and she looked older than everyone else, in a somewhat frumpy blue top that was stretched out around the neck, and dirty, faded and ripped jeans, with her oversized feet exploding out the bottom announcing themselves to the world. Alex took his time and found himself admiring her oversized feet. He marvelled at the sensual curves of the seemingly misshapen toe and the bluish veins bulging from underneath her fair and pink feet. With her slightly darkened toenails curved at a weird angle, perched at the edge of her crooked and near-monstrous toes, her deformed feet stood out from the rest of her in a very interesting, almost exciting way. Alex never saw the allure of her feet to be fetishistic in any way, but it was somewhat of a unique selling point, if you would, that she had that made her stand out from the rest of the girls.

"That one in the blue top?" Alex asked Ammar, eyes still planted on her feet.

"Yeah, that one, I heard she's a wild one," Ammar said, almost licking his lips.

"Who told you that? And wild as in how and what kind of wild?" Alex quizzed Ammar.

"I don't know, I guess she is open-minded? Like you can talk to her about anything kinda girl." Ammar shrugged.

Unimpressed by that, Alex rolled his eyes for a moment before casting them back to her feet, now curled up neatly under her legs as she sat cross-legged on the cold hard floor.

She noticed Alex looking at her and smiled bashfully at him. Alex squinted his eyes to do a smoulder, smiled back at her as he tilted his head to the side playfully. She smiled again, this time brighter and with teeth, and Alex saw to it that he met with her after class.

Ammar and Alex made plans with Aisha, Nurain and the twins to hang out outside the Eunos MRT station nearby for a quick cigarette and a drink. Hilda, the new girl, was asked to come along and soon, they were all seated on the stone benches outside the station, sharing cigarettes, taking turns chugging canned beer and generally goofing off. Well, the boys were the ones goofing off and peacocking while the girls sat back and chilled. They hung around each other, talking about nothing in particular, as Alex used this time to size Hilda up. Alex stood about three meters away, one hand in his pocket, a cigarette resting between his lips, watching Hilda with interest as she showed off to the rest of the group on how to blow smoke rings. He took a deep breath, as if preparing for it to be taken away as she tilted her head back and looked upwards, exposing her long, pale yet sensuous neck pulsating in cadence with her jaw to produce imperfect little smoke rings rising out of her pursed and wrinkled dry lips from the cigarette she shared with Aisha. His mind recorded and replayed every decibel of the rough, almost gravelly tone of voice that somehow sounded both masculine and feminine to him. A voice that was both commanding yet with a strong silvery singsong quality that entranced him. Alex imagined using his fingers to tuck the stray hairs sticking out from her temples into the back of her deliciously curvy ears and inadvertently fantasized about sticking his tongue into them. Her face looked like a chimera straight out of *The Island of Doctor Moreau*, one that was half-human and half-eagle, with eyes that completed the face with an intense predatory look about her. Her slightly hunched posture made it look as if she had folded wings adorning her back and was swooping in for the kill. With a forehead that was wide and high, Alex thought that boys could find more than enough space to play football on it. She stood up to be almost a head taller than Alex, with her skinny arms swinging awkwardly as she walked. And her walk, it was as if she had been trained to walk while holding a big and heavy bag in between her thighs because she had a very uncomfortable gait about her, almost like a bow-legged flamingo walking to avoid getting its feet wet. She had slightly misaligned teeth sitting in a discoloured row, some overlapping each other as if vying for attention from the things outside of her mouth.

But therein lay the reasons why Alex was starting to be very smitten with Hilda. She seemed to be perfectly imperfect. All her physical quirks and her grotesque characteristics, on any other person, would turn them into a monstrosity that was highly flawed, with mutations, aberrations and hideous anomalies. However, she carried the maelstrom of organic debris very well and owned them like a baboon made perfect. Everything about her that was ludicrous and unnatural, were the very things that made her perfect in his eyes. By all accounts, she was not attractive in a conventional sense, and in the depths of Alex's mind, there was a stirring debate about whether she was human in the first place. But Alex just loved the way he felt when he looked at her. He felt at peace, even as she sat there in her dazed, faraway look in her eyes, smiling in the distance, the world felt right for him.

Only Hilda could have those hideous things on her and make them look gorgeous and attractive.

Only Hilda could have the things that people would call hideous and monstrous and still make them into something that was sexy and alluring.

It was as if Hilda was the black hole Alex needed to hide from a world that demanded everyone to be painfully perfect.

Hilda abruptly stood up and said that she had to go home early because her father was very strict with her, and Alex, snapping out of his internal drama, took the opportunity to walk her to the bus stop and asked her out on a proper date that weekend, to East Coast Park beach, for a walk, the after-dinner kind, in the evening. She smiled that bashful smile that Alex was starting to love so much, gave him her number and said okay to his date.

In the days leading up to the date, Alex and Hilda spent inordinate amounts of time hanging on the phone talking to each other. She played up her girly and bashful tone of voice while Alex flirted with her sometimes into the wee hours of the morning. There would be days where they would make a date on the phone, late in the night when both parents were asleep just so they could whisper into each other's ears of the things they planned to do and of often frivolous things they wanted to do with and to each other.

"Oh, your neck is very sensitive and ticklish to the touch, you say? Well then, when we meet, I am going to play with your neck and the folds of the skin there, *no hands!*" Alex would whisper to her.

"Oh, and I will love every minute of that. And you know what I will do once you are done? I am going to stick my tongue in your ear," she whispered back, and Alex could tell that she was smiling through the phone.

"I am imagining what your skin will feel like on my hands. I think I cannot be touching you," Alex said with a slight tinge of regret.

"Why is that?" Hilda asked.

"Because I know it would feel so good, and if I did touch you, I wouldn't want to let go of you ever," Alex said, very happy to have set up this particular line very well.

"You're quite a sweet one, aren't you?" she asked rhetorically.

"Yes, I am, but also dangerous, because too many sweet things can cause diabetes, and I wouldn't want that to happen to you," Alex said, again in an almost scripted fashion.

Hilda giggled, and as her voice lowered into a come-hither smoulder, she wished him good night and that she could not wait to finally be with him on their first date this coming weekend.

Alex tore through the week in a daze with both eyes on his date with Hilda on Saturday. He ran as many scenarios and tried to script as many things as he could to anticipate Hilda's every response and every move, just so that he could come away from it in a positive light. Because if he could not get her to be his girlfriend, at least he would create a good enough impression for her to introduce him to her other friends, ones who could be the greatest arm candy he could ever imagine.

Saturday finally came, and the one thing Alex had learnt was to never show how excited you were with the date, so he purposefully dressed down in a black Kreator T-shirt, jeans and his well-worn maroon kicks. He arrived on time and waited outside the ECP McDonald's by the benches, cold like a stone, a portrait of nonchalance. Hilda floated by awkwardly but like an immaculate dream made of breath and skin, wearing a dark blue floral top, hanging loosely off her bony shoulders and the same dirty blue jeans she wore when they first met. She had her hair done, and what was limp, lifeless and with an unhealthy gloss to it, now was coiffed with care, voluminous and luxuriant. Her freshly powdered face was radiant in the soft evening sun, and she looked and smelled fresh out of the shower. There seemed to be an unearthly, ethereal glow around her as time slowed down to a standstill. Alex stood up to greet her, and Hilda returned his greeting with a tight and glorious hug. He could feel the softness of her feminine flesh melting into and all over him, which stirred in him the emotions he felt when he first made physical contact with Zubaidah. The only difference was that the emotions were now conditioned to make their way to below his waist and to stir the loins there instead.

She took his hand and went to walk side by side toward the beach. Alex found it very difficult to tear his eyes off her because she looked resplendent in the soft evening light, as the sea breeze blew softly into her, causing her hair to flail about sensuously. He enjoyed the sight of her top, blown into her body, revealing her skinny form, which took all of his strength to not run his fingers along her shapely silhouette. She spoke softly to him, but all he could hear were the distant rumbling and the gurgling waves emanating from his crotch as he got dizzy with the scent of her perfume mixed with the salty sea breeze. He gave the occasional grunt, a scoff and a chuckle, but never engaged Hilda in deep conversation, and Hilda didn't mind either. She didn't mind that no one listened, because she just wanted to talk as she looked far ahead into the distance.

Even as they held hands and swung their arms in cadence to each other, walking together almost in step, there were no two other people that were further apart than they were at that moment. There was Alex, now lusting over her, with a porno movie playing in his head involving himself and Hilda, while Hilda looked every which way but at him as she spoke in random words that were seemingly devoid of context and meaning. Just standalone words, words spoken for the sake of being spoken. If they both had speech bubbles over their heads, they would be empty even as their faces and bodies remained animated. There was something empty and incomplete in this picture of budding young love, like a prayer without faith recited in a temple with no God. Nevertheless, they were an emptiness, an abyss that was supposed to exist in that particular time and space. They were the antithesis to everything that existed on that plane, an emptiness devoid of God's love, but one that was supposed to be there.

Both of them soon arrived at an old Amber beacon tower and Hilda suggested that they go hang out in the tower where they could get some privacy and enjoy a good view of the sunset. At the top of the lookout tower, Alex initially sat on the ground opposite Hilda, because he just wanted to drink every inch of her with his eyes. Hilda asked, "Why are you sitting there? Come sit next to me, darling." Alex stood up, took a deep breath of the cool evening sea breeze and sat next to her. He sat there, distracted by a familiar voice booming from the ground when without a word, Hilda lunged at him and planted her lips on his. Alex was stunned at first but reacted quickly by opening his mouth and sticking his tongue into hers, something she enjoyed.

It was his first real kiss.

It was initiated by the girl.

The same girl who then proceeded to teach him how to kiss.

And where to kiss.

The neck, the ears.

Alex felt the thunderous boner working its way up from his crotch as they spent the rest of the day feeding off of each other's tongues. He wanted to get home quick and to jack one off before coming out to meet Hilda again, but he hung onto Hilda's lips with his and recorded every moment in his spank bank. They spent the next few hours making out and sucking on each other's faces, taking small breaks in between to cuddle as they sat on the concrete floor that was covered with a thin layer of beach sand. Alex would pick up and play with random twigs or dried leaves off the floor, but Hilda would tell him off, saying, "It's dirty, right, and those fingers and hands are going to touch me, you know, so please keep them clean!"

In between making out, Hilda would be speaking to him, words that didn't make sense to him one bit, and Alex would drift off into the distant blue and orange sky that accompanied the setting sun on the horizon. Hilda didn't seem to mind that Alex had drifted off as she continued to speak, like a lone deejay speaking on air on late-night radio. Alex thought of Zubaidah, Azizah, and wondered which one he could call his girlfriend. He looked forward to the day when he would be able to say things like, "Oh, my girlfriend…" or "Yeah, I was with my girlfriend…". For months now, despite the attention he was given by girls his age at the tuition centre, he always imagined being someone else's boyfriend, holding hands with a mysterious girl with long hair, a yellow top, face always unseen. That unseen face began to slowly take shape, and it soon almost appeared to be Hilda's face.

That chimeric imperfect face.

That half-human and half-eagle face.

That face, complete with the intense predatory look.

The face that launched a thousand ships from inside Alex.

The face that made Alex want to show the shape of his heart.

However, Alex was soon snapped out of his reflective stupor by Hilda's face planted on his as her tongue snaked its way into his mouth again.

186

And so it was for the next few weeks, Hilda and Alex, hardly speaking or communicating to each other, but they made out with a passion and hunger that eclipsed the world as they knew it. The only words said by her were to tell him where his hands were to go on her body and where he needed to put his tongue. Once in a while, she would ask if he had eaten before turning into a ravenous beast and devouring him for the next few hours. And all that they were about involved looking for quiet, far off places for privacy so they could make out and indulge in mutual heavy petting. And on the phone, they would be discussing where to go so they could make out. She didn't care if Alex washed himself or not, and he didn't care if she brushed her teeth or not. Or even if they wore clothes from yesterday that smelled like a kitchen that was flooded with a stale mix of curdled milk and flat beer. They just wanted to taste each other and for them to never stop making out. It was all about that long kiss, the tongue in each other's mouth, his arms around her body, and her hands on his crotch. The sound they made as they sucked on each other's lips, the wet squish and squelch of their mouths and the muted, guttural moans that came from deep inside their throats. It was, in a sense, the purest form of teenage love, no drama, no emotion, and much like teenagers, their emotions came from their clenched fists or from below the waist.

As hot and heavy as they began their relationship, it soon began to fizzle out as Hilda and Alex drifted apart in a matter of months.

Three months, to be exact.

They stopped calling each other, Hilda stopped stealing glances at him, and in Alex's mind, and the face of the girl in the yellow top began to fade to a faceless, grey void. He wondered in secret if he had something to do with Hilda walking away from him. Putting up a branch, nonchalant face in public, he wondered and often despaired at the fact that he was losing Hilda. Maybe if he did wash himself that one time, maybe she would stay longer? Alex informed Ammar and his bevy of groupies about the state of his relationship, but that just further isolated him from Hilda, who seemed to be unhappy that word of their fling got out. Not knowing how to deal with this unfamiliar sinking feeling in his chest, Alex threw himself into his songs and his books. He identified with the familiar chest-thumping, gut-wrenching emotions felt in 'Still Loving You.' He threw his hands in the air, walked alone on the beach, his face a mask of pain and anguish as he imitated Jon Secada in the 'Just Another Day' music video. Right down to the unbuttoned white shirt flapping in the wind and ripped jeans. As he threw himself into his books, he read about the candle, or was it the star that shone the brightest, would be the first one to fizzle and die out, and he compared that to that fling he had with Hilda. However, the common theme in all his relationships with the opposite sex tended to be that it was the girl who made her move on him, and it shaped his perception of what courtship and flirting should be in his later years.

However, the biggest lesson that he took from all of this came from Ammar's words in consoling him, which were: "Don't worry, dude, easy come, easy go. As easy as they come, it is easier for them to go. But not to worry, there are plenty of them, so don't be too sad, have fun and be happy, okay?" This reinforced the idea that had already taken root in him years ago, and in the years to come. And as much as he denied it and though he never admitted it to anyone, Hilda was the best thing that happened to him and the closest he had ever come to loving and being in love with someone. This was easily the saddest part of how he loved and who he was, that this was the most serious and real relationship he had ever had with a woman, and it was all downhill from there.

# 14.

"**D**on't worry, I know you'll adore him," Charmaine said with a whimsical twinge in her voice.

"Then why don't *you* date him?" Carol shot back, sneering in disdain at her best friend.

"Not my type," Charmaine said as she dismissed Carol. She did this every now and then as a power move, in her attempts to challenge and out-alpha Carol. Sometimes it worked. Most of the time, not so much.

"Then what makes you think he will be my type?" a near exasperated Carol fired back.

"Darling, you don't have a type. You just like men. Men in crisp white shirts, sleeves folded."

*Yeah, she does know me very well.*

"Smart men who are a bit of a dork, but ultimately strong and respectful."

*Who doesn't love a strong, respectful dork?*

"The assholes with hearts, those are your type."

*Yeah, I like them assholes. And hearts. Or hearts with assholes.*

"And you can find bits and pieces of that in almost every man, honey. The rest, you can develop in them," Charmaine lectured Carol. "Are you listening to me, woman?"

"Yes, yes, Madam. Anything you say, Madam," Carol said as she rolled her eyes.

She did not really mind that her best friend Charmaine set her up on a date with a total stranger. She could use with a date or two lately after the horrible make-holiday-plans-on-the-first-date encounter. She was fast getting tired of dating people who inevitably ended up pissing her off, making her laugh for the wrong reasons, socially awkward weirdos, or people who were absent when they taught flirting and seduction in school but still wanted to get into her pants. But how bad could this man be? He had been vetted by one of the few people she trusted, and the one she coughed up should be of some standard.

"Alright, tell me about this Joel again," Carol asked.

"Well, I don't know him, per se. He's actually Harry's friend, and he comes by every now and then to game and to fix our computers. He is a nice guy, good at what he does, and always has this air of authority about him. And my initial impression of him is that he is someone confident, but not cocky. Old enough to be self-assured but still young enough to be curious and willing to experiment," Charmaine went on in a roundabout manner, which in reality said nothing about this Joel person.

"Wow, you just said a whole lot of nothing, so much so that I feel like giving you a fistful of something. You don't even know the guy, and you want me to go on a date with him? What the hell am I to you, your performing doll for your perverse entertainment?" Carol protested, vociferously, in vocabulary and volume, but half-heartedly in tone and intent. Because she knew that deep down, she enjoyed the attention that Charmaine had given her and that Joel would be giving her.

"Dude, I know. And I'm sorry, but you do need a Joel right now. The last thing I want to be is best friends with a crazy, single cat lady who smells of cat. I am thinking of your matrimonial happiness and future here," Charmaine, with her tongue-in-cheek wit, quipped.

Carol understood where Charmaine was coming from, and she really didn't mind it, she just wished that her best friend put in more effort for her. As much as they had been best friends for over ten years now, Carol really could not stand one of Charmaine's dominant traits: how she made everything about her. Carol would come to her place and confide in her about anything, Charmaine somehow made it all about her. Once, Carol felt lonely and down on her birthday, so she asked Charmaine out for some company and to confide in her. And as the conversations wore on, Carol realised that Charmaine had steered it to how lonely and unfulfilled she was with her fiancé Ryan and how she felt he never stepped up to be the man of the household. Or of how Charmaine developed and entertained harmless crushes with the much younger co-workers and the delivery drivers that came and went at the office. Give her fifteen minutes, and your problems would disappear in the face of her moral conundrums as well as her own frustrations and lack of fulfilment.

"I just feel so lonely on the shelf, you know, Charm, and especially so on my birthdays," Carol would say.

"Yeah, I know exactly how you feel. It is the same for me when Ryan goes on his business trips or works late or just is never around the house when I need him. I know life can be hectic for us all, but he is not making an effort in the relationship, I feel. I feel it is just me who is working hard at this and that he is just cruising. Even in bed, he has stopped trying…" Charmaine would be ranting and raving.

Carol found herself listening to Charmaine's litany of complaints instead of airing hers. And after a few hours, nothing got solved, no one was happier and they were back where they started, Carol being alone and lonely, Charmaine being frustrated. But in this battlefield, each other was all they had, so Carol, and to some extent Charmaine as well, held their tongues and continued to be each other's porous rock formations.

"Alright, fine, but I want you to do all the coordinating for me. Just tell me when and where to show up, and I'll show up looking like my fine self, and  I don't want to be doing any work this time round. Also, he is going to have to work hard to impress me." Carol laid down the law for Charmaine.

And so it was for Carol, whose revelry and mirth lay in the hands of her best friend. But it was a welcome change of pace for Carol; it was like having a personal assistant taking care of her daily affairs. Well, just this one affair really, but Carol still appreciated the convenience of it all. Charmaine had them on a date at a Les Bouchons in Ann Siang Hill where the drinks were expensive, the ambience heavy with sexual tension, punctuated by songs from a carefully curated playlist with romance in mind. Carol showed up in her casual shabby chic outfit, in a concerted effort to look like she didn't really care who showed up or how this night turned out.

*Who'd have thought that so much thought was needed to look like you didn't care?*

*But really, I have zero expectations tonight.*

*He is going to have to work real hard to fuck this up for us tonight.*

As soon as she settled into her seat and her surroundings, she spied a painfully normal-looking man walking in who fit the description Charmaine had given to Carol. White shirt, sleeves rolled up, form-fitting grey pants and well-coiffed hair.

*He actually put in effort. Nice. Madam likes this so far*

"Hi, I'm Joel. You're Carol, right, Charmaine's friend?" he asked nervously.

Carol tried very hard to stifle a chuckle at his boyish nervousness and replied, "Yes, you are about right, I am Carol Charmaine's friend," she said as she smiled and shook his hand.

*Clammy. He cannot be THAT nervous right?*

He fumbled a little bit as he sat across from Carol but soon gathered his senses and got over the initial awkwardness and nerves. It was a matter of time before they were having a lively conversation about food, music, cars, diets and workouts.

*This is going really well. I never figured us both to be having a scintillating conversation, let alone see the beginnings of a good time.*

*This feels good.*

*He might just end up getting laid tonight.*

However, Carol did notice something of a weird habit that Joel seemed to have – he kept looking at his mobile phone. She stole a glance at one of those moments and realised that he was actually rejecting phone calls.

*Good. He needs to focus on me tonight if he wants to have a good one.*

However, as the night wore on, over dinner, over giggles and laughter, over the many clinks of their wine glasses, he fidgeted with his phone a lot more and was starting to get worked up over it. Carol, too, was starting to feel a more negative energy emanating from her dinner partner and was wondering what it was that was so important that needed his attention despite his efforts to ignore it.

"Look, Joel," Carol finally said. "Someone obviously needs to talk to you about something important. Your phone has been ringing, and you have been ignoring your phone the whole night. So answer the damn call, take care of what needs to be taken care of, so we can finally get back to our night. I am just starting to have a good time, you know," Carol commanded.

"Sorry, it's just my mum. Okay, I will pick up her call, settle her first and then we can focus on each other, okay?" he stammered.

"Okay, go, settle this," Carol said dismissively as she waved him away, leaning back into her seat almost petulantly.

He picked up his phone, excused himself and stepped out of the restaurant and was soon deep in the throes of a conversation with his mum. Where he was outside the restaurant, Carol could see him clear as day, and he seemed agitated, almost upset as he paced about the sidewalk near the entrance of the restaurant and gesticulating wildly at times. Carol could see his face slowly turning crimson red as beads of sweat gathered and formed a film of sheen on his forehead that soon trickled down his temples and eyes.

*Poor thing. He looks like he's having a bad night.*

*I hope all is okay, because Madam would still like some dick tonight.*

*He looks quite cute when he's angry, actually.*

*Maybe this is what Charmaine meant by loving his mum. That is pretty cute.*

*I wished I could have the same level of affection for my mum.*

*Okay, now is not the time to go there, Carol.*

Joel soon walked in, still flustered and somewhat out-of-sorts.

"Everything okay?" Carol asked, half hoping for him to avoid it and not answer.

"Yeah, everything's okay. My mum is being very needy and emotional these days, especially when I am not around at home much. You see, Dad passed on five years ago and Mum doesn't really know how to handle it. He has always been the one taking care of her, spoiling her, so now she feels abandoned, and as much as I hate it, I have to be my dad to her in a way. So it is very tough on the family. She keeps faking an illness and calling the ambulance or going to the Accident and Emergency room just so she can get people's attention. And she spends her days lying down in bed watching TV complaining about how my siblings and I are never around, or about this "mysterious pain" on both her legs…" he said as he went on and on about his mum.

*Okay, unnecessary exposition.*

*Shut up already.*

*So NOT the time for this.*

*Well, on the bright side, he does seem to have a strong affection for his mum.*

"She is still worried about me and spends her time worrying for me. I get slightly out of breath because I take the stairs up, she freaked out thinking I have a lung ailment…"

*Okay, enough, I get it.*

"Once, I couldn't come visit her and couldn't pick up her calls because I had a headache, she sent this long essay of a text message about how I never had headaches before, and she is worried that it is brain tumour…"

*Alright, I am very close to not wanting to be a part of this.*

*What am I, your family therapist?*

And so it was for Carol that the evening became a therapy session for her partner, who was still having Mum issues and letting it out on her. On one hand, she felt like she should contribute and maybe he could find a way out of this mess of a wilderness that was familial relations, but on the other hand, she kinda wanted him to suffer a little bit for putting her through this. Even as she spent the rest of the evening nodding her head, grimacing sympathetically, and feigning interest in making an effort to solve the problem.

*Okay, I am running out of sympathetic words to say.*

*Maybe I should just grunt sympathetically.*

*Is there such a thing though?*

*I know, I will just go "awww" and "uh-huh" and "hmmm," that should buy me some time to space out from this emotional drivel.*

She was in the midst of tilting her head in a lame effort to focus on Joel's tirade when in the corner of her eye, she saw a puny hurricane in the form of a little old lady with a slightly hunched back, gesticulating wildly at the maître d'. It was then when she saw the sheer horror grasping Joel's face as he recognised the voice and the little old lady.

It was the mum!

It was his mum!

He looked at Carol, his face a mask of terror, mouth agape, hoping to quickly squeeze out an apology, but the angry, shrill shouts from the now very agitated old lady pierced the chill and laid back ambience of the restaurant. Terror soon turned to shame and embarrassment as he realised that the old lady hurricane was headed his way.

"How can you do this to me, boy? How could you leave me all alone at home in the dark? You left me to die at home alone with no food! Don't you love me anymore? I am your *mother!"* screamed the old lady who was herself like a whirl-wind of doom and despair. "You said you were going to be home by nine p.m. What time is it now? It's almost ten p.m.! You know how worried sick I am because of this? How could you leave me wondering what in the world happened to you all alone at home?"

*What the hell?*

"And you! You hussy, what are your intentions with my son? You want to take his money? You want to take him away from me? Over my dead body, you skank! You are going to have to pry him from my cold dead hands!" she continued as she turned her rage toward Carol.

*What the fuck is going on here?*

Carol was too shocked to react and as she was wont to do, she just stared blankly with the wheels and gears turning furiously in her head, trying to make sense of all that was happening, mainly trying to decipher whether this was reality or a dream. And how, if this was reality, could this happen?

*This has got to be a prank, right?*

*Is this even real?*

"You think you are good enough for him? In your shabby clothes. What are you, a whore? A drug addict? *Both?* How dare you take my son away from me? *Give me back my son!"* the old lady screamed frantically, causing a maelstrom of a scene that everyone wished would just dissipate and blow over.

*Did Charmaine set this up, and is she just around the corner laughing her dead ass off at this?*

Overcome with disbelief and incredulity, Carol shook her head and blinked repeatedly with a faint hope that this was all a figment of her imagination, or that she would wake up, rolling in her comfortable sheets and laughing off that weirdo dream about a boy named Joel and his overbearing and frantic mother. Unfortunately, it was not to be because this was as real as it got for her. She cast her eyes to Joel, who seemed to have melted into a pool of embarrassment, face in his hands and shivering with rage.

Or was it weeping?

*Oh my god, is he crying?*

*I think he's crying!*

*Oh shit oh shit oh shit! What do I do? What should I say?*

The old lady's frantic maternal shouts faded in her mind as she tried very hard to process what was going on when a splash of cold fluid knocked her out of her thoughtful stupor as she realised that in her rage, the old lady mumma bear had taken his glass of red wine and emptied the contents of it in her face. Now no longer a deer in headlights and seething with a blinding rage of the ages, Carol got to her feet, flipped the dinner table with one hand and threw all that was on it – plates, glasses, cloth, food, dignity, serenity, self-control – all over the bare concrete floor in a deafening din of crashes and bumps. However, the noise she created snapped Carol out of her blinding rage, and she tried very hard to regain some semblance of composure. The sudden explosion of activity also stunned the little old lady, who was momentarily silenced and took several steps back in fear as the table had literally been turned against her.

Carol straightened herself up, put herself together, still with rage in her eyes, and said to Joel, "I am going to the ladies room, after which I am walking out of this place and out of your life. I want you to forget that I exist, as I will forget that you do. You will not call me ever, nor will you say hello to me should we bump into each other on the street. When I die, I do not want you to be at my funeral. My world is complete and fulfilled without you and your mum. So goodbye, and please don't make this difficult."

She walked away from the table toward the ladies room as the mum's voice still lingered in the air. A voice no longer coated with rage. It was a strangely calm, soothing tone of voice, the voice of a mother comforting her beloved child. Carol shuddered as she went into the ladies room, locked the door behind her, leaned on the sink and stared at her wine-soaked face. Determined to not be spitting vile rage, she quietly washed her face and wiped down her wine-stained top.

*Man, what a psycho.*

*I cannot imagine the years of therapy that guy needs to go through to get over this.*

*Maybe she does this all the time, and maybe he likes this.*

*She probably has a shrine at home dedicated to her beloved prince of her womb.*

*I think he mentioned his father is no longer around, right? Yeah.*

*And he did mention that she wants him to replace the father?*

*Oh my, that is such creepy, weird. But that's what he said.*

*My gosh, maybe they sleep in the same bed together.*

*She does look like she did breastfeed him till he was fifteen and sleep in his bed till he was eighteen.*

After she was done ruminating, she walked out of the ladies room, eyes focused on the counter, ready to make her payment and get out of the place. She made a beeline to the staff behind the counter but was told that the bill had already been paid for by the old lady who came.

*Well, at least she paid for my dinner and drink tonight, so it's not so bad.*

"Ma'am, I have also been asked to convey this message to you by the lady who came by to pick up her son," Assistant Manager Leo, according to his nametag, said to Carol.

"Okay, what is it?" Carol replied.

He winced hard and hesitated as Carol mentally braced herself for an uncomfortable exchange. "Well, she said, in these exact words…" he said gingerly as he pulled out a piece of paper from his breast pocket. "She said, err, she wants me to tell you, ummm…"

"Just out with it, Leo, tell me what she wants you to say," Carol said with a smile that betrayed the annoyance in her tone.

"Okay, err, how about you just read the note she dictated to me?" Leo said.

Carol folded her arms and stood her ground with a firm "No," largely because she wanted to make Leo work a little bit and not to let him off easy. He hadn't been very attentive and helpful tonight anyway.

"Well, err, she said that, errrr, you will burn in hell with all the other whores who has tried to take her son away from her, and that she will hunt you down if you ever try to speak to her or her son again as well as, ummm, this, 'I will rain on you fire and fury of biblical proportions, the likes of which that has never been seen before, should you —'"

"Okay okay okay, I get it, Leo. Thank you. And I am sorry for what has happened to your place. It was never my intention to cause trouble."

"Oh no trouble, Miss. No trouble at all, it's not like you conjured a hurricane out of thin air. We know you're not Storm," Leo said with a smile.

"Haha, thank you, Leo, you have a good night tonight."

"You too, Miss, and don't be troubled by this, there are so many guys out there like this one tonight, so this can be a pretty normal thing."

Carol shuddered as she walked out. Now *that* was a frightening thing to behold: an army of angry old mums protecting their adult sons.

**15.**

Alex sipped his black coffee, leaving the cup hovering just below his nose to savour the aroma and filling his senses with all manners of olfactory pleasure. He looked intently into the eyes of the person – or at least he thought it was a person because it could've very well been a human-shaped wall – opposite him. His head instinctively nodding at regular intervals, whose face was a blurry mass made up of sad expressive eyes attached to a pale orange balloon. He must have spaced out while someone was talking to him, and slowly his eyes went back into focus where he saw and was reminded of what had been going on with him.

It was a lovely sunny Sunday morning, and he had been out early for breakfast with a former colleague named Tanya, from the days when they were both journalists at the Starbucks in Parkway Parade. They hadn't met in years and had been catching up on each other's lives since breakfast and were now having coffee as they continued to update each other. Only he was getting bored of it. He looked across and focused on Tanya. She had a face that seemed to be perpetually painted with sadness. Even when she smiled, and she had a very bright and cheery smile, there was always a very strong tinge of sadness about that smile. Maybe it was her droopy cheeks, or her full, heavy lips weighed down by gravity or a lifetime of discontent. Coupled with her hunched posture, she looked like she permanently needed a pick-me-up or a new, better life or was about to start her shift ringing the bells at Notre Dame. She had been like that for as long as Alex had known her, except for the short bob she was sporting on her head now. And the weight that she had put on over the years.

Alex spaced out again amidst the drone of her monotone voice and the incessant buzz of humanity surrounding the cafe and recalled a time when he slept with Tanya. Both of them shared the same birthday, and it was the one time when they decided to celebrate it together at a bar. Friends came and left in a blur, and all Alex could remember were the numerous shots of alcohol they shared together and licking her face every chance he could. He couldn't even remember the sex, which was usually because he was that drunk, or she wasn't that memorable.

Or both.

But he did remember her licking ass real well and how she let him blow his load in her mouth, down her throat without much protest. Well, the alcohol helped with the lack of protests, but other than that, there wasn't much to remember, let alone enough to give him a nostalgic boner. Well, there was a slight hint of a half-boner actually; he was, after all, a hot-blooded male.

Being dragged back, almost kicking and screaming, to the present, Alex smiled and nodded just to show her that he was paying attention. The steady stream of human traffic seemed to be getting heavier by the minute, with discordant music from the different shops around laying on top of the buzz of humanity in a cacophonous mix, and Alex was soon feeling the excruciating discomfort of being amidst urban chaos. The cool air conditioning did nothing to alleviate his discomfort as he shuffled about in his seat. Again, he ran his eyes over Tanya, and from what he could decipher, what seemed to be under that tent of a Sunday dress was not what he would want to have and to hold on a day like this. Minutes seemed to crawl and was almost at a standstill; he could feel tiny beads of sweat taking its time, in an excruciatingly slow evolution from an empty pore slowly being filled up with a microscopic bead of sweat, getting bigger and bigger by the minute, and trickling down his temple, manoeuvring around the microscopic crevasses and valleys on his skin. He had to fake taking a phone call from his mobile phone to break the dreary, insufferable not-date. Even the fake phone call couldn't save him, so Alex decided to put to the sword this abortion of a meet up and he just said, "Tanya, sorry, I'm late, I really have to go now. It's been nice catching up with you though, don't be a stranger, okay?"

Tanya looked disappointed, and Alex couldn't tell if that was her default or that she was truly disappointed. Nevertheless, she smiled a smile as bright as she could muster, got to her feet, hugged him and bid him farewell. Alex could feel the soft mush of woman caving in around his arms, a kind of mush he somewhat enjoyed from day to day, but he wasn't feeling it. It did feel like he would leave an Alex-shaped dent all around her fleshly matronly body. Tanya hung on to his body as long as she could before Alex broke off the hug, tilted his head at her and smiled before turning around to walk out of the now bustling shopping mall.

Bright rays of sunshine burnt his eyes as he winced hard and frantically fished his sunglasses out from his pocket. Seconds later, he felt the searing heat and dense humidity violently embracing him. Even after years of living in this weather, he could never get used to it. "Climate change," he often whispered to himself, but today, it was just a very angsty, "Fuck!" It took him a little while to gather his senses and get his bearings, stumbling like a drunk returning home late from a night out. Nevertheless, composed and cool, he began his strut down the stairs, looking resplendent in the morning sun in the clothes he slept in the night before: his faded and very worn out Grey Scale T-shirt, skinny-fit black track pants that had almost faded down to a grey, and his well-worn running shoes. It made him look somewhat fresh from the gym, or sloppy sporty chic at best with his tousled hair, a crown of laziness and large sunglasses covering a very cranky face, a face that had to wake up at 8 a.m. on a Sunday morning just to have a mediocre breakfast on a bad not-date. He really felt like being dramatic and dropping to his knees onto the white hot concrete floor, raising his torso to the sky screaming, "Why hath thou forsaken me?" But there was no one for him to perform for.

He trudged on, one hand in his pocket, the other rubbing his neck and scratching the back of his head, just so he had something to do with it, when, in the corner of his eye, a yellow flash appeared in his vision, bright enough to catch his attention, radiant and incandescent to make him turn his head to look, and look he did.

He thought he had seen her again.

His Lyna.

The bright blonde hair now in a short bob, well-coiffed but still with random strands shining in the morning light, dancing in the breeze. The pale alabaster skin reddened by the sun covered with a thin sheen of sweat and slightly reddened in the heavy tropical weather. She was wearing a canary yellow shift dress that clung tightly around her with her taut sinews still very clear, despite the weight Alex saw she had put on. She was scurrying hurriedly to get somewhere, and Alex only had enough time to catch a glimpse of her profile, so he wasn't sure if it was indeed his Lyna or a doppelganger.

So he decided to follow her and hope that they would eventually come to a common stop, like a pedestrian crossing, a bus stop or a taxi stand, somewhere he could tell his heart that this was or wasn't the woman for him. He just needed that visual assurance. So, like a predator, he stalked her, followed her across the road, through Roxy Square and to the other side. But she kept walking, once in a while looking to her left and right, giving Alex a glimpse of what she looked like, but it wasn't enough for him.

He needed to be absolutely sure.

Her pace quickened, and it was all he could do to keep up with her as she tore through the streets of Katong. She soon turned into an old, dilapidated mall that desperately needed a facelift, and he followed her. Inside, it was as if time stood still, with discoloured tiles and storefronts that looked like they were still in the early eighties. The dank smell that hung in the air came from the air conditioning system that was put in place in the eighties, giving it a distinct, almost mouldy scent to the mall. Most of the shops were closed, and it was not well lit in the mall, but he caught a glimpse of her dress disappearing around the corner at the top of the escalator. He followed it but lost sight of her on the second floor.

Alex looked around at the closed shops and peered into the darkness of the second floor. He felt like he was in a post-apocalyptic game looking for a sign as zombies and monsters lurked in every corner. He deduced that there was nothing here on this floor for a woman like her, so he decided to go up another floor to see if there were any leads for him. He climbed a disused escalator, looked around an open door with carpeted steps, bathing in soft, ethereal, orange light, leading upstairs to an unknown, unearthly realm. He gingerly walked through the door and up the cream-coloured carpeted flight of stairs when he heard very faint singing, buoyed by a subtle beat. He stopped in his tracks, strained to listen to the songs, but to no avail. The air suddenly became cold, and the sweat that covered his body and face felt like icicles across his skin. His eyes scurried about looking for a sign of what this place was. The only way he could find his yellow angel was to keep going up the stairs.

He continued to climb up and finally came to brand new, big double doors with golden handles. The singing grew louder and more discordant, the music now clearer, like a clear and shiny mirror lifting a reflection of an ugly toad to greater heights of beauty that it did not belong to. He saw a rustic sign hung on the door that read, "Cornerstone Church."

He saw it.

He read it.

But he was booty blind.

So he opened the doors and walked through it.

Alex, who never believed in any religion, opened the doors and walked through it.

The man who harboured a devotion to pussy and the skirt at almost the same fanatical levels of a religious person, opened the doors and walked through it.

The music and the singing blasted through the doors and hit him much harder than the cold air did on his sweaty skin. So hard that he winced and cringed at the decibel assault he faced. The room was dark, but as soon as his eyes adjusted to the light, he immediately knew what was going on. It was the church's Sunday Mass, and the congregation was singing praise and worship songs to a live band playing on stage.

The place was a refurbished movie theatre, with the padded seats set on a sloped floor, the highest part at the rear. The stage lay right in the front and on it were live musicians, eyes closed, playing and swaying to the music of love and devotion, a singer, front and centre, mic in one hand, the other raised with her fingers moving about as she got lost in the moment. He looked around and people, the congregation, were on their feet, swaying to the hypnotic music, eyes closed, hands in the air, mouths agape, singing passionately but out-of-tune to the songs. But they didn't care, they were in the house of their Lord and saviour, Jesus Christ. And if he knew it, Christ was not one to judge you on the tone of your singing voice. He, or specifically his followers, would judge you for everything else. Alex saw men and women, young and old, children and teenagers, losing themselves to the worship as his eyes scanned the dim lighting for his canary yellow angel.

She was easy to spot amidst the sea of worshippers. She sat right by the aisle, her canary yellow dress shone in the darkness, her shimmering skin radiant in the darkness, her glow bringing light to the darkest recesses of the universe. In the house of God, Alex was sure he had found his true love, his once in a lifetime. He gussied up and strode toward her, saw that there was an empty seat next to her, sidled into the empty seat and was prepared to come face to face with his goddess.

Unfortunately for him, it wasn't Lyna that was standing there, just some run-of-the-mill Christian worshipper, arms aloft, eyes closed, and body swaying to the music in sheer and utter devotion to the Word of God. She did look very much like Lyna, but this stranger lacked the self-assuredness and badassery that Lyna carried with her. Up close, this cheap copy of his love of a lifetime suddenly began to take on the look of a hobbit at the bottom of the bottle, beaten, bruised and battered. Disappointed, Alex huffed and puffed as he sat on the cushioned seat, slumped, his head resting on his half-clenched fist wondering what to do next.

*In the morning, when I rise, give me Jesus.*

Alex sank deeper into his seat and was fast becoming aware of the daggers being thrown at him through the eyes of other worshippers for being seated. He cut a petulant yet forlorn figure in the darkness, with only the lights on stage shining on him. His scowl could barely be seen in the low lights but could surely be felt a thousand miles away.

*Give me Jesus, you can have the world, but give me Jesus.*

The band on stage was actually quite good, with the sound mixed very well. It wasn't too loud, nor were they playing with a sonic imbalance as he was able to hear every single note from the instruments with no one instrument being too loud or dominant.

A new song came on. This had to be a medley. A thirty-minute medley. Or it could just be that the band loved playing to an adoring crowd.

*Give thanks with a grateful heart to the Holy One, give thanks because he's Jesus Christ, His Son.*

Alex stewed in his discontent and began to see what a waste of a day this was starting to be. Arms folded like a child throwing a hissy fit, he sat still, unmoving, with only his tapping foot moving not in time to the music but in a brewing frustration.

*And now let the weak say "I am strong." Let the poor say, "I am rich"*

Suddenly, in a flash of inspiration that largely came from below the waist, he snapped onto his feet, raised his arms and began swaying to the music. Not to worship the one true saviour. He sang loud with eyes closed not from sheer and utter devotion to the Word of God. Alex just wanted to get laid with the cheap Lyna copy so it wouldn't be that much of a wasted day. His intentions were clear only to him, his deceit hidden beneath a holy veneer of spiritual piety. Hands still in the air, he joined hands with her and swayed with her in what looked like a dance of faith and religious fervour. She took his hand and joined in what seemed to be a spiritual coming together of strangers in the name of God. That singing segment of Mass lasted thirty more minutes, with the songs drawn out to include audience participation, breaks worked into the songs. So it was thirty blissful minutes of holding hands with his copy girl.

The songs finally ended and the band stopped playing as Alex turned to look at her and said, "You're a new one here, are you? I've been coming here to worship for about three years now, and I've never seen you before."

It was a lie.

"Yes, I am quite new here. I just came here for worship about two months ago, having come to this island about six months before that," she replied with an easy smile that revealed an almost perfect set of white teeth.

"So, who introduced you to this church?" Alex asked.

"No one, I just saw a crowd here and followed. Was quite surprised that there is a church here, because coincidentally, I have been looking for a church to worship in." She spoke in an accent that he could not place.

"Ah, you were a stray sheep, Glad you have found the flock to follow, and the Shepherd for you to look up to," Alex said in a concerted attempt to insert as many religious-ese as he could to make him sound more credible.

"Yes, you can say that I was a stray. Thankfully the house of God never turns away the strays," she said as her eyes shifted and rested on the large crucifix hanging above the stage, the same stage where a pastor was giving his weekend sermon.

Seeing that, Alex said, "It's awe-inspiring, isn't it? That image. That image of a God who died for us, who sacrificed everything for us, and only wants us to love Him and each other. Sometimes I feel there is so much love coming from Him and me that I feel that I am going to explode, that the world, the universe just cannot handle the love that I have for Him."

Lies.

Nevertheless, her face brightened in admiration and awe as she turned to face him.

"I feel the same way too! Every time I look upon the Cross, I feel overwhelmed with love for Him. Sometimes I cry and I cannot contain and envision just how much love there is for Him," she said in a voice that had a mix of childlike innocence and excitement, almost breaking with emotion.

Alex grabbed both her hands, smiled as he looked deep into her eyes and said, "I am glad that I have found a kindred spirit in the house of our Father, his Son and the Holy Spirit. I almost feel like we were supposed to sit next to each other, as the Lord has willed it to be so."

Deceit.

"What is your name?" Alex asked her.

"My name is Sophie. I am from…."

He interrupted her, "Hi, Sophie, my name is Aaron. in the Bible, Exodus 4:14, it means a teacher, and a mountain of strength. And you don't need to tell me where you come from, because it is all God's earth."

Untruth.

"This has never happened to me before, I hardly ever meet anyone in church. Usually I just worship and revel in the presence of the Lord before I go home. But, there is something about you, Aaron…"she said as her voice trailed off, looking deep into his eyes as if expecting a kiss.

Alex was glad to have been able to throw her off just enough for her to mistake her love and devotion for her God onto him. Not all of it though, just enough for her to see him as more than a random stranger from the street. More than just a fellow worshipper in the congregation. She began to see him as a superior. And, as the story of his life, he unknowingly did this, blissfully unaware of the effect he could have when he said or did certain things to people.

They were now seated facing each other and in a world of their own, ignoring the hundreds of other worshippers in the congregation with the pastor in prayer. As far as they were concerned, they were fast becoming each other's answered prayer. Alex, the asshole who now seemed to have lost his heart, who just wanted to get laid. And Sophie, a lonely stranger in a strange land just looking to belong to something bigger than herself, to someone stronger than herself. Alex adjusted his posture to conceal the burgeoning boner he was developing at the prospect of pussy in the pews. Sophie looked at him the same way she looked at the large cross hanging over the stage when the lights went out, signalling the next segment of the program, more singing and worship. They both stood up, still holding hands and began to sway to the music of the Lord.

Alex, usually a patient hunter of the flesh, was suddenly overcome by an urgency he hadn't felt since he was in his early twenties. He just wanted to close the deal right there and then. So he let go of her hand and put it on the small of her back and began lightly caressing it. Sophie did not protest but seemed to enjoy having both spiritual and fleshly pleasures at the same time. It was like having a threesome or a moresome where multiple partners would satisfy your needs simultaneously. As he slowly caressed her with two fingers, he soon laid his whole hand on her back and began to slowly, sensually rub her back in time with the beat of the music and the intensity of the verses and the chorus. He glanced at Sophie and her face was a mask of pain, a mask of pleasure, a wince and a grimace painted with a smile as well as the slightest, faintest touch of orgasm. Her mouth slightly agape, he could almost see the pools of saliva collecting in the corners of her mouth before she gulped it down. Doing this to her, this act of pure sin gave Alex a boner much more thunderous than he ever had, a boner that was bursting through his already skin-tight track pants. He almost had to slap himself from caving into the temptation of dropping his pants right there and then to please himself in the house of God.

Alex continued to caress Sophie, and Sophie loved every minute of it. Consumed by lust, Alex moved his hand further down her back and onto her ample yet saggy bum. He squeezed and caressed it as he felt her G-string underwear through her dress. He left his hand there to linger with a handful of flesh, just waiting for it to turn into a mouthful of flesh. However, her eyes shot open as if snapped out of her lustful stupor. She stopped swaying and without looking at him, she hissed, "Not. Here!" Her face was now painted with disappointment as she shook her head in disapproval of what had just transpired.

He turned cold with fear as his hand shot back to his side as with a wave of terror washed over him. For he too snapped out of his lustful stupor and realised where he was. He stammered an apology out as he excused himself, and Sophie wordlessly moved aside to let him pass as he made his way to the men's room to collect his thoughts. Once there, he washed his face, leaned on the sink and looked himself in the mirror, and it was exactly at that point where his heart grew back, beating harder and growing larger than his boner. He was then brutally attacked by his conscience and left reeling as he looked at his wet shimmering face in the light of the men's room on the mirror and was utterly disgusted at what he saw. The lies, the deceit, the shameless use of God's name in lust, and the disrespect he had shown in the house of God. Most of all, he was utterly ashamed at the way he slithered his way into Sophie's good graces. In all of Alex's flings, one-night-stands and sexcapades, he never had to be deceitful because he always chose women who were similar to him or had a similar agenda as he did, so it could always be boiled down to it being a mutual exchange of goods and services. A payment rendered for time spent and workmanship. It was always an exercise devoid of emotion, and he never had to tug at the heartstrings of his prospects to get them to fuck him like it was his last night on earth. But here he stood, having been blinded by booty, consumed by lust, and slithered his way into the heart of a pious woman, a virtuous woman.

So he did what he did best: rationalize this whole situation through his own faulty lens of logic and reason. And his best solution to this murder of a situation was to walk out of the church, because it wasn't like he would ever be back here, and he didn't even give Sophie his real name. He would walk away from this disaster, and everyone would be none the wiser.

So he did.

He walked right out of the mall into the blazing heat that could very well be the burning flames of hell for him and never looked back. He swore to never come near this place again, and lucky for him, it was in an area he never went to anyway, so it was all good. He just hoped that no one recognised him on the streets in the near future from the short time he was there.

As he walked briskly away from the scene of the crime, his mind took him to somewhere strange, somewhere he had never been before. As he pounded the pavements in the blazing tropical sun, he was brought back to a specific point of time at the airport where he saw the *Mademoiselle*. He remembered her strong arms, her demure smile and the almost perilous meeting of souls that was fleeting enough for him to want more, but long enough for him to be comfortable with it. His pace slowed to a languid stroll, almost as if the hand of the Mademoiselle herself sat reassuringly on his shoulders and was soothing his weary soul. He swore he could also smell the Mademoiselle perfume.

And, yes, Sophie would wonder where that slimy loser went and would eventually figure out she had been sold a batch of snake oil, but there was no harm done, really. No hearts were broken, no one was hurt badly. She would get over it and probably at the moment she realised "Aaron" had disappeared, but for Alex, it might take a while longer for his conscience and his best friend to let him get over this episode. And on some level, Alex didn't want to get over this, because in the weeks to come, he found himself stalking the mall that housed the church from a cafe next to the mall. He did it just so he could get a glimpse of Sophie and was very happy whenever he did. Because he felt that she was the closest thing to Lyna that he could ever be close to, and the last thing he wanted was to forget how she looked. And this allowed him to keep the memory of her, her physique at the very least, fresh in his mind.

**16.**



Carol stared intently at the sizzling slab of red meat cooking on the grill still, like a statue carved on a pedestal, standing frozen as the people walked by. Her eyes flitted between the meat and a timer being held up by Charmaine sitting nearby, both women frozen in their position, poised and ready to strike at something, anything. But it was the clock that struck first, striking 8 p.m. on the dot, which meant it was time to flip the meat, which Carol did expertly while Charmaine grimaced and winced at the imaginary thought of hot oil splashing onto her skin and in her eyes.

Charmaine was not much of a chef, and to be honest, not much of anything in the kitchen, except an eater. Especially the things that Carol whipped up, even if it was a store-bought macaroni and cheese from the microwave, Charmaine would wolf it down just because it was made for her by Carol. Carol, on the other hand, while no Michelin-star chef, had cut her teeth in the kitchen while studying in Australia and had made many a fancy meal herself, so she knew her way well around any kitchen. Carol's latest obsession was to cook the perfect steak, nice and pink in the middle, almost scorched on the outside and sealing the juicy flavours in. Both Carol and Charmaine decided to get together on an evening off to catch up on this, update each other about their lives and bond over meat, brussel sprouts, aioli and a bottle of wine. They were not the kind of friends who talked to each other every day, with both leading busy professional and social lives. Well, it seemed to be only Charmaine who was the one socially busy with her new fiancé and meeting up with his side of friends and family. That pretty much left Carol on her own most of the time, and Charmaine often joked that she would try to meet up as often as she could because she was Carol's adult supervision, a notion that was often met with scorn by Carol, even if it was always in jest.

Both the notion and the scorn.

Nevertheless, they enjoyed each other's company a lot more now than before, because whenever they met, it was quality time, and no time for frivolous and inconsequential small talk. Even as issues, challenges, problems are sorted out, they often spoke of and discussed in depth their pet topics. And both seemed to enjoy this sweet spot of friendship they were in at the moment.

"Wait, so how was Tinder? Did you manage to meet or hook up with anyone?" Charmaine asked as she sipped her glass of red.

"Oh. My. God! That guy was so fucked up! You know what he did? He planned a two-week getaway for him and me, and presented it to me with PowerPoint slides and a spreadsheet right after we finished dinner. I didn't even get to order dessert first!" Carol lamented as she smacked the grill with the tongs in utter annoyance.

Charmaine threw her head back and cackled in uncontrollable laughter, her body shaking sensually for Carol to see, and she slapped the countertop repeatedly in utter disbelief and unbridled joy.

"Great, good, good, laugh at my misery, ya bish. Remember, I am cooking your dinner, you won't know what I put into your meat," a disgruntled Carol said.

Charmaine's gleeful laughter slowly died as she struggled to compose herself. In her quiet moments, she did feel guilty at finding some form of pleasure at Carol's misadventures in dating. It had even increased her popularity among her other circles of friends as she related to them Carol's dating efforts and failures, regardless of how graphic they could be. Carol knew that, and she didn't really mind, because it wasn't like she was the butt of the joke, and she was glad in some way her misfortune had brought laughter and joy to some people.

"Okay okay, sorry sorry." Charmaine gasped as she caught her breath. "How the hell do you meet with these kinda weirdos though? Is it true that whatever it is that you put out to the universe, the universe will return it to you? You know, the law of attraction thing I heard about in some New Age seminar bullshit I had to attend at work."

"I really have no idea what I am 'putting out' to the universe, to be honest. All I know is that I do put out from time to time," Carol said with a wry smile as she tended to the last of the grilled meat, taking it off the grill to rest on the wooden chopping board as she got started on sautéing the brussel sprouts in olive oil, with bits of garlic, chilli flakes, and sea salt. Charmaine grimaced at the sight of greens being prepared as she was not much of a vegetable lover. She only ate it because as always, it was Carol who prepared it for her. Charmaine had felt a strong affection for Carol, since the day they met in the office on Carol's first day at work, some fourteen years ago. Both had been about the same age, fresh out of university, so they banded together. And since they had lunch that day, both had been inseparable; even as life brought them along different and diverging paths, they somehow remained in touch and continued to pour their hearts out to each other. Both were wildly different in terms of characteristics, with Charmaine having a more lackadaisical and unfocused approach to the many things she had on her

218

plate, many of which remained incomplete, while Carol was more organised and maintained a laser focus on one task at a time before moving on. Their common ground had always been their sharp, caustic wit and bitchiness and their inability to suffer fools and men who often did not show them any regard when it came to their professional or general capabilities. You could say that despite being almost complete and polar opposites of each other, they complement each other as they were on the opposite ends of the same spectrum.

"I do feel for you, Care, you work so hard, and once in a while when you wanna find someone other than me to connect with, you get these weirdos," Charmaine said as her voice turned serious laced with sympathy. "And it is *always* weirdos, right, that you end up going out with?"

"Well not all, remember I told you about Khairul? He's actually quite a nice guy, hot body and all. But the micro penis was a major deal-breaker for me." Carol recalled in horror the time she walked out on the tiddly dick, leaving it alone at the hotel. "Oh shit! I have a big ass bone to pick with you, asshole! Remember Joel? Joel who 'loves his mother'?"

"Yes, what was it with him?" Charmaine asked.

"You seriously don't know?" Carol asked incredulously, throwing a fresh clove of garlic at Charmaine.

"Oi, bish! What, what?" Charmaine protested.

"That fucker is a momma's boy! Yes, he loves his momma, but his momma loves him much more! So much that she showed up on our date and yelled at me for taking him away from her!" Carol exclaimed as she repeatedly threw cloves of garlic at Charmaine.

Charmaine, choking on her wine, tried hard to cough, laugh and dodge the cloves of garlic thrown at her. She must have coughed and hacked out both her lungs before she gained composure and said, "Oh shit oh shit oh shit! I had no idea!"

"How the fuck could you introduce me to him!" Carol yelled at Charmaine. "Last warning, Charmaine! Last, fucking, warning!"

Charmaine laughed a laugh of a thousand years and apologised profusely to Carol. "Okay, I promise to be tougher in my vetting process as your lead lady-in-waiting, Queen Carol," Charmaine said in jest, although that had a tinge of truth and seriousness to it.

Carol laughed along with Charmaine because that was the only thing she could do whenever she thought back to the nuclear holocaust of dates she had had, with and without Charmaine's help.

Dinner was served, and they both buried their faces in their juicy steaks, inhaling it because venting was hard work. Especially when it got serious. In between grunts of gastronomic lust and sighs of post coital approval, not much was said as they devoured their dinner in what looked like a grim suburban ritual of blood sacrifice.

"Care, if I get fat, I am so blaming you!" Charmaine said in between mouthfuls of meat and wine. "And I am gonna stop with calorie counting just for tonight. I am going to rip it up at the gym tomorrow. Why, why do I let you do this to me?" Charmaine complained as she wolfed down another mouthful of cow.

Nevertheless, despite the complaints and concerns regarding calories, carbs, gyms and weight gain, their plates were polished clean in record time.

"You know, Charm," Carol said as she finished clearing her plate at the dishwasher. "I know this is a flight of fancy and useless romance, but I want to meet someone who makes me sing, or at the very least makes me play a song in my head, you know what I mean? That one quality in a man, that elusive X-factor, that, that…" Carol's voice trailed off as her eyes glazed over, gazing out into the darkness of the evening.

"Stop it. Stop it! Stop it with that fucking X-factor, that, that…'one quality.' You know, whenever you wax lyrical about that, I never understand a word of what you're saying. Hell, I don't think you even know what that means! I think you're using that as an excuse to stall for something to happen to you or for you, or you really don't know what you want, Miss I Got It All Figured Out and in Control!" a very irritated Charmaine scolded Carol. She impatiently rapped her knuckles on the countertop and elaborated, "You need to decide and nail down a specific type of man you want. Be as shallow or as deep as you want to be, because then it will be easier to paint a mental picture of him and measure that to every guy you meet. Also, easier for me to help you introduce to you to your type of a man instead of bringing to you one Joel after another."

"I *do* know what I want in a man, and I am not using it as an excuse to fuck around or to stall for something. I know what I want, I just find it hard to describe it to everyone, and with even you, the girl who knows me best, and I can't properly articulate it. I have a specific quality in —"

"Yes yes yes, I know, you want someone to make you sing," Charmaine interrupted mockingly.

"Don't you dare mock me, you cow," Carol hissed. "Just because Tim fell landing with his dick inside you, doesn't mean that you got it all," she scoffed as her eyes threw daggers into Charmaine's face.

"Okay, okay," Charmaine backed off. "Okay, you do know that there are people who spend a whole lifetime and then some looking for that *one* but never do find them, when all this while, the actual one passes them by and they are none the wiser?" she added.

"Right. But I am not just gonna settle for *okay*, or *right*. I mean, I am potentially gonna spend the rest of my life with that person, I think I am right to be very picky about it, and if that one elusive quality I am looking for is something that a lot of men do not live up to, then I am happy for them to be just disembodied dicks with voices at my beck and call," Carol said as she stood up and poured herself her second glass of red wine.

"Oh, so you just wanna be all slutty and loose for the rest of your life? Like Cheryl and her bevy of pretty boy toys from China and Korea? You wanna be like her when you turn fifty-five? A sagging sack of skin propped up by strategic pins, needles and knives? I don't think that even if we put together our resources, we can afford the work she did on herself. I think she even got her vocal cords done." Charmaine spoke of a marketing manager they both knew from their old workplace.

They laughed for a little while before a moment of silence descended upon them. The air was heavy, and on a very still night, the smoke from the cooking still lingered in the kitchen, covering it with an eerie mist as the smell of burnt meat hung around like an unwanted house guest. Carol could hear the gulps in Charmaine's throat as she drank her wine and the dull clink her glass made as it made contact with the coaster on the hard surface. In the silence, their breaths synchronized, much like their periods when they were hanging out a lot together. Carol sighed as she took another sip of the exotic Kindzmarauli wine from Georgia. She leaned forward, both elbows on the sparkling clean countertop, eyes gazing into a faraway place with her kitchen-stained white top, coloured with streaks of oil and bloody beef juice that made her look like a warrior in silent contemplation after a big battle. Her hair, tied in a bun at the back of her head, sat in a lazy mess as her feet started to get sore from cooking all day. All Charmaine could hear were the sounds of the neighbourhood, children laughing, dogs barking, vehicles passing by and her neighbours' footsteps dragging by outside the apartment. And all Carol could hear was Scorpion's 'Still Loving You,' which she began to hum during the break in their conversation. She recalled the time when she was on a date at the airport, and she chanced upon a man who, without doing or saying anything, made her sing. She didn't know who he was, she couldn't even recall properly what he looked like, aside from his biceps and his tight khakis, but somehow this mysterious man had managed to embed himself into her mind and would pop up every now and again, and, as he was wont to do, makes her sing. It was months ago and somehow she found herself thinking about that man and wondered if he was her once in a lifetime that had passed her by.

"Is that the song you're talking about? The song that will play in your head, the song that you will sing, when you meet that one?" Charmaine whispered, her voice lowered, suddenly gravelly and hoarse.

"Yes, this," Carol replied.

"What is it with you and this song?" Charmaine asked.

"You remember Aunt Rachel and Auntie Sam? The two tattooed aunties you followed me to visit at the hospital last year?" Carol asked Charmaine.

"Oh, yes, the two lionesses of sass, the OG queens of shade! I love them! How are they? Are they alright?" Charmaine asked in earnest.

"Not so good actually, but I'll tell you more later. But yeah, it was them who introduced me to rock music, and one song led to another. I came across that song one day while I was studying Maths one day. And that song stuck with me all day that day. It was also the day when I met Mark, the first boy I had a crush on. So I always relate that song to love, and to being in love. I know it's weird, it's a song about a failing relationship on the verge of a breakup, but it is that kind of passion and longing I want to have in a man, and for a man to have for me," Carol explained at length.

"Mark? Tell me more!" Charmaine asked.

"He was this boy I met a long long time ago, back when I was in secondary school. I was taking a break from studying and took a walk around the neighbourhood when I walked past this bunch of football boys; his friends and he were hanging out at the nearby patch of grass. And you know how boys behave like monkeys around girls, jumping around, loud and obnoxious. But Mark was different. He was cool, nonchalant and almost didn't care. But he cared enough to come and say hi to me as I walked by. He walked with me that evening and even walked me home. And we ended up exchanging numbers. Till today, I don't really remember what exactly happened, but all I can remember was 'Still Loving You' playing in my head as he spoke and as we walked that evening."

"What happened then?" Charmaine probed.

"In the next few weeks, we ended up talking on the phone for hours on end, and of course we ended up dating. Our first date was to this small record shop in some weirdo shopping mall where the uncle allowed us to listen to any cassette album we wanted. We spent hours there that day listening to rock music and would spend hours more in the weeks to come at that record shop together. He loved the same type of songs I did, and he, together with that record shop uncle, would show me many more bands of the same kind. And I remember the day he asked me to be his girlfriend.

He bought me chocolate ice cream with a cherry on top, in this weird tall margarita glass from some seafood restaurant downstairs at that weirdo shopping mall, sang the lyrics of 'Sweet Child O'Mine' and then asked me to be his sweet child at the record shop. All this while, the uncle at the shop was looking and smiling. Quite unusual, I know, but it was, well, sweet. And he was sweet too, we had a good time together, and he was always so kind, caring, and thoughtful. He always said the right things at the right time, and our families loved having us around," Carol recalled with a glint of nostalgia in her eyes and longing in her voice.

"He sounds weirdly dreamy. What next?" Charmaine probed further.

Carol took another mouthful of red wine, as if bracing herself for an impact of having to confront her past, and continued, "We were perfect for each other at the time, but it ended, just like that, I don't know why. He called one day to say he is going away, and he is not coming back. I thought he was being melodramatic because of having to serve national service, but a friend told me that he didn't have to serve. His friends said he was sent away to study overseas by his parents. Or was it that he had to return home to his parents. Other versions I heard was that his parents divorced and that he chose to stay with his mum overseas. Even as my mum and dad asked me what happened to Mark, I never knew how to reply. And till today, when they do ask, I still don't know what to say other than it ended. So yeah, then it was me who is now singing 'Still Loving You' in the hope of him coming back to me.

"So, it is probably because I never had much of a closure from Mark, even as I got over him and what happened. Ever since then, how he made me feel, the songs I hear and sing when I was together with Mark are the benchmarks for any relationship that I go into, and for every guy I meet," Carol said with openness that could only be seen with Charmaine.

"Aww you poor dumbass romantic. Still doesn't explain why you get all the weirdos dating you and you putting their three-second micro dicks into your mouth and hands," Charmaine, whose face was flushed red with wine and whose gastronomic bloodlust was satiated, whispered menacingly.

"Fuck you, you cow, I was being serious and baring my heart and soul to you," Carol hissed back at Charmaine, not defensively but more in annoyance.

Charmaine laughed heartily as she dodged a handful of ice that was thrown at her by Carol and apologised in between fits of laughter. Carol loved how both of them could go from being at each other's throats to feeling such love and affection for each other in an instant. Most of all, she loved how they could be apart for an extended period of time but would always pick up where they left off, as if no time had passed since they last met. *This is probably what having a best friend is like*, Carol thought. *Better still, this is what having a sister is about*, something she never had a chance to experience, being an only child.

Her mum always said to her that she had sisters in Aunt Rachel and Aunt Sam because they were adult kids. She could see how Mum would say that about them, but to her, Aunt Rachel and Aunt Sam were more than just friends. They brought rock and roll to her, taught her about boys, warned her about life and showed her how to be tough, independent and strong. Like how the only person she should ever rely on was herself, to always watch your back, or at the very least, always prepare yourself for the worst case scenarios, and to keep a tight circle of friends. The times they spent together at the salon, at family gatherings, and — as she grew older — at bars and coffee shops, Carol learnt more about life, about how to be a woman, about how to conduct herself, than any school with the most highly trained teachers could ever have taught her.

And then there were the bar wenches Eve, Natalie and Alice, more women who looked out for her as she made her foray into adulthood, the corporate world and toward independence. Women who taught her to never rely on handouts and to stand your ground in the face of the male-dominated world of business, and how she needed to work twice as hard as a woman to be half as successful as the men in the business. Lessons that had helped her thrive amidst strong challenges at the workplace, or at the very least, these women were there for her with a plate of piping hot fried rice and an ice cold pint of Guinness or a glass of whiskey sour. Not a bad bunch of teachers to have and to be taught by as she took on the characteristics these women exuded, the strength and resilience, but also the vulnerability, the gnawing insecurity despite being placed in a strong position, a certain paranoia that drove some to being better and others to insanity.

And now, she had Charmaine. More likely she had taken on Charmaine, whom she would mentor every now and then and teach as the other women had with Carol. She had had to nurse Charmaine through three messy breakups, been her late night professional counsel on negotiating office politics and in flirting and seducing the men she had her eyes on. They hardly ever got it right, but therein lay the beauty and fun of their friendship. She often wished that Charmaine could have seen Aunt Rachel and Aunt Sam at the height of their youth and badassery, tattooed, hot snarky lips and swinging hips swaying to Def Leppard's 'Pour Some Sugar On Me,' instead of at the twilight of their lives, vulnerable and frail by their bedside, writhing in pain, one cancer-ridden, the other suffering from debilitating heart failure. Carol knew it was a matter of time before she would lose two major influences in her life to age and disease, but it was neither something she wanted to nor was ready to deal with. And it was then that thought came flashing into her mind.

*Is that why I am out of sorts with myself and meeting these weirdos?*

*I cannot deal with the fact that Aunt Sam and Aunt Rachel are sick, so I am lashing out, dating and just fucking any weirdo that comes by?*

*I am in such a need to feel good about something that I am willing to do anything, or anyone, just to feel good about the situation.*

*A situation that renders me helpless to do anything to ease the pain of these two women I love so much?*

Carol finally told Charmaine about Aunt Rachel and Sam, poured her heart out about their illnesses, their struggles with their illnesses as well as their rapidly aging and breaking down bodies. Most of all, Carol confided how she feared losing the two women she had loved so dearly for a large part of her life. Charmaine listened intently and finally understood Carol.

"Is this why you're getting around these weirdos? It's because you yourself are out of sorts?" Charmaine asked gently, in a very maternal and comforting tone, as if reading Carol's mind.

"Is it because you find it hard to confront their mortality, as well as your own, that you are lashing out, desperate for something, anything to make you feel good about yourself, or the situation? And maybe, the worst of all, you feel helpless, with all the strength you have and the knowledge that you have amassed, you are still unable to help the ones who matter most to you?"

"I don't know, Charm. Maybe yes. Maybe not. I really don't know. All I know is that I don't feel as good as I usually do about things, about myself, and haven't been since I took you to see them in hospital. And now, getting updates about them and how some days they seem to be better, and how they would take a turn for the worst on other days, I just cannot take it anymore," Carol said as she buried her face in her hands. "On one hand, and I feel fucking guilty saying this, I want them to just let go and die so they won't suffer anymore. That seems to be the logical, humane thought to have. But the more I think about it, the more I feel their deaths have less to do with releasing them from their suffering than it is about us who are suffering, watching them like that.

"About me."

"That part of me who just cannot accept that they are that frail and sickly. That little girl who grew up watching the two aunties kick ass, but now having their assess handed to them by Father Time. The girl who cannot stand the sadness and helplessness as I watch them wither away and die. It's very selfish of me to say that, right?" Carol said as her voice began to crack.

Charmaine did not say anything but just welcomed Carol's weary head to lie on her shoulders as her body shook in fear. No words needed to be said at that moment. As a heavy silence descended upon them in the kitchen, they both sighed a deep sigh. Charmaine's mind racing and gears clicking, thinking how she could help her best friend through this, and not just by sending positive messages, vibes and memes via social media. But truly as a friend, a sister, a confidante. She then realised that she was already being a friend, a sister and a confidante. She was there to comfort her in her time of need, and there were neither words nor vibes and memes needed. Carol just needed to know that her shoulders were there for her to bury herself in. Charmaine put her glass down and wrapped her arms around Carol, cradling her, protecting her, giving her maternal instincts a good workout as she wordlessly consoled an increasingly distraught friend in need.

Carol closed her eyes tight, rested her head on welcoming shoulders that were very familiar with her head. She shifted and buried her face in Charmaine's shoulders in an effort to suppress the tears that threatened to roll down her cheeks. She hated to cry, and to be vulnerable, but if anyone should see her be all that and more, it had been and should be Charmaine. Her eyes closed, face cradled by Charmaine's reluctantly strong yet reliable shoulders, Carol quietly hummed the melody of 'Still Loving You,' as an image of a man began to take shape in her mind. She was brought back to the time she was on that Tinder date with Lawrence at the airport, where she saw a man. It was the regular-looking man in a short-sleeved maroon shirt, sleeves folded up to reveal taut biceps, almost screaming to be released from the grip of the fabric. He wore brown khaki pants, with a matching belt and Doc Marten boots. He looked normal, almost unremarkable, and he did not stand out in the crowd, but there was something about him. He was, by all accounts, strange and bordering on creepy, sniffing the air, sighing and hovering over her at the Starbucks, but there was something about him that triggered in her a familiar sensation. A sensation she recalled from years ago when she was with Mark.

The sensation, that feeling, that memory.

The one who made her sing Scorpions' 'Still Loving You.'

## 17

"**D**ude, this beer sucks, no wonder it's so cheap!" Alex lamented as he crushed the now empty blue beer can.

"What beer is it, Foster? Oh, it's Jester, hah!" Ian laughed. "What the hell brand is this? I've never even heard of it. See what you get when you scrimp and save on the good things in life?" Ian said mockingly as he gently sipped his glass of white.

"I am so not scrimping and saving just on a self-imposed austerity drive. I need to save money, dude, I wanna go back to gallivanting in the Euros again," Alex replied as he cracked open a different can of beer.

"Oh, you going to that side of the woods again? Why?" Ian asked. "Oh no. You're not going to search for that little Russian trollop you're so madly in love with? Why why why? Why her? I don't really know her and I haven't even met her, yet I am very annoyed by her."

"I thought, of all people, you would get it. She is my once in a lifetime okay," Alex said as he chugged his beer.

"No, I don't get it, what is there to get? She left you high and dry. Yes, it was for her family, but she has no excuse to leave it hanging as it is now and for not getting in touch to either end it for closure or pick up where you guys left off," Ian lectured him, in a very familiar spiel that he had spat out to Alex's face many a time "She better be dead or dying in a frozen tundra somewhere in Siberia, and only then will she have an excuse for jumping off this earth."

Alex looked out the window with a faraway look in his eyes, reminiscing about the first time they met in the hotel room. The first time they fucked off the books. The first time they met at her new condominium. Ultimately, it was last time they met at the bar that was the memory that burnt itself into his heart, the one memory that clung onto him like a cancerous wart on his chest.

"Dude, look at me!" Ian barked as Alex snapped out of his nostalgic daydream.

"You are not sitting there and thinking about her. I did not come here to hang out with you and to indulge in your broken dream. Hell, your dream is not just broken, it's *gone*. And you need to move the fuck on!" Ian continued to bark at Alex.

Alex sat there in silence with no retort and no comeback because he knew that Ian was right. He really needed to get over Lyna and to stop measuring every girl he met with how Lyna was.

"You're right, man. Her memory and the idea she represents is like an all-consuming wildfire, bright, the flames dancing seductively, licking all that stands between her, but, in truth, it burns everything down to a blackened, charred husk of nothingness."

"With all that said, you are still pining for her. With pairs of balls you've grown, you would drop it all to the ground in an instant if she tells you to, wouldn't you?" Ian said as he mocked Alex's spinal growth spurt.

Alex nodded and quietly agreed with Ian. He still wondered why someone he just wanted a free lay from had such a hold and sway over him.

"I think I love her, dude," Alex finally spat out loud.

"No, you're not. You're in love with the idea of her. You're in love with what she represents, and what it means for you to have her hanging off your arms. You're in love with how she makes you feel, and what she makes you look like," Ian scolded him, like Mrs Janet D'Silva did when Alex was nine years old and had forgotten to do his homework. Back then, he had Rahman to comfort him, to protect him. Not anymore. "No, you are not in love with her. She is just a trophy for you. The whore you managed to convince to not charge you and sleep with you for free. She is no different from the auntie at the shops who gives you free expired bread and discounted over-ripe avocados. And you can't wait to show her off to everyone."

Ian was very frustrated and wanted to rip Alex a new one, because for months now, all he had heard was "Lyna this, Lyna that," how she was his once in a lifetime, and that "none can equal her splendour," "sleeping with her is like having four women in bed," and Ian has had enough. It was starting to feel like Ian was the one who needed to break up with Alex. Nevertheless, he realised that Alex needed to get out of this funk and he hated seeing his best friend stuck in this vicious cycle of self-loathing and grief, as much as Alex claimed that he was alright.

Ian poured himself another glass of wine from Alex's wine cabinet. Both were having pyjama sessions at Alex's apartment, eating and drinking in their pyjamas, lounging on the sofa looking at a switched off flat screen TV. Dinner was a simple slab of barely cooked meat and toasted Italian bread dipped in infused olive oil, and was long gone and their plates washed and dried. Dessert was a simple bowl of ice cream, wolfed down in record time as the bowls sat on the coffee table, licked clean, so now they were working their way through a bottle of exotic wine. Ian was sitting  languidly yet resplendently on the massive orange-coloured wingback armchair like an aristocrat lording over his realm, a glass of wine in hand, legs crossed, swaying to a silent beat, elbows resting on the armrests like a stone, a strong, scolding stone. Alex was slouched on his sofa, his usual pose of late, legs wide open, one arm barely hanging on to his wine glass on the armrest, the other slumped on his side, docile and waiting for instructions to scratch him. He looked like he just wanted to melt into the sofa and be someone's piece of furniture for the rest of his life. *Preferably Lyna's piece of furniture,* he thought as he quietly sipped his wine.

"It's not like I'm not trying to get over her. I am, I've been trying hard to get back on the saddle and get out of this funk," Alex whined.

"Oh yeah? How'd that turn out? Let me see, vaginal odour, melting face, olive oil weirdo turning you into a tossed salad, and *not* in a good way, and then what else do we have, oh yeah, the tranny. Did I miss anyone?"

"Yeah, I forgot to tell you about the backpacker girl with the skid marks."

Ian choked and spat his wine in laughter, badly shaking with glee and almost breaking the wine glass he was holding. "You did not tell me about this, tell me tell me! Wait, do I need to prepare a bucket next to me in case I puke out my dinner?"

Alex rolled his eyes and recounted the story of the time he met Sara, the unhygienic backpacker who badly needed a wash in Bangkok. And therein lay the basis of their friendship: Alex living his life, doing his thing, getting himself into a weird, sticky situation, getting out of it, and recounting it to Ian who laughs his ass off at it. Alex weirdly enjoyed the fact that his misery had made someone laugh and was almost infamous in some of Ian's other circle of friends.

"You know what you should have done? Asked her if she wanted to take a shower with you. How is that for romance and foreplay?" Ian said in between fits of laughter.

"Yeah, and she will wipe me down with the garbage water face towel from Hell instead of having a proper shower," Alex said with a shiver down his spine.

Both laughed heartily as the wine flowed more freely and moods began to lighten.

"You know, I thought it was difficult for gay men, but guys like you make our experience seem like playschool," Ian said.

"Dude, gay men have it easy, okay. Because it involves men, and men are promiscuous. So getting laid is like getting a coffee. It's not a chore, it's a choice with you guys," Alex shot back.

"Yeah true, but getting dick and buggery are not all that we want okay. We, like you straight people too, want connection, that feeling of a million butterflies in our stomach, the romance and the love," Ian pined.

"Yeah noted, with thanks," Alex said mockingly. "What I am saying is it's easier for men. Gay men, straight men, they are essentially simple dumbasses. And in a gay relationship where both parties are like-minded and equally promiscuous, then it can make things very simple. Now, add a woman to it, and things will get complicated beyond imagination," Alex replied.

"No, you idiot," Ian scolded him. "It is when emotions are involved, that is when it gets complicated. And gay relationships do involve a whole lot of emotion too you know. So stop it with your disparaging of the fairer sex. Misogyny is not a good colour on you, dude."

"I'm just saying that you guys have it easier because men are less complicated, that's all," Alex said as he began his ideological retreat.

"And I am correcting you in that it is not women who complicate things, but emotions that do. Men in gay relationships have emotions too. As much as all men, gay and straight, are promiscuous, we all have emotions, and they do get involved. So what I am saying is, *that* is exactly where it gets complicated. For both gay and straight relationships.

"You know, when was the last time I was on a proper date?" Ian continued. "A real date, coffee, drinks, a meal, conversation, without being asked to go back to my place, have sex and not see each other again? It has been thirteen years since I had a date like that. Thirteen fucking years. Because now, all my dates end with, 'So, are we going to go back to your place for sexy time?'" Ian complained as he rolled his eyes hard.

"Wait that would be my dream date!" Alex laughed, but deep inside he knew that wasn't what he wanted either.

"You stupid cow, stop thinking with your dick and see this from my perspective, you horny idiot. I don't want meaningless sex anymore. I want to be in love, I want that connection and chemistry, I want that slight tingle of romance. I want to be in a loving, respectful yet irreverent relationship. And I am sure you want that too with your Russian trollop or whoever it is that is renting a space in that convoluted head of yours, mate," Ian said, his voice starting to sound shrill and frantic before he realised how close he was to losing control and chilled the hell down.

Alex leaned back into the couch, played with his glass of wine and looked at Ian. They had known each other for nine years now, and both had risen quickly in each other's esteem with their penchant for steak, good wine and the occasional promiscuous behaviour. They tolerated and understood each other's quirks and idiosyncrasies, the kind that would freak other people out. They never judged each other's lifestyle choices no matter how questionable it might seem but would provide honest counsel when the situation called for it. Ian, and another one of their friends Marzie, took pride in being Alex's adult supervisors, to curb his often salacious appetite for debauchery that would very often land him in hot water. Alex respected Ian's counsel, even as he disagreed with it and the arguments they got into. The frequent clash of ideas never dented their friendship but strengthened it to the point where both were able to confide in each other about anything in a somewhat bizarre but supportive emotional three-way. And now Alex could not imagine his life without his favourite homosexual, just as Ian acknowledged that life would never be the same without him listening to and laughing at Alex's shenanigans before counselling him like a baby brother he wished he had.

Alex stretched out on the sofa and let out an almighty yawn before getting up to fix himself a whiskey old-fashioned, his go-to drink when he wanted to take it up a notch for the evening. Or as Ian would say, his old-man drink to drown out the day. As he stood there mixing his drink, his mind replayed the events of the past few months in his head. The transsexual experiment, Tabitha, the skid-marked backpacker, the near-blasphemous pick-up at the church. He chuckled to himself as he recalled those memories and how mortified he was at that point. However, he soon saw a pattern emerging. When things got out of hand on his encounters with women, his mind would usually drift to his happy place with Lyna frolicking in the background. But ever since his brief encounter with the Mademoiselle at the airport, she seemed to have taken Lyna's place. Not frolicking or in slow motion, but sitting up, legs crossed, in a form-hugging burgundy dress, her hanging foot swaying to an idle beat, the rest of her motionless, expressionless, like a stone whose mere presence was enough of a mockery or an inspiration to him. He kept his mind's eye on her now very familiar face, her every feature and flaw now more recognisable, her faraway voice humming that familiar tune still ringing in his ears. Her movements limited, her words few, but usually none, yet she was able to maintain an imposing presence in his mind, even if it was only for a few seconds.

Alex stood still like a stone by the kitchen counter, with mixers and other bar top paraphernalia littered across the counter, resting his elbows on the matte red stone counter. He tried to focus on the Mademoiselle, trying hard to recall who she was and where they met. He didn't think that they had slept together because he wouldn't not remember it unless something untoward happened during their tryst. He was very confused but excited at the same time, like a dog wagging its tail, panting hard, tongue hanging out in anticipation of his new toy.

"Oh dude dude, you remember Hilda? The one you told me about, how you had a crush on her way back when back in the day?" Ian suddenly remarked.

Alex snapped out of his Mademoiselle daze, turned to face Ian and said, "Oh yeah, last I heard was that she got married, popped three kids out and is now in matrimonial bliss in Texas or something. Yeah, what about her?"

"Oh, she's back in town," Ian said, as if it would be something of importance for Alex.

"Is she still married, or she left that fella in the lone star state? If so, are you telling me this so that I can swoop in and be the new father figure to her children, and be her daddy figure?" Alex said, words dripping with sarcasm, but not denying that there was a part of him that wanted that to be true.

"No, I am just telling you that she's back in town. And stop being such a predatory opportunist please. We're talking about someone's family here, okay," Ian retorted.

"It is of no importance to me that she's back in town, dude," Alex snapped back. However even as he did, he also wondered if she still looked like a chimera, one that he would love to have a proper date with, and maybe even another chance at wooing her this time without weird adolescent hormones interfering in the flirting. It was eons ago that he went on that date with her on the beach, yet he still remembered almost every minute detail like it was yesterday. Alex remembered the way her hair fell across her face, how her skin seemed to shimmer in the dusk, how her smile seemed to light the dark pathway they were on.

"Wait, how do you know her?" Alex asked.

"Oh, we were in college together back in the day, when she rode her big-ass, off-road bike ferrying me around campus. This was in ninety-six, if I have my dates correct. And you mentioned her to me several times about how you dated her once," Ian replied matter-of-factly.

Alex grunted audibly, exhaled and ignored Ian. Because, as he was wont to do, he wanted to indulge in a touch of nostalgia and recreate what happened in his mind, but the image of the Mademoiselle, like a legion of infantrymen storming the gates of a castle, came barging into his mind, sitting still, judging him on a throne, subtly shaking her head in disapproval, drumming her fingers on her lap, judging him for his seemingly unsavoury choices of his imagination.

"Okay, so why are you randomly mentioning her to me? Right after we talked about dating and hooking up," Alex said, still unable to let it go.

"Because as far as I know, she is your first love, right? I wanted to remind you about how that feels like, maybe it will trigger something in you and inspire you, or something, I dunno," Ian replied.

"Hah, if you're talking first loves, then you'd have to go way back to primary school, dude. It was 1989, with this girl Zubaidah from the school near mine. We'd meet at the bus stop every day after school. Man, we were tight! We held hands, our dates would be every Saturday at the public library where we would read books together, followed by lunch at the A&W for waffles, ice cream and root beer float," Alex said whimsically, a faraway look in his eyes as he recalled the innocent times he had with Zubaidah.

"How is this the first time I'm hearing about her? What happened to her? Your stupid ass dumped her, right?" Ian quizzed.

"No, I liked her very much. She just disappeared. We had drifted apart a little bit because I was sitting for the national exams that year. But it was only for a few months, and when I wanted to see her again, she was gone. According to her entourage, she had stopped coming to school even before the exams started, so I don't know. No one knows, it was as if she upped and left," Alex said with a very subtle tinge of sadness in his voice, one that Ian could sense.

"Okay, if you tell me that Zubaidah, or even if I take it and stretch it far and wide, Hilda, either one of them, is your once in a lifetime, I can understand. They could very well be your once in a lifetime, but please, not that super dodgy Stalin-esque lizard-witch who pimped her colleague out to you," Ian scolded Alex.

240

"Yes. No more," Alex mumbled as the image of the Mademoiselle again came wafting into his mind like a cool breeze on a hot and balmy tropical afternoon.

# 18.

"You gonna be okay there, hun?" Charmaine asked, a sympathetic look scratched across her face.

"Yeah, I'll be fine," Carol said as she shrugged off the emotional weight whose coils had been tightening around her insides like a serpent wrapped around its prey.

Both were at the front door as they bade each other good-bye after a night of emotional catharsis and self-reflection. Carol was unsure if she felt better because she was finally by herself, something she had gotten very comfortable with, or the fact that she had unloaded on Charmaine the issues plaguing her lately. She stood by the open door longer and watched as Charmaine walked away, her matronly hips swaying clumsily in her strides as her grey capri pants clung tightly around them. Carol noted how Charmaine didn't seem to walk nor strut around, but she seemed to scurry around like a librarian on duty, clipboard clutched close to her chest. Yet the sway of her hips seemed to be very pronounced, and as Charmaine disappeared down the steps at the end of the corridor, Carol sighed deeply as if bracing herself for another unwelcome night of loneliness.

She reached for her keys nearby, locked the very imposing, painted-black wrought iron gates before she closed the heavy vintage wooden door. She turned to look at the house that she bought and poured her heart and soul into so that it felt like a proper home. The walls were painted a cool lime green and stood in contrast to the deep purple on other walls. The  dark wood flooring gave the house a rustic country feel to it, and the vintage furniture pieces, which she called the accent pieces of her living room, enhanced the exotic, modern beach resort aesthetic that she wanted. A prince's ransom was put into achieving the look, as well as countless sleepless nights poring over samples and photos from magazines and online. All to build a house she could call her own, that reflected the complex multi-faceted sides of her.

*Why did I do it all like this?*

*It's not like there is anyone who can appreciate this,*

*Well, other than Charmaine.*

*Shut up, Carol.*

*Self-pity is not a colour that looks good on you.*

She scanned the kitchen and decided that Charmaine had done a very good job of clearing the dishes and cleaning the kitchen. Stoves tops and all seemed to sparkle a lot more than when Carol cleaned and scrubbed them. Charmaine even looked graceful and elegant as she toiled in the kitchen, sometimes even on her hands and knees. It was an elegance that Carol could never achieve and not something she strove for anyway. She was just happy for the kitchen and her house in general to be clean enough to be free of unwelcome insects and rodents. She walked over to the windows, shut them for the night, but stopped herself before she got into the shower for a quick wash before she retired for the night. It was her nightly ritual, a set of things that needed to be done before she could put herself into the right frame of mind for a restful night. Quick shower, a thorough brush of her pearly whites, mouthwash, face wash and moisturiser.

That was set number one.

Once that was done, she could proceed with set number two, which was to close and secure all windows and to double check that she had locked both the gate and front door. Not that she needed to be paranoid, living in one of the safest countries in the world, but it was something she had been doing since she was a child. To ensure that everything was secure and locked down before she could be at peace. What followed next were the lights and electrical outlets that were not in use to be switched off. Her laptop, which had been playing music all night from her Spotify playlist, was finally silenced, and she breathed in the sudden silence surrounding her flat. Making a concerted effort to not even look at her internet browser, she quickly shut down her laptop and turned off the lights in the hall. The room descended into darkness but was soon bathed in the light coming from outside, the orange street lights, the bright white from other units and the red-hued glow coming from the distant city skyline. Carol stood in the darkness for a moment, giving her flat a visual onceover to ensure that everything was in place before having a final look out the window, as if bidding goodnight to the world outside before shutting the casement windows tight and locking them. All eight of them surrounded the house, and once the buzz from the outside world had been shut out, an almost deafening silence seized the flat and hung heavily in the air. Just the way Carol liked it. In the darkness, she strode confidently to her bedroom, a journey she had made a thousand times alone.

Shutting the door behind her, she turned on the air conditioning and stood at the foot of her bed for a few minutes to let the room cool down from the balmy tropical heat that had enveloped the flat before getting into her pyjamas and getting under the sheets. She enjoyed the biting cold in the room while she kept warm under her sheets and the final set of things to do before bed. She rubbed bare calves against

244

her sheets, something that her mum said she had been doing since she was a baby. It gave her comfort and relaxed her and was the final act that would signal her arrival to slumberland. With the wine still swirling in her head, the ever-increasing cold gripping the room tightly, it was a matter of minutes before she was out like a light. There wasn't even time for thoughts, reflections, nor flights of fancy.

She soon found herself in a strange orange-hued, sepia-filtered world. It smelled like a stale kitchen because she was in a kitchen. It was a kitchen that looked like it was in the fifties, with a stained, single-door fridge, discoloured white tiles on the wall, and cream-coloured kitchen cabinets, some of which were worn from use. She looked around apprehensively as the silence rang loud in her ears. But she wasn't confused, because she knew why she was there, and that was where she was supposed to be at that point. She leaned against the old fridge and waited, when Sandra Oh came barging in, dressed in hospital scrubs, panicking.

"We have a problem. The cadavers we bought from that guy for practice tonight did not arrive! I can't believe you talked me into trusting that seedy little crone with the white van!" Sandra exclaimed frantically as she paced about the room, stomping on the wooden floor. Carol wanted to say something but felt that she didn't need to; she was exactly where she was supposed to be, and that was all she needed to do. She watched as Sandra paced frantically and thought out loud about cadavers, body parts, internal organs and ointments. She looked down and saw that she was also wearing hospital scrubs and sneakers, leaning against the kitchen cabinets waiting for something to unfold.

She must've blinked, because she was then transported to a graveyard. It was still an orange and sepia-hued world with rolling hills dotted with pale tombstones, some weathered and worn, some covered with moss, and mounds of earth as far as her eyes could see. She stood at what seemed to be at the edge of the forest, right where the greenery ended and where the graveyard began. There seemed to be a very thin layer of mist rising ominously from the ground and lingering, some swirling, as if dancing to the music of the dead, some like pale tongues licking the heavy air.

But Carol was not afraid; in fact, she was at peace. She enjoyed the silence, the occasional rustle of the branches of the trees swaying in the breeze, the way the wind whispered softly in her ears and caressed her skin. The smell of grass mingled with wet soil and the aged bark, branches and root of the trees, all combined to a unique musk of nature lingering around her as if welcoming her to this neck of the woods. Carol looked around, and everything seemed still, waiting for her command. Carol took a tentative step forward and the rustle of the leaves she stepped on seemed to throw the entire picturesque tableau into life, with the sound of the earth being punctured piercing the air. She snapped her head toward the sound and saw Sandra with a shovel in hand, still in her scrubs that was now dirty and covered in wet earth, digging into the ground. Next to her lay a pick axe slumped on the ground after what seemed like a hard day's work, and mason jars of all sizes littered the area around Sandra. Carol took a closer look and saw that the mason jars were filled with a human's internal organs, a brain in a bar with the unmistakable fleshly curls swimming in an unknown clear fluid, a deep red slab of meat which she assumed was a human liver sloshing about in a bucket filled with liquid, an unborn foetus seemingly alive but very much dead, floating in what looked like a stasis chamber of a mason jar. All of this did not seem out of place for Carol as she just looked at the things and Sandra, busy at work.

"Well, are you just gonna stand there or are you gonna help? You do know that this is all your fault, right, Missy?" Sandra barked, in a high-pitched, panicked voice. Carol shrugged, looked away and took a step back into the forest where she heard a faint sound bleeding into the air around her. She closed her eyes, trying to focus on the sound, and she could barely make out a beat, a melody. It was clear that a sound, a rhythm, a melody was hanging in the air, but trying to catch it was like trying to eat a bowl of soup with a pair of chopsticks. And that made her increasingly frantic as her breath quickened and her head began to throb as she tried to grasp that mysterious sound while trying to drown out Sandra's incessant ramblings. She tried to take a step toward the melody, but she was unable to move. She seems to be rooted to the spot, with Sandra barking in one ear, the melody in the other, her eyes searching for something, anything that she could see as a visual anchor. But all she could see were rolling hills of tombstones that seemed to mock her. She felt a strange weight on her shoulders that was causing her to sink into the soft earth. She looked up into the orange sky that was holding its breath as the sun retreated in the distant horizon and she felt like the sun setting, slowly sinking into the earth.

She smiled to look away when a gust of cold air slapped her hard. Her eyes were heavy as lead as she forced them open to realise she was back in her room, safe and snug under her sheets, with the air conditioning like a winter demon giving out periodic gusts of cold air.

Man that was a dream and a half.

She lay in bed and drank the silence of her bedroom, a silence that hung heavy, and broken occasionally by the low hum of the air conditioning. Her room was an island of peace when compared to what went on in her dream.

Shit. It's only 3 a.m., nice, on a day I get to sleep in as late as I want to, I get woken up at 3 a.m.

I need to pee.

But it's so nice and warm here.

Wonder what the dream meant though.

She wondered about the significance of the body parts, cadavers and the sepia-tinted atmosphere of her dream as well as the setting of the forest and the graveyard. Most of all, she wondered about that strange melodic sound she kept hearing in the dream. A sound that was fast fading from her memory.

And Sandra Oh? I need to watch less TV.

Okay, I do need to pee.

Carol lay in bed for a few more minutes, listening to the moans and groans made by her old flat. She used to get scared of these nocturnal noises as a child, but she outgrew them at age twelve. By sheer will, she pried herself out of bed, and her body was soon enough assaulted by the freezing cold air latching on to every inch of her skin. She shivered in the cold embrace of the air, put her arms around herself and skipped out of her freezing room into the heavy, balmy living room and heaved a sigh of relief. After washing up, she cracked open her kitchen window and looked out into the night. A block of flats obscured the view of a park from her home, so all she could see was a giant blob of white concrete with precise corners, punctured with little black holes that were the windows to the apartments. She breathed in the cool night air, and it tasted of the early morning dew with cigarette smoke mixed in.

Carol looked up into the night sky and saw that the sky was of a deep crimson hue as if blood had been splattered across the sky. The waxing gibbous moon appeared an angry orange, like the lesser son of the great sire that was the sun.

Beautiful. It's been a while since I took note of nature. Maybe that was what the forest and the rolling hills were about.

Carol continued to stare blankly into the night sky. However, she wasn't looking at anything or anyone in particular, she was just spacing out when she was reminded of the sound, that melody, that faint tune she heard in her dream earlier. The sound had faded deeper into her subconscious and try as she might, she still could not grasp what the sound was. She tried humming a tune, any tune, with the hope that it would lock into the time signature or the melody of that mysterious sound, but she was just unable to as the tune faded further into oblivion.

I hate this. It's like a musical worm has crawled in my ear and is now keeping quiet just to torment me.

She heard the distant rumble of an engine coming to life, the almost noiseless slither of the tyres of a bicycle rolling over the tarred roads, a shrieking of mice scurrying near the bins – the cacophony of the suburbs that drowned out the melody she had in her head. Giving up, she slammed the window shut in a huff and stomped back into the ice-box of a bedroom. She flew into her bedroom and dove under her sheets and tried to get back to sleep. She tossed and turned for a few minutes before a stillness descended upon her that brought along a restful slumber.

She heard that sound again. It was a high-pitched wail of seemingly random but repeated notes. There was nothing but darkness around her and she seemed to be swimming in a place where time and space fused together in a primordial soup. But all she could focus on was that sound. The high-pitched notes seem to ring prominently before melting into the swirling darkness and reverberate across the space in a low, unrecognisable rumbling of a drone before picking up its pitch in an infernal cycle of sound waves. Tired of being frustrated, Carol gave up and instead tried to relax and enjoy her moment of bliss in the darkness. And the moment she decided to let it go, the sound reverberated louder than before, clearer than in her previous dream. It was the sound of Scorpions' song. The unmistakable guitar intro to 'Still Loving You.'

The melody was now clear as crystal and Carol, always happy to be listening to the Scorpions, relaxed as a smile broke across her face and began humming to the tune as she sat back and enjoyed this ride seemingly between space and time. The song was on repeat, and Carol was happy to indulge as light began to slowly ooze out of the cracked walls of darkness and soon, Carol found herself dressed in an oxblood cowl-neck top, khaki capris pants and maroon Converse sneakers. The outfit combination was somewhat inappropriate as the darkness unravelled around her, and she found herself standing by an empty freeway, as if waiting for a ride. The song reverberated through the invisible walls of her dream and hung all over them when she saw a black sports car hurtling down the road at breakneck speed. However, it seemed to be in slow motion the nearer it got to her, and true enough, everything seemed to move with a heavy sludge.

Everything except her.

She scanned her surroundings as no thoughts entered her head. She could see a forlorn building in the distance, but nothing much to look at, and there was nothing she could think of. It was as if an invisible force was holding on to her vocal cords and her mind tightly. The same invisible force that directed her vision to the black sports car as it came closer. The car looked like it could run her over, but Carol was not afraid that it would. She looked at it coming in slow motion, mind blank as she noted how dirty and grimy the car was. It was covered by a thick layer of dust and caked with dried sludge that seemed to be torn off as the car hurtled past her. Her eyes fixed on the car when she felt another pair of eyes trained on her. She focused her vision and realised that the driver of the car had his eyes on her. He had fire in his eyes set in a bronzed face that almost appeared faceless. A face that never stood out in any crowd.

A familiar face.

The face of a man in a maroon short-sleeved shirt, sleeves folded up to reveal the taut biceps almost screaming to be released from the grip of the sleeves. His face had no distinguishing feature and was as if it was a sentence that had been redacted, yet naturally bronzed and shimmering, and there was something about him that invoked in her a familiar sensation. A sensation she recalled from years ago. Her face scrunched into a serious scowl as she tried to find her voice when the song hanging in the air grew louder. So loud it latched onto her vocal chords and released them for her to sing the tune of Scorpions' 'Still Loving You.' She sang in her mind with gusto as their eyes met, as she saw the deep brown eyes, almond shaped. When the car drove painfully slow past her, it was slow enough for Carol to notice a tilt of his head, a smile and his full lips pouted into a smirk.

Carol opened her eyes and found herself still humming Scorpions' tune, her mouth dry as the air in her cold room. Her breaths were raspy and gravelly and it was some time before saliva coated her mouth and she felt normal again. Rubbing out the sleep from her eyes, she stretched out from underneath her sheets and lay in the darkness. Her body is toasty warm but her face cold.

It's that airport man again. And at that hotel, as well?

What kind of magic and sorcery is this?

What, is he somehow a tenant in my mind now? Popping up every now and then?

Aside from his biceps, he is not exactly someone I'd lust after.

I mean, if he were to talk to me in a bar, I'd entertain him, if he wore a nice white business shirt with good forearm action.

But he does not look like someone who wears business shirts to work.

Oh, look at me being all judgmental and all.

There is something about him though, that is as far as I could tell.

Carol rolled onto her right side, her most comfortable position to sleep and imagined another warm, naked body embracing her from behind. She closed her eyes and entertained that fantasy as she instinctively hummed that now infernal Scorpions song. And as soon as that happened, that bronzed, painfully normal looking face with the head tilt and pursed-lipped smirk came barging into her mind.

Damn it, there he is again.

What the hell, brain, are you okay? You need a break?

Or is it a case of what the hell is the universe trying to tell me here?

Looking at the clock, she realised that it was almost 5 a.m., and usually time for her morning run. She had decided to put it off for this morning on account of her day off, but since she was wide awake now, and in order to get this mysterious smirk out of her mind, she decided to pry herself out of bed to go for that run at this unearthly hour. A flood of cold air came awash over her body as she quickly reached for the remote control to turn off the air conditioning. Goosebumps formed all over her as she ripped her pyjamas off and fished out her sports bra and running tights. She skipped out into the warm and balmy living room, took her keys, put on her running shoes and went out into the crisp early morning.

There were already people about to or had started their day. A woman who most likely just rolled out of bed and into her work garb was waiting for the lift, and in the lift, a much older man wearing a crisp white, short-sleeved shirt and high-waisted grey pants, with a manly musk of perfume and cigarette greeted them.

Girl, you need a better morning routine.

And Uncle, who gave you permission to be so sexy this early in the morning.

She stole a glance at the older man and saw a bald pate sitting atop a face carved in pain and sadness. A face that was almost ready to die.

Poor thing. He would look so much better if he smiled.

Out on the pavement by the road, Carol saw that the suburb was slowly awakening, with streets becoming increasingly noisy and the lights from the other flats flickering.

She opted to not do any stretching to warm up and decided to shock her system into the workout. So she plugged her inner ear buds in and took strong, confident strides on her way to her usual five-kilometre run. As she usually did, Carol looked dead ahead on her long runs, not caring of the things that happened in her peripheral vision. She was focused on her breathing, taking that one more step as her feet became increasingly heavy and looking for the next landmark that would indicate the finish line was almost over. It was a very easy way for Carol to clear her head as it was only her, the road, her protesting lungs and her feet, all in a singular cell in conflict with each other. An occasional cough, hack and spit interrupted her steady breathing, but it was nothing out of the ordinary. Her knees sounded out in meek protest, but ultimately silenced by her persistence. That early in the morning, it was difficult to work out into a sweat, despite the humidity in the air that often made Carol feel like she was drowning when breathing hard. Nevertheless, with the focus of an athlete, she powered through the run, getting into a nice comfortable rhythm of step and breath, blocking out other thoughts and sensations. Sometimes she felt like floating in the air as she got into her running zone with her focus only a hundred meters in front of her.

She had forgotten that she had music in her ears, as she often felt that life came with an accompanying soundtrack, but it was Klaus Meine's voice that broke her focus as he sang the opening lyrics to 'Still Loving You.' Without thought, she hummed the song in her mind, and as soon as that happened, that painfully normal, bronzed face with cheeky brown eyes and the pursed lips took shape in her mind. And then came the head tilt and the smirk. She blinked her eyes hard and tried to shake his image out of her head, but to no avail.

Fuck! This has to stop!

What the hell happened that he is now planted in my subconscious?

Is this some form of PTSD?

Carol broke her stride and came to a sudden stop. She bent over her haunches, facing the pavement she pounded earlier as she coughed and hacked almost a lung out. She struggled to catch her breath after that as she clasped her hands behind her head, stood upright and breathed in as deep as she could. Even as this happened, that head tilt and smirk was still in her head, mocking her. She spat out a large chuck of mucus in disdain and wiped her mouth dry with her wrists.

Such lady-like behaviour.

Who the fuck cares, I just had a workout.

She lingered on the pavement a little bit longer as she caught her breath, and her body cooled off from the run. She took a slow, leisurely stroll home and this time, she entertained the image of that bronzed man in her head.

Why are you here?

She was not upset that she was thinking of some stranger she had not met. She was just puzzled at how it was possible for her to be thinking this much of him.

How the fuck did you get here anyway?

She had only seen him twice, and she was confused by the effect he was having on her.

What is it about you that got me thinking of you?

She knew nothing about him, just the playful head tilt and the irreverent smirk.

Who are you?

**19.**

Alex sighed deeply as he slammed the door of the taxi behind a drunk and giggly Ian. He stood by the road for a few seconds, staring into the air as vehicles whizzed past him in a blur, often blowing exhaust fumes in his face, cutting a forlorn figure under the orange streetlight. The heavy humidity in the air together with the fumes choked him out of his brief daze, and he scurried back to his apartment to do a quick clean up and get ready for bed. Thankfully, there wasn't much of a clean up to do after their very simple meal of meat and wine, but Alex still needed the house to be cleaned and fresh before he went to bed. It did not matter that he was filthy and smelled of the kitchen, but as long as the house was clean and sparkling, he was happy. Alex played some music on the sound bar on a playlist creatively titled "Cleaning" and went about cleaning his island countertop obsessively, scrubbing the surface down to a spit shine. Alex somewhat enjoyed cleaning and running because those were the only two activities that gave him time to switch off his brain and to function fully on autopilot. And since most of his thoughts came from below the waist, this gave him a break from having to think about sex, Lyna and increasingly, the Mademoiselle.

And at this point, he just wanted to be alone, no thoughts, no words, just lost in his music. He had a strange, faraway yet empty look in his eyes as he went to work on the kitchen sink with the grace of a powerlifter hobbling about at the gym he had been going to for the last twenty-three years. He washed his hands as well as his face and hair in the kitchen sink, too lazy to properly wash up. The cold water bristled on his face and feeling suitably clean and refreshed, his eyes scanned every inch of the now sparkling kitchen countertop. Ensuring that the kitchen sink was clear of any gunk or build-up, he sat on the kitchen stool as he took in Gary Moore's 'Still Got the Blues' guitar solo, eyes closed, lips pursed and head slowly bobbing to the slow, soulful blues beat. One of his habits was that the song, any song that was playing on air, in his ear, in his mind, needed to end before he could do the next thing on his list. So woe was him if he found himself in the car listening to a radio music marathon, because nothing got done for an hour.

Gary Moore's guitar solo ended, and the sound drew to a close as Alex got up and prepared himself for bed. He closed the windows and checked that the doors were locked and switched off the lights. Bathed in darkness, he strode confidently to the boudoir and jumped into his low platform bed, crawled under his sheets, and with the wine still swirling in his head, sleep came to him easy.

The song Sway by Bic Runga dancing sensuously in the air, heavy with the smell of eucalyptus and pine, interlaced with exhaust fumes. The ballad swaying in the air, heavy with the smell of eucalyptus and pine, interlaced with exhaust fumes. The roar of engines from the bus caused Alex to snap his head in that direction, reminding him what bus he was supposed to take into the city. The air was a crisp early winter, with every breath visible with wisps of vapour.

The second line of the song slithered in the air like a deliciously licentious pole dancer across the smooth floor.

Alex felt warm and snug in his thick hoodie, thermal track pants and socks, and a skull cap covering his head down to his ears. Looking like a typically seedy kerb crawler, people walking by gave him a wide berth and gave uneasy glances at him as he leaned back, hands in his hoodie pockets, waiting for something or someone. He knew, but yet he did not. He just existed at that bus stop as the world flew on by at almost breakneck speed. He gazed lazily at the branches swaying languidly in the cold breeze, his face caressed by the cold fingers of the air and the occasional slap of fumes by the rushing vehicles going by. He crossed his legs and soon his foot swung to the beat of the song in the air.

Alex got up to shake off the cold and was pacing around the bus stop when a very dirty and grimy 1967 Ford Mustang Nurain pulled up at the bus stop, engine in a low menacing rumble. The car was caked in urban and city grime that was so thick it was difficult for him to tell what the original colour of the car was. Aside from the dirt, it seemed to be a well-maintained hunk of steel. The driver's seat was empty, and Alex felt right to jump right in and drive off. Foot on the accelerator, the car let out a low, sexy groan that got louder and sexier the harder he stepped on the pedal. Alex could feel the early stirrings of a thunderous boner coming up just sitting in the seat and pushing the pedal.

It was warm and toasty in the car, the heater working well, busting out hot air tirelessly in a low drone. Alex took off his skull cap, tousled his hair, and then took off his hoodie. In his worn out Bad Religion T-shirt, hair artfully tossed, driving the car, he looked aloof and nonchalant, dangerously cool and detached. Looking down his legs, he saw now that they were covered in some kind of worn denim and not his black thermal track pants. Adjusting the seats and the mirrors, he sped off down the highway, destination unknown.

Alex cruised by what was turning out to be a highway that snaked along the coastline, and he enjoyed the crystalline green waters periodically broken by white waves, framed by the azure sky clear of any clouds. The early winter seemed to have made way for a mid-spring day as the warm rays of the sun appeared in the sky. He felt happy and at ease but for a brief moment, as the spell was broken by a loud, jarring and high-pitched fart of an engine coming from a small motorcycle. He looked to the front and saw a small scooter ridden by a woman wearing a white robe, cloth flapping in the wind. She wasn't wearing a helmet, and he could see her wild yellow hair blown almost parallel to the road. Annoyed at first, that soon made way for indifference as he went back to driving what he felt was the best car he had ever driven.

With Bic Runga's tune still hanging in the wind, Alex felt at ease.

In the corner of his eye, he noticed a similar woman, wearing the same outfit, with the same yellow hair, riding a similar motorcycle, seemingly flying right next to his car. Looking around, he found himself being flanked by the two motorcyclists, who finally turned to look at him. Alex felt a brief chill snaking down his spine and cold fingers wrapping itself around his heart when he saw their faces. They were a mirror image of each other, and they had big, empty ghostly eyes, with pure evil emanating from those orbs of death. Their mouths curled in a demonic sneer with chapped crimson lips framing rows of sharpened canines and fangs and a blackened tongue flapping in the air like a hound of Hell. Fear gripped him initially before it was washed out again by his nonchalance.

Logic seem to have been torn apart.

The harlots of hell sped up and were no longer flanking him and almost disappeared in the distance when Alex was overcome by a strong desire to follow them and hunt them down. For what purpose, he didn't know, but all he knew was that they knew something he did not and it was up to him to beat that out of them. Demons or no. So from a languid cruise down the coastline, the engine of his car roared as he sped off to chase the two harlots, still not knowing why exactly. Weaving in and out of traffic and ignoring a speed camera planted along the road and ignoring the flash seen in his rear-view mirror, he continued headlong down the road. In the distance, he could see the harlots now no longer riding their motorcycles but spreading their white, tattered wings and flying down the road, closer down by the coast. His eyes widened in surprise as they took flight but was still determined to give chase.

Now it all threatens to turn sour when in the distance, he could see a worn down, dilapidated building that stood out in an empty field of grass and pools of mud. The tendrils of smoke and mist hovered over the field and around the base of the building, giving it an air of foreboding and disquiet. He saw the last flapping of white cloth disappearing behind a large and dark opening of the building that looked like its mouth. From where he was, the building looked like it had a face tainted with sorrow and regret. The windows were its eyes, sometimes flickering with life, but dark and brooding most of the time. The large opening down the middle of the ground looked like its mouth, agape with horror, was in a perpetual silent scream. The peeling paint off the walls were like leper skin falling off, a once glorious and handsome face now wasting away in decay.

Alex made a beeline for the building, hurtling down the now empty freeway, the mid-spring day having turned into a dull, dour and depressing grey, the sun hiding behind dark clouds, with rays of light barely seeping through the clouds. The air had become dank and heavy and every breath seemed heavy and Alex felt like he was drowning, and it was all that he could do to keep the car in control. It was no longer a pleasant, languid drive down the coast, and it was as if the car was being weighed down in a bog, and no matter how much he put the pedal to the metal, the car seemed to have slowed down to a glacial pace. Alex took his eyes off the building and off the road to look at the dashboard of the Mustang to see if there was something wrong with it, but all seemed to be functioning well. He looked up and in an instant, everything was silent. He could no longer hear the roar of the Mustang engine, the clangour of the machinery and not even his thoughts. It was as if the air had grown limbs that curled around the sides of his head to cut out all sound. Alex felt immobilized, and for the first time, his nonchalance and his indifference deserted him.

For the first time, he felt the cold fingers of fear coiling around his heart and that terrible chill snaking down his spine and spreading to his extremities. His breath quickened, yet it was difficult to breathe. He wanted to scream, but an invisible force seem to have gotten hold of his voice in a vice-like grip. Frozen in fear, in a car that had been hurtling down the road, Alex instinctively shook his head hard hoping that things would somehow change for the better. However, the only change that was brought about was a faraway sound, a high-pitched melodic wail that soon began to manifest itself with a rhythm and beat. It was a sound he was familiar with, yet unknown to him at the same time. That sound, that mysterious melody had soothed his soul, and the rising fear in him earlier had abated as he was able to breathe again. That sound became clearer and crisper and he soon realised that he knew the sound and was very familiar with it. And as soon as he realised that, his voice returned and he found himself humming the opening guitar intro to 'Still Loving You.'

Amidst the now grey-hued, almost depressing landscape, he noticed a spot of colour not far ahead. It was like a wine stain on a grey sheet that got bigger as he drove closer to it. As the splotch of deep red became clearer, something else caught his attention.

A smell.

The smell.

The strong, boner-inducing scent of Chanel's Mademoiselle came seeping into the car and it was as if he had driven through a force-field of Mademoiselle. It was as if he was making entry into a planet's atmosphere that was all Mademoiselle. The early stirrings of a boner he had earlier now seem to be inflamed once again, and he felt the familiar tightening and the pleasurable pain as his crotch pushed hard against his pants. He took a huge whiff of Mademoiselle as his eyes cleared and his vision sharpened.

He saw her. Standing by the freeway, as if waiting for him, and he expected her to raise her hand to flag him down.

As the second verse of Still Loving You rings louder in his head.

She was dressed in an oxblood cowl neck top, khaki capris pants and maroon Converse sneakers. The outfit combination stood out in a sea of depressing grey right by the empty freeway. She stood there like a stone, resplendent in her colours and a sight to behold amidst the dullness and decay of the surroundings. The song now reverberated loud through the invisible walls of his dream and bled all over the air as the vision of perfection shone bright in his eyes. He loved everything about her as he saw her, her posture, and as time slowed to a standstill, he could see and love her statuesque shoulders, the thick veins that ran down her bicep, her artfully tousled hair both frozen in place and dancing in the wind.

He drove past her in what seemed to be a glacial pace, and their eyes met.

Alex, smitten and bashful at the sight of his Mademoiselle, tilted his head to the right, smiled at her and followed it up with a quick pout and smirk and ended off with a nod of approval, when everything started to dissolve into darkness and he soon felt his face smacked by a gust of cold air that left his face bristling. He opened his eyes and found himself under his sheets, warm and snug, face cold from the air conditioning, eyes still full of sleep, a raging boner in his boxer shorts. And even as the smell and sight of his Mademoiselle faded, the song still played in his head as he hummed it to its end.

As he lay in bed, he couldn't get the Mademoiselle out of his head and wondered how she would feel if he rubbed his boner against her smooth alabaster skin. He chuckled at the thought, even dismissing it, but his boner did have a mind of its own and demanded his attention. He initially imagined and fantasized about his last romp with Lyna, but his brain, stubbornly, painted an image of the Mademoiselle coming through the bedroom door, dressed in sexy oxblood lingerie and bathed in Chanel's Mademoiselle. Alex played along with the image in his mind and let it unfold. He imagined the Mademoiselle strutting around his bedroom and stopping at the foot of his bed and standing there, watching him, as if waiting for a sign from him. Eyes still closed, Alex pulled his boxers down from under his sheets to his knees and felt his hot, thundering boner in his hands that throbbed hard at the sight of the Mademoiselle in his mind's eye. Alex focused on her shoulders and arms, fetishized them in his self-pleasure. He could see her pale face bathed in the suburban lights coming in from his bedroom window and saw that she was smiling with her eyes, just the way he liked women to do. He imagined running his nose and tongue all over her smooth skin wrapped tightly around sinuous muscle, smelling of Mademoiselle, and that brought him to the familiar heights of pleasure. He imagined planting a deep, wet sloppy kiss on her crimson lips as her fingers slithered down his skin and tenderly grabbed his now engorged penis. Warm and comfortable under his sheets, his comforter now pulsing visibly and steadily, eyes closed, his face a mask of pleasure and serenity which was soon broken and contorted as he reached his climax. His comforter pulsed harder and more frantic with his hands under working hard to reach his climax before a gasp followed by a series of grunts and groans as he writhed in a pleasure that almost lasted forever. He felt the hot liquid snaking down his fingers as he squeezed and clenched hard to intensify the pleasure, his body quivering in the final throes of pleasure, and as soon as it had begun, the waves of pleasure stopped, and he realised the real need to clean up, or at the very least, wipe himself dry of his spunk.

With a sigh and a pained grunt, Alex rolled off his bed, turned on the lights and began to scrummage around the room for a towel to wipe himself down. He also saw that he had stained his comforter sheets as well, and since he was already up, he decided he might as well change the sheets too. The thought of him voluntarily swimming in his fluids alone in bed was no longer something he was willing to let slide. *Maybe it is an age thing,* he thought, and that he no longer needed to tolerate circumstances that he could easily avoid. Nevertheless, he went a step further, where instead of just wiping himself down, he decided to take an early morning shower and maybe get a head start on the day. After he was done changing his sheets from his favourite yellow and grey combo to a deep burgundy, he stood up straight to stretch and to warm his muscles up. The cold room had already warmed up from the exertions before, and his skin no longer bristled in the cold air. He put on his workout playlist he called "One more rep, you fucker," taking in the loud blast beats of

Pete Sandoval. Alex was a picture of contrasts, movements slow, deliberate, and serene. His breaths now loud, but long, smooth and deep. He loved feeling the stretch and the burn, especially in his lower limbs. Still naked from the waist down, he went about his exercises and giggled at how he must have looked like to people watching. But it was a necessary evil to do, the stretching, not being naked from the waist down. Because the years of lifting and pumping iron had taken its toll on his body that he was now told to do at least three minutes of full body stretching every day.

By now, the movements were all from muscle memory, and he was able to enjoy the burn and the songs without having to put in much thought about what exercise to do next. He enjoyed the guttural growls of David Vincent barking incantations in the 'Lord of All Fevers and Plague.' He nodded his head in time with Lemmy Kilmister's gruff yet soulful rendition of 'Whorehouse Blues.' He felt a guilty stirring in his soul at Taylor Swift's heartfelt and sincere singing of 'Love Story,' which was chased down by Lady Antebellum's 'Need You Now' to nail down his guilty pleasure. He bobbed his head, pursed his lips, smiled and giggled through the very eclectic yet carefully curated playlist, each song having some specific and deep meaning for him.

However, as Metallica's 'Wherever I May Roam' faded, Alex felt a slight unease creeping into his body, and it was as if the stretches had opened his body up to a surreptitious invasion of disquietude. The wailing wah-pedalled guitars and the barking vocals formed an unlikely melodic duet that brought the song into a fade-out as a sense of dread descended upon him. The next bit of music that resounded out of the speakers made him realise why the doom. It was the familiar high-pitched plucking of guitar chords from that one guitar player, who was then joined by another in a melodic duet of rhythm guitars, when the slightly nasal, high-pitched lament bled out of the speakers.

The first lines of 'Still Loving You' rings in his ears again.

The song made him stop in his tracks as the memory of the dream he just had replayed in his mind. He had forgotten about the Mademoiselle, who had been the object of his self-servicing affection just a moment ago, but the thought of her came rushing back, and now, instead of a thunderous boner, Alex tilted his head to the left, smiled to himself, a smile as sweet as he could muster alone in his bedroom and twisted and pursed his lips into a contorted sneer as he nodded his head. Amidst the questions and puzzlement swirling in his head about who she was and why she was the object of his affection lately, he also felt an overwhelming calm and a tinge of happiness washing over him at the thought of the Mademoiselle.

He revelled in the mystery and celebrated the strangeness and the seemingly random turn of events his subconscious had brought him. As he hummed the power ballad, feeling the burn and stretch in his muscles, and as the initial stirrings of an erection began to throb and warm between his thighs, a silent "Hi, darling" slipped out from his lips, and that was all he needed to continue fantasizing about the Mademoiselle as he banished Lyna out of his mind in the midst of stretching his hamstrings.

Nevertheless, it was easy to cast Lyna out of his mind now.

Because now every woman looked like the Mademoiselle.

Yet he barely knew her. Not sure how he could find her. Not sure if she would even talk to him. He writhed in this pool of uncertainty and doubt, yet heavily laced with an unknown surety and an unwavering swagger of calm confidence. Despite the disquietude he felt drizzling down upon him earlier, he could feel his nonchalance come creeping back into him, making him feel that familiar comfort. It was like he had received assurances from the universe that it would all be alright if he was willing to be driven by the invisible forces of fate for once in his life.

I need your love, and the closing words of 'Still Loving You.'

# 20.

C arol shifted uncomfortably as she perched perilously at the top of a bar stool, her heels anchoring her as it hooked onto the leg rest, making her that little bit more secure and just slightly comfortable. She hated being at that bar. The tables and stools were mismatched in height, making it very almost painful for her. She hated the thumping EDM bass and the random noises that seemed to pass off as music these days and the one-word uttered throughout the song passing off as 'lyrics.' And she hated having to put on her work face on a Friday night to have drinks with colleagues she already had to tolerate for five to six days every week, at company events and trips. She hated having to spend her birthday with these bunch of materialists whose religion was the almighty dollar. Worst of all, she hated herself for not telling them it was her birthday.

She never liked to make her birthday a big deal but would appreciate it if someone did without her asking or telling them to. So she never purposely revealed her date of birth to anyone, especially at her workplace, but somehow word got out from the company admin or a random message on social media that someone managed to stumble upon.

*Urgh, why the hell am I here on my birth-fucking-day?*

*I could be in a late-night spa.*

*I could be in a tub with a nice glass of wine.*

*Or better still, in bed with someone.*

*Yah, at the rate you've been at, who would be in bed with you early?*

*Your best bet is Charmaine.*

*Your worst would be all the other guys you have been seeing the past few months.*

*Hah.*

*Small dick, three-second man, talk too much, and one who would most probably have his mum join us in bed,*

*Ewwwww.*

"Cheers, everyone!" The raucous voices of her colleagues shattered her inner thoughts and the peace that came with it as everyone raised their glasses and clumsily clinked them into each other's in a weird nocturnal social ritual. She obliged them and took another shot of honeyed whiskey that her boss loved so much. Carol spaced out right after the toast as her colleagues rambled along talking shop even on a Friday night, and that was another thing she hated. Her colleagues didn't seem to know how to switch off and had their lives revolve around everything that was work-related, which she saw as a sad state of affairs for them. She had tried to engage them about their hobbies and passions with one of her senior colleagues, Song Da, who stated that his passions and hobbies were his family, his work and drinking alcohol, to rapturous laughter and firm approval. Another colleague, Mandy, a portly matron in her mid-thirties, stated that her life revolved around her clients and serving them as best as she could.

*Man, these people need a life.*

*I'd say they need to get laid, but it would be a waste of fluids.*

*Man, I need to get laid.*

*I should be getting birthday sex right now!*

Carol wanted to excuse herself, pick up her things and just walk away from this tepid pool of misaligned human values, but she felt obliged to stick around at least till someone got plastered drunk. And so far, the most likely candidate was portly Mandy, who seemed to have a need to drown something in her with alcohol. Maybe it was her insecurity that needed to be drowned out as she let alcohol take the wheel. She had been chugging her drinks at double the rate of everyone else on the table. She was drinking faster than she was eating her crispy anchovies.

*Yeap, Mandy is gunna get sloppy drunk tonight.*

*I hope I don't have to take care of her when that happens.*

*As much as I want to stay and watch her make friends with the floor, I think I would rather be banged on the floor.*

She hadn't noticed the lights flashing on her phone earlier indicating a message was sent to her. She read the message, and it was Charmaine asking, "Babe, you doing anything tonight?"

"I am with work people. Not busy, just hanging. What's up?"

"I have the rest of the night free, thought we could go somewhere and chill."

"Yeah, I'm with these fuckers." Carol secretly took a photo of her colleagues on her mobile and sent it to Charmaine.

"Urgh, don't you hate those fuckers? Why are you hanging out with them?"

"Because free food, free snacks and free booze, darling. No girl would turn that down."

"You mean no TEENAGED girl would turn that down, you are an old adult!" Charmaine's message read, followed by three laughing emoticons.

Carol smiled.

"Shut up, bitch. Girl needs to eat sometime okay. Plus the soft-shelled crab here is awesome!"

"Yeah, you tolerated those fuckers for soft-shelled crab. Sure. Sure." Rolling eyes emoticon. "I know it's good, but I know you well, bitch. You just want company. Call me then! Why do you have to wait for me to ask you to come out?" Angry face emoticon.

"Deep sigh," Carol's sent message read.

"Okay, shut up, you ready to come out?"

"Yeah, I'm ready to split the joint. Where are we meeting?"

"Alright, Concorde Mall, 30 minutes okay?"

"Okay, sure. What's happening there?"

"Shut up and just meet me there okay?

"Who else will be there?"

"Just you and me babe." Kissy face emoticon.

Middle finger emoticon.

Rolling on the floor laughing GIF.

Carol got up, excused herself to go to the ladies room to wash and touch up her war paint and to straighten herself out and prepare for an easy exit. It was a surprisingly smooth getaway, because while many of them went off to smoke, there was only Melissa, a junior associate who just joined the team three months ago, left to watch over the table.

"Something important just came up, tell the others I need to go," Carol barked at the glorified intern who didn't dare to question Carol and just nodded meekly as Carol gathered her things and flew away from the bar toward the taxi stand and boarded the vehicle waiting there.

Carol sat in the backseat of the car and stared emptily at the city lights bathing her in different hues, thankful to have been able to slip away from those fuckers without much drama. She sighed deeply as her fingers twitched, and she felt a certain emptiness in her chest and mouth, which were the initial pangs of cigarette cravings, having quit the cancer stick for a few months now since her bout of bronchitis. She was glad that she didn't replace that vice with another, well, not like it was a real vice to begin with. She barely smoked more than four cigarettes a day, and a pack of cigarettes would last her a week.

*So good that Charmaine read my mind.*

*What is this place she's taking me to?*

*If I remember correctly, the Concorde Shopping Mall has developed into quite a seedy joint that looks like it never got out of the eighties.*

*Maybe she wants to do one of those late-night spa sessions.*

*But aren't those notoriously sordid and usually for men?*

She could hear the disembodied voice of the cab driver trying to make conversation with her, but all she could see were the blur of city lights hurtling past as the cab wove through traffic. Carol closed her eyes and silently made a birthday wish. Her world now cloaked in darkness as the sounds of the city and the cabin driver's voice was drowned out by her daze, she focused on her voice making the wish.

*Well, this year I wish…*

But she could not go on. Not for a lack of trying or inspiration. But the darkness and void was replaced by that familiar song again, and Carol just chuckled at herself for allowing that. She knew what would happen next if she entertained that song and allowed it to go on, but not tonight.

*Sorry, not tonight.*

She was very surprised that the cab driver was still talking to her. Well, more like *at* her. Had she been unknowingly grunting and 'hmmm-ing' her replies? Regardless of that, she was relieved when she got to her destination, tapped her credit card at the machine and got out of the cab and into the balmy humidity of the urban night. She then realised that she had about thirty minutes to spare before meeting Charmaine, so she decided to go on a quick walkabout on the urban terrain. The mall was empty, with all the shopfronts on the first floor having their shutters down. Empty aisles bathed in a dull fluorescent light, giving the mall a dour and dated air to it. The aging central air conditioning had been switched off barely twenty minutes ago. So a quiet chill still hung in the air and her every step seemed to echo loudly against the bare walls. She could hear the distant, muffled thump of bass beats rumbling in the air and she realised that she could have stepped into a place where time had stood still since 1988. The mall was constructed with a typically eighties aesthetic, with five donuts stacked on top of each other, connected by four escalators at each side and a glass "bubble" elevator, with an open atrium in the middle where you could look up at the floors and shops in the mall. Carol stood in the centre of the atrium, the dull fluorescent lights reflecting off the cheap marble floors and looked up the different levels, and she was suddenly awash with nostalgia. She was taken back to Joo Chiat Complex, to the R&S Salon, with Aunt Sam and Aunt Rachel.

It all came rushing back to her, the smell of the complex strangely similar to the one hanging around the Concorde Shopping Mall. A flood of colours and sounds accompanied her treasured memory of the R&S Salon as she happily swam in the pleasant childhood memories, the dull thumping of the bass now silenced by Warrant's 'Heaven' and White Snake's 'Is This Love.'

But it was The Carpenters' Yesterday Once More that played loudest in her mind.

She remembered Aunt Sam and Aunt Rachel and felt a tinge of sadness at the passing of Aunt Sam and promised to herself that she would spend more time with her ailing Aunt Rachel. In fact, that became her birthday wish.

*I will spend more time with Aunt Rachel and try to bring her happiness and colour to her days.*

Carol could feel a tsunami of sadness welling up inside her, threatening to sweep her away in a tide of emotion, only to be stemmed by the verses of Yesterday Once More, a song that brought her peace.

But she swallowed hard and took a deep, gasping breath as if she had been holding it in her ride along the cavernous halls of yesterday. The stale air filled her lungs once again, and she stood there squinting her eyes at the weary fluorescent lights of the mall, the warmth of the songs of yesterday rapidly losing its effect on her body.

She recalled every smile, every playful smack on the head they dished out to her, every song they taught her on the guitar, every song they sang together and every guitar lick they bobbed their heads together to and every riff they raised their horns to and every shade thrown at her regarding Carol's choices in her social life and her sometime questionable musical choices.

*I wonder if Aunt Sam is looking at me and approving of the choices I have made.*

A faraway voice came floating into her thoughts. It was too subtle to hear at first, but became louder, yet muffled like a wasp buzzing under heavy felt. "Excuse me, Miss, are you okay?" A gravelly, weary voice seemed to suddenly stifle the sounds and voices in her head. It was an elderly security guard with a torch in hand, with the sad face of an old man neglected and ignored by those he loved so much.

"Sorry, yes, I am okay. I am waiting for my friend here," Carol stammered as she slowly drifted back into an increasingly insipid and grey present.

"Oh okay, good. Maybe you want to sit over there while you wait for your friend? It's more comfortable than standing out here in the middle of the whole world", the old man said with a slight chuckle.

"Ah yes, okay, will do. Sorry, didn't mean to cause trouble".

"Oh, no trouble at all, young lady. It's not very often that an old security man like me gets to talk to a pretty lady like yourself," the old man said as she turned away bashfully and smiled.

*Is Uncle Security Guard hitting on me?*

*Urgh no, come on, he's just being nice*

"Okay, thank you, Uncle. You have a good night," Carol said as Uncle Security Guard walked away and waved at her without turning to look.

*Okay, now where is this woman?*

She went to the stone benches not far away from where she was standing, felt the cool, smooth stone on her thighs as she sat on it, fished out her mobile phone and was about to send a text message to Charmaine when she heard that familiar shriek.

"Oi, woman! Here here!" Charmaine cried out, gesturing for Carol to come over to her. She stood in the shadows in what looked like a lift lobby cloaked in darkness.

Carol rolled her eyes, smiled and went to Carol. They hugged their usual hug and Carol said, "So, where is this place you're taking me to?"

"Firstly, happy birthday, bish!" Charmaine exclaimed as she kissed Carol on both cheeks. "And where we're going, *is* my gift to you tonight," Charmaine continued with a glint of mischief in her eyes and rolled into the corners of her mouth as she smiled.

"Should I be afraid?" Carol joked.

"Well, if it all turns out well, I reckon you should, but in a good way"

"What the fuck does that even mean?"

"Stop with the questions and come with me, okay?" Charmaine said as she took Carol's hand into the darkness of the lift lobby. The doors opened, and they were bathed in the bright, cheap lights of the lift, and they entered in silence.

"I don't like this, Charmaine. I don't like how quiet you are," Carol said nervously, half in jest.

"Just – just….*Shhhh*!" Charmaine commanded her.

Carol stood in the lift, staring at their reflection on the lift doors and shuffled uncomfortably. Charmaine had a creepy smile plastered all across her face, which made Carol even more uncomfortable, so she began to whistle, random whistling sounds at first, which soon developed into the familiar melody of Scorpion's –

*No, NOT TONIGHT!*

The lift door opened soon enough, and Carol saw that they were on the eighth floor and the lift landing was bathed in a pale orange light, the floors carpeted with a cheesy animal print and at the end, straight ahead, were big double doors framed by two towering potted plants. She stepped off the lift gingerly before Charmaine grabbed her hand and excitedly pulled her out and opened the doors for her.

Carol soon saw that they were in a club, with a very tacky name, Naked Gun. With neon lights flickering off the walls, the doors opened to two large billiard tables, each brightly lit by a behemoth of a ceiling light hovering just over them. The green of the tables seemed soothing at first, but the flickering neon lights that pulsed beyond the tables were jarring to her. Charmaine pulled her past the billiard tables and to the bar with a large, bright and flashy backdrop of different manners of alcohol bottles on display. The bartender, a cute, skinny twink of a boy, dressed in weird white straps wrapped around his torso, smiled at her sweetly as she stumbled past the bar into the seating area. The bar was strangely empty, save for the wait staff she saw flitting about, serving no one particular. The seating area was punctuated with booth seats, with very high back rests and angled in such a way that it was impossible to take a peek at who was sitting there. There wasn't even any music playing, and as they took their seats in the booths, a pair of wait staff came and brusquely asked for their orders.

"Just get us a bottle of your 2008 Kindzmarauli chilled, please. And two glasses," Charmaine ordered. Carol was surprised at how the usually quiet retreating wallflower had become confident and assertive tonight.

"Wow, is there something you want to tell me about yourself, Charmaine?" Carol asked as she chuckled.

"Enough about me, because tonight is all about you," Charmaine said as she giggled.

An army of waiters soon came by and fussed over them with the wine, bringing snacks and some strange equipment for a night club laid out on the coffee table in front of them. Carol saw, among other things, a small flashlight, surgical gloves, and a riding crop.

*What in the name of hell is this club about?*

The wait staff poured them their wine as both ladies raised their glasses to each other and clinked them in their usual toast as they said, "Stroush." The word had no meaning actually, and it was just a sound they made when it was just the two of them in a toast to each other. Carol took a sip and realised that they were facing a rather large stage that looked like it was made of mirrors from the floor, wall and ceiling.

*Interesting.*

Charmaine still sat in the corner, with that goofy smile across her face, not saying a word. Carol looked around the club, bathed in soft orange and white lights, with cheesy elevator music playing ever so subtly on the speakers. And noticed that there was someone else in another booth, another pair of women, who seemed to be dressed to the nines. They seemed to have noticed Carol looking at them and turned their heads to look and smiled. Carol smiled sweetly as she raised her glass at them. "Okay, Charmaine, what the hell is this? Look, if you –"

"Shhhh," Charmaine interrupted her. "Just sit back, enjoy the wine and the snacks, and you'll find out soon enough, okay? I'm sure it will be worth your while. Trust me," Charmaine said with that familiar glint of mischief painted all over her face now.

"Alright, fine," Carol huffed as she sat back, one foot anchored on the tip of the coffee table, the other resting lazily underneath her.

*They would do well to play some real music here though.*

*I'm getting bored.*

*The wine is good though. Trust this bitch to get my wine tastes to the tee.*

She looked at Charmaine and wanted to initiate a conversation with her out of boredom, but Charmaine waved her

278

away and put a finger on her lips, shushing her as if she was a child.

She was about to get up to do something, anything, when the house lights went down, smothering everything in an uncomfortable darkness. In the darkness, Carol waited anxiously for what was about to happen next.

A flash of bright light soon exploded on stage, and the whole club was bathed in a flash of white light. A shimmering disco ball descended from the ceiling, reflecting multi-hued lights dancing across the walls and floor. Carol was shocked by the sudden explosion of activity, heart racing, and as she stood there trying to catch her breath, the stage of mirrors was now being filled with men. Young, pretty, fair-skinned men, some skinny and slim, some ripped with muscle, some lean with hunger, all dressed in the same white straps that wrapped around their tight bodies. All of them were wearing similarly white boy shorts, barely able to contain their pulsing boy flesh. Carol thought they were dancers and that Charmaine had brought her to a male strip club, but that wasn't to be because if they were dancers, they would, well, be dancing. But instead, they just stood there, on stage, and posed in various positions. Some standing straight, arms by their side, bellies sucked in and chest puffed out. Some stood with arms folded, their weight on one leg, relaxed and confident. Some were in weird nineties boyband poses with hand gestures, bright smiles, and only two were dancing at a time. The dance, if you could call it a dance, was just a random bobbing of the head and hips in time with the pulsing bass beats.

It was then that Carol realised why the stage was made of mirrors. She could clearly see every nook and cranny of almost *all* the men on the stage. Focusing on the mirror at the back of the stage, she could see how taut their butts were, as well as how strong their backs were. She just had to look at the mirrored ceiling to see their broad shoulders and see if any of them had a bald spot developing. And looking at the mirrors on the stage floor, well, she could see all their junk from a different, weird, yet interesting angle. And the men seemed to know who was being looked at by whom and where they were being looked at because they would pose accordingly. Carol also noticed that the men had a coloured circular plastic coin pinned to their hips with a number printed on them. Still taking all of this in, processing it, she noticed the other ladies whispering something to a wait staff and smiled gleefully. The staff then shone a laser pointer to a man on stage who then proceeded to disappear behind the other booth. And it was then she realised where she was.

"So, ma'am, which of our men would you like to accompany you tonight? You can choose one for forty minutes, an hour, or for the whole night," one of the wait staff, Jolene, whispered in her ear. "I would suggest number nineteen. His name is Lance, and he is very popular among our clients here. He's from Japan, and there he worked in a much larger establishment like this and even then he was very popular. He is our star investment here."

Carol realised that she was in a "hanging flower joint" for ladies where she could pay for the company of the men or hosts there. To hang a garland of flowers was to call one or several of the men over to join her at her table for drinks, joyful banter and light intimacy. Each "session" could be anywhere from ten dollars to thousands of dollars! Also, the amount of attention and affection the lady received was proportionate to the price she paid. It was a slightly more elegant and sophisticated form of prostitution, and by no means a crass trade of flesh; the only difference was that the currency used in this economy was mainly time, attention and affection given.

Carol reeled in horror at the thought of being in such a seedy place. More so that Charmaine knew of this place! She had read about this and scoffed at it, saying that it was a place for lonely housewives and ugly hunchbacks. And now, she was one of them, either a lonely housewife or an ugly hunchback. Her eyes widened in fear and anger at Charmaine, who was still in the corner now giggling uncontrollably at Carol's face.

"What the fuck is this, Charmaine?" Carol shrieked almost desperately at her.

But her voice was drowned out by the thumping club beats, and the horror plastered across her face was just fuelling Charmaine's laughter. She was rolling in gales of laughter as she slapped her knees in sheer glee.

Carol stood up, took one final, shamefully lusty look at number twenty-two, the one who among all had caught her eye, and gestured to Charmaine to come outside. Charmaine at first ignored her but realised how serious the situation was when Carol reached in to grab her arm and dragged her out of the club.

Now as they stood in the deathly silent lift landing, when compared to the booming bass of the club inside, Carol punched Charmaine on her arm and screamed, "What the fuck were you thinking? You think I'm that desperate for company that I need to pay for these – these fuck boys to come entertain me?"

"But I – "

Carol refused to give Charmaine a word in.

"I am very mad and disappointed at you, Charm. My. Best. Friend. And you do this shit to me? What makes you even think that I will be okay with this? Oh my god, you think I am a desperate, lonely slut, who drifts from one fuck boy to the next?"

"No, I never, I just —"

"Who the fuck gave you this idea that I will like this? That I will be into this? Okay, this is what I want you to do now. You are going back in, you are going to pay the bill, you are going to bring me the bottle of Kindzmarauli we barely had time to drink before this place exploded into a nest of vice. And you are going to ask Jolene how much it will cost me to spend time with number twenty-two. *Now!*" Carol shouted to Charmaine.

Charmaine was confused at first, and was close to tears, but soon, that familiar mischief came crawling back across her face as she turned and disappeared behind the big double doors. Yes, all while yelling at Charmaine, Carol could only think of number twenty-two, his smooth pasty skin, his skinny boyish build and the pretty face. She just wanted to have him in a gilded cage, feed him fruits and sunflower seeds and just watch as he performed for her. She folded her arms, and paced the lift landing in front of the club for what seemed an eternity before the door opened and Charmaine stepped out, a bottle in hand and a face painted with sadness.

"Your number twenty-two has already been taken by the other lady in the club. But Jolene recommends another guy, number twenty-eight. She says that —"

"Then no, I'm done for the night. It's twenty-two or nothing. Let's go home, Charm," Carol said.

"But why? Let's go in and look at them some more, and you might change your mind," Charmaine protested.

"No, I'm done, but, if *you* want to stay and ogle at them you go ahead, I am done ogling," Carol said firmly.

Charmaine had no choice but to follow Carol, as much as she wanted to stay on and look at pretty boys vying for her attention. It was the one night she had left free for Carol, and the one night she could live vicariously through Carol. Because Carol was more than just her best friend, the sister she never had. More than just a confidante.

Because in Carol, she saw the excitement, the sin that she was not brave enough to admit to, let alone commit.

They went their separate ways by the road outside the mall.

"We good, yeah?" Charmaine said in a tremulous voice.

Carol smiled, cupped her hands over Charmaine's cheeks, and kissed her. "Yes, darling, we're good. I know you meant well. Just that, next time, run it past me first, okay? No surprises."

"No surprises. Got it."

Charmaine had her partner pick her up from the mall, and as Carol waved her off, she took a walk to clear her head. She chuckled at the foul but ultimately well-meaning effort to cheer her up. But ultimately, she found herself alone still, humming Scorpion's –

*NOT. FUCKING. TONIGHT!*

21.

"**M**edic!" Long shouted from across the barracks. "You coming with us later? Please come, we have many many ladies for you, more ladies than you can count!"

Alex opened his weary eyes, turned his head, unwillingly, toward the sound of Long's voice and mustered from within him the best nod he could muster at that time of day. Alex, with his platoon, had just finished a three-day-two-night mission at his reservist duty with 657 SIR. They had been digging trenches in Lim Chu Kang, simulated an attack on enemy positions in Yishun, defended theirs fiercely and marched through the night in Mandai, lugging his fifteen-kilogram equipment pack in the last seventy-two hours, with only four hours of sleep in between. He was all manners of hungry, thirsty, tired and sore. Even the cold hard floor of Jurong Camp felt like the comfiest mattresses the world could offer. But at least it was dry, and a welcome change from the wet splotches of mud and puddles he had to lie in when in the mosquito and insect orgy of a jungle. He was even too tired to get out of his filthy army fatigues and was just lying there swimming in his own sweat, tears, mud and blood. He looked up at his bed, and she seemed to be seducing him to lie in her with her pristine white sheets, soft spring mattress, warm olive green blanket and firm pillows like the breasts of a matronly wench. But he knew well enough to not tarnish the purity of the bed that had cradled him in her arms dutifully for the past week. It didn't really matter to Alex anyway because every inch of him ached to hell and back; even breathing hurt.

Nevertheless, he slowly but surely and almost expertly, peeled off his items of clothing one by one with minimal effort and movement. He slid his mud-caked boots off, handsfree, by slowly shimmying his ankles and using the other foot, the same went for his socks, soaking wet. His feet wrinkled, and it was as if they had aged half a century. It didn't stink, surprisingly, and he thought maybe even germs and bacteria were too tired to latch on to his skanky feet. Still on the floor, he began taking off his camouflage pants followed by his top, and soon he was lying there on the cold hard floor in nothing but his baby blue Bonds briefs. Still too tired to lift himself off the floor, he became the laughing stock of the platoon who gathered around him like hyenas crowding around a wounded wildebeest at the Serengeti. They were pointing, laughing and poking at him, and he should be annoyed, but all he could hear was a cacophony of disembodied shrieking and guttural moans. Finally, after what seemed like an eternity, Alex managed to pry himself off the floor, wrapped a towel around his waist and limped to the common bathroom to wash himself. He spent almost thirty minutes under the cold running water as if it was his body and soul that needed cleansing. He slathered himself with soap and shampoo and scrubbed himself raw with a small face towel, and when he was clean and dried, he felt like he had lost several kilos in weight. His mood lifted, his felt immensely lighter on his feet, and it was as if all the weariness and fatigue had been washed away. Now he was ready to speak to Long about the upcoming night festivities.

"Aye, Long, so what's the plan later?" he asked as he languidly strolled, hands in his pockets, to Long's side of the barracks.

"The plan is, Mr Medic, to meet at this place in Geylang called New Shanghai at nine p.m. Dinner, pre-drinking, will all be at your own time and own targets, just as long as you show up at the New Shanghai at nine. I have already booked for us a room with snacks, several towers of beer and two bottles of whiskey. The damage for that works out to a hundred fifty dollars per person. Bring extra money because the ladies they have there will burn a hole in your pocket, and you be most happy to let them do that." Long fired off  the instructions to Alex, instructions that he had been very used to firing off during his many a time at the club.

"Wah, you sound like an old grizzled veteran of the club. What kinda club is it?" Alex asked with a tinge of innocence in his voice.

Long giggled and explained, "It's a karaoke bar, you pay for the room, food and booze. You also pay twenty dollars for the hostesses to sit with you, and you can pretty much have your way with her, short of banging her right there and then."

"Interesting."

"And if you feel like getting takeaway, typically the girls would charge you two hundred dollars for the night. And you also need to pay for the hotel stay, so that works out to two hundred fifty per night for lady company, on top of the one fifty you paid for the room, food and snacks. So, all in, we're looking at five hundred dollars per person damage for the night. Not too bad, I think, considering we only do this what, once a year?" Long rattled on.

"Yeah, not too bad at all."

"So how, Mr Medic? You coming or what?"

Alex took a moment to consider; especially after the failed night out he had at the Thai disco with Long, he was rightfully sceptical. Well, technically Long was not at fault – it was he who chose to go home with that old crone – and Long had nothing to do with it, aside from bringing him there. But the thought of easy pussy again clouded his judgement, and he agreed to get on board and spent the rest of the afternoon with the other boys shouting, *"New fucking Shanghai, fuckers!"* as they went about packing their things and cleaning up before leaving the barracks and not see each other again for a whole year. Even during the out-processing of the main body, Alex and the boys just could not resist shouting, *"New fucking Shanghai, fuckers!"* and giving each other high fives and fist bumps. They scattered once they were able to leave, and Alex took a leisurely drive home, showered once more, and took a nap, drummed up a quick meal before heading out to run a few errands that should take him just nice, to half past nine in the evening to meet Long and the rest. Fashionably late but not too annoying.

Alex rocked up to *New fucking Shanghai* and knew instantly he was going to have a very good time that night. Long had reserved a private room on the top floor of the establishment, and they were the only people there, so they had the run of the entire floor. Alex felt his thighs burn a little bit as he climbed the stairs. He got to the fifth floor and was greeted by a skinny, barely legal teenager with a scrappy moustache trying his best to look mean and imposing. He opened the door and waved Alex into the room, already raucous with off-key singing, bales of laughter and the loud cackling of hostesses. Alex stepped in and saw that aside from the television playing karaoke videos for the boys to sing to, there were no other lights on. It was as if he stepped into a theatre in the middle of the movie. His eyes soon adjusted to the darkness and saw a very simply furnished room. It had wall to wall sofas on three sides of the room, with the one side of the room reserved for the fifty-five-inch television and karaoke equipment. Looking at the people already in there, he saw Long with his familiar Bruce-Lee-sequel hairstyle sitting on the couch, manspreading wide, his arms around the two dangerously young and scantily clad hostesses, his left hand resting languidly on a breast, his right on another. Andre was sitting up, one hand on the mic and singing his heart out to a familiar tune from the seventies that Alex couldn't be bothered to identify because his eyes were on the juicy little trollop hanging off Andre's torso like a baby koala hugging a tree. Andre had his shirt hiked up to his shoulders and the girl was suckling on his nipple as if in a feeding frenzy. And then there was John, a portly middle-aged married man on the sofa, eyes closed, planting light kisses on his chosen hostess, his hands in between her knees as far as Alex could see, but he was pretty sure it went further up.

The decor on the walls were of eighties kitsch and it smelled like the place hadn't been washed since the sixties: cigarette ash, stale beer, damp carpets and of course, pure unadulterated lust. And once he had gotten his bearings with high fives and fist bumps all round, he fished out eighty dollars from his pockets and demanded his share of woman as he sat on the sofa. Two sweet-looking women came in, stood some way away from him waiting for his approval. Raring to go, he couldn't care less what they looked like; it was too dark to care anyway. He just wanted some service, some loving and to cop a feel of a boob, a nipple and a labia. The women went about flanking him on both sides, took his money and took his hands to explore their young bodies. They would stop to explore his with their tongues and hot breaths, stopping only to pour him beer and to feed him sliced mangoes. Alex felt like a king and was surprised at what just two hundred and thirty dollars could get him.

Nevertheless, once the novelty of having two non-English speaking women nibbling at his ears and other accessible body parts wore off, it got very tedious to even be there. So after a while, and a few shots of beer from glasses too big to be called shot glasses but too small to be called mugs, Alex got up and out as he pretended to take a call. He walked down to the bar and found himself just standing there, taking a break from all the attention he had been getting.

And it was at that point where he noticed by the bar a rather modestly dressed, unassumingly gorgeous woman nursing a glass of bourbon, with the bottle within her reach. His first thoughts were that she was definitely a working girl, a hostess. But she definitely wasn't dressed like one. The manager, Jacky, came out and struck a conversation with him as he lit a cigarette. He offered Alex a cigarette which he politely declined. So naturally, Alex asked Jacky who that woman was and whether she was a customer or staff, and he gave the best answer a curious boy could hope for.

"Oh, that's Bobo, and she's our talent manager," Jacky replied nonchalantly. Alex's eyes lit up and fireworks went off and exploded in his head.

She was their China girl scout!

Their mama-san.

The gatekeeper who kept the ugly ones out and let the pretty ones through.

Fuelled by some morbid curiosity of the business in the seemingly legal flesh trade, and by the seemingly exotic job title, Alex asked to be introduced to her.

"Bobo, come, come!" Jacky said in a loud and brusque voice. Almost rude. "Come, Bobo, this is our client, Alex. Alex, this is our talent manager, Bobo."

They shook hands, and she soon poured Alex a drink and asked for him to join her. Alex found that she was well-educated, had a law degree and spoke perfect English. Hailing from Harbin in China, she regaled him with stories of pretty porcelain village girls from the far reaches of the Middle Kingdom, and painfully naive and pure mountain girls from the most obscure of provinces. Alex listened intently and also discovered that her father was a snakehead in the seventies and the eighties, and according to her, it had become some sort of a bizarre family business, just that hers appeared to be more legal.

Conversation and bourbon flowed freely, and they discovered that they were having a very nice time chatting, as Alex forgot that he was there with his mates and easy pussy. But he didn't care anymore, because he had Bobo, who by all counts was more interesting and stimulating than any of what the non-English speaking hostesses could do with their tongues and fingers in the dark. Once in a while, he would pop into the room and touch base with Long and the others, but he soon got tired of running up and down the stairs, so he paid Long his share of the night's festivities and spent the rest of the time with Bobo at the bar. As the night wore on, she soon invited him to have supper with her at the dim sum place just round the corner and they took their conversation there. They had a good time, so at the end of the night, well, more like at 6 a.m., they obligatorily exchanged numbers and promised to keep in touch.

Alex didn't get laid, and it was still a good night.

It was a once in a lifetime.

However, they didn't speak for a few months following that evening. Not even a text message. But one afternoon, bored in a staff meeting, Alex found himself scrolling through his phone looking for nothing in particular and came across her number, messaging profile and her profile picture that induced a semi-boner in him. So he sent her a speculative text message and soon enough. the both got back in touch. And it was a matter of time before they started fucking. So, they stayed in touch, touched each other, and it was nice, comfortable with no complications. It was almost like his relationship with Lyna but with less emotions and complications. She was happy for Alex to be too busy, and he did not have to see her as Alex was happy just knowing she was around.

They didn't need each other, just happy to know they'd be there when they wanted the other. It was a sweet arrangement to have, almost business-like, and it reminded Alex of how it was with Olivia, the Thai amulet saleswoman and his only-when-in-town girlfriend.

One day, Bobo was in town recently, but instead of staying in her usual rental studio apartment, she decided to get a hotel room at a nice, no-frills hotel in a great location. She called after work and asked if Alex wanted to do dinner at the Hong Kong Cafe they went to whenever she was in town. However, Alex wasn't in the mood for supper really, so he declined, and she suggested that they just meet up anyway, which was code for "let's fuck." Not one to turn down a booty call at 11 p.m., he tore himself from his lesson preparations and flew down into town to see her.

They met.

He took her back to her room in a condo on Lorong 26.

They kissed.

She stuck her tongue into his mouth, and it was at that point where things started to get a little bit weird.

She pulled her face back slightly, but with her tongue still sticking out, and she began to lick all four of his sharp canine teeth. She not only ran her tongue at the sharp point of his canine teeth, she even pushed her tongue hard on it. She smiled and giggled as if she had her hands on precious gold as she molested his teeth. She flicked his tongue away as he tried to playfully lick her probing fingers. She pulled his lips back, went in real close to inspect his canines, and he could feel her fingers running along the sharp points of his teeth, and her pushing her tongue into the sharpened point of his canine. And it went to the point where she asked him to bite into her tongue with his canines, not his front teeth, but his canines.

Perplexed at first, but he obliged nevertheless. Not wanting to hurt her, he just nibbled at her tongue hard. But she leaned back, slapped his head hard till he saw stars and asked him to bite into her tongue *like a man! Harder!*

So he did! And she seemed to really like it. After that bit of foreplay, she fucked him hard and furiously like a ravenous tiger that night, and it was good.

As they both lay in bed, soaked in sweat after their exertions, spent in each other's arms, she took his hand and bit him on the palm, on the area called the Mount of Venus. She bit hard enough to leave an angry red bite mark on his palm, but not hard enough to break the skin. Alex wasn't fussed and ignored her antics simply because he was used to having women bite him. But something else happened that night that made him take notice.

She stuck her hand out, and asked Alex to bite into her palm. This time, he bit hard. And he kept biting until she winced in pain and let out a small cry and when he felt her withdrawing her hand slightly. She then looked at her palm, and using the sheets, wiped off his saliva from her palm and ran her fingers, almost lovingly over the bite mark he had left on her palm. Alex looked and saw deep, angry welts, crooked like his teeth, and her palm was painted crimson by the rush of blood there. He looked at her in awe as she caressed the bite marks his crooked front teeth and canines left on her palm, and she lovingly kissed the bite mark.

She looked at Alex with her bright eyes and her gorgeous smile, her luscious lips framing her perfect teeth, and said, "I like it."

"Like what?" he asked.

"Your teeth," she said as she sidled over to plant a huge wet kiss on his lips and pinched his nipples, something she thought he liked.

"Explain, please," he said as he subtly winced in pain.

"Because you remember Lily, darling?" she asked.

Alex vaguely remembered a Lily in that dark cavernous ka-raoke room with Long and Andre. He nodded.

"Because of something she said to me yesterday," she continued.

"She say, you, darling, you are not handsome, not tall, not rich, dark skin.  She say you are not what a lot of girls from China or anywhere would like because of how you look. But somehow you have this quality, this something that she finds very attractive. She mentioned to me that your smile is very dirty and with your crooked teeth, but she like looking at you, and that she feel happy when you are around. Even when you don't talk to her, she feels good and secure. You make her feel good."

Alex tried hard to make sense of what she was saying, but his thoughts were interrupted.

Bobo continued, "So I think about you a lot when she told me that. And that's why I called you to come out tonight because I wanted to see you. And, she was right, I like what I see. Your teeth, even though they are crooked and weirdly shaped, they are very nice, very different and only you can have it. You put those exact same teeth, your piercing eyes, your thick lips, your nose on anyone else, and they will be called monster. So I really think that only you can have things people will say that are not nice but make them nice, only you can have the things that people will say are ugly and monstrous but make them look beautiful on you."

Alex finally got the gist of it, and when it sunk in, he started to feel a little bit uncomfortable at where this conversation could be going. So, not wanting to be drawn into a whole emotional talk about feelings, and where this relationship was going, Alex kissed her deeply and ran his mouth and tongue over every inch of her body and eventually fucked her hard into submission and to keep her quiet. As Alex climaxed onto her face this time, they got into the shower together and began to wash each other clean, a very erotic and intimate act that both of them enjoyed doing together. No words were needed as they went about to wordlessly scour each other of the sins they had committed. But this time, Alex decided to skip their post-shower snuggle under the sheets in their warm bathrobes and used the "family breakfast outing in the morning" excuse to leave her room and to go home. She appeared to know the drill all too well, gathered his clothes for him, helped him dress, gave him a very tight hug like it was the last time they would be in each other's embrace, and kissed him deeply before they parted ways. As he walked along the corridor away from her room, Alex was still trying to figure out what she tried to say.

This was what he had understood from what Lily and Bobo said so far: both were trying to say that despite his physical shortcomings, they could still, very easily, find the things that made him very attractive to them and that somehow he was able to make them feel good and secure about themselves. How or why that was so, neither women could explain. Nevertheless, both women found something in him that they found to be attractive for them, traits that only he could possess, and features that normal people would find unattractive; on Alex, they somehow became attractive.

Or something like that. Alex found himself swimming in uncertainty and doubt on whether what Bobo meant it as a compliment or as tactic number fifty-six in the China girl playbook to latch on to a foreign prospect who could give them a brighter future away from the remote mountain villages of China. Was that her way of telling him that she loved him and was looking for something more than just fucking when she was in town? He still felt good nonetheless, that there were women who could say that he was attractive in his own unique way, even if they were women who were paid to flatter and often deceive.

These thoughts were swirling in his head as he drove home at three in the morning. It did not matter that he had to be up for work in two hours' time, or the fact that he hadn't been sleeping much in the past few months. All he wanted was for this to continue for as long as it remained feasible. But he knew that Bobo would sooner or later, someday, just fall off the earth without warning. Or find someone who she really wanted to be with. Or move on with her life.

*That's how the cookie crumbles, I guess.*

# 22.

"You see, Mark, everyone does financial planning. Financial planning can be broken down to two broad areas. The first is risk management, and the second is wealth management," Carol said, firm yet welcoming, as she began her presentation on the basics of financial planning and management to her prospect.

"Let's look at the first area, risk management. This part of your portfolio essentially ensures that should anything unfortunate happen to you, everything will be taken care of. What risks are we talking about? Risks of illnesses, accidents and…" In the corner of her eye Carol saw the notification lights of her phone blinking green, meaning a call was coming in. She picked up the phone and saw that it was her cousin Anne calling. A deft swipe of her thumb rejected the call and she continued, "…and hospitalisation. Now, in order to have a very comprehensive risk management portfolio, there are *five* areas you need to include. The first one is income protection. Right now, as you are earning an income, everything that you do…." She saw the green light blinking again and saw that it was Anne again, and she deftly rejected it again. "…everything you do revolves around the income earned. So, if you were to fall sick, or suffer a severe injury that prevents you from working and earning that income, this part of your portfolio helps you by replacing your income earned. How?

By giving you a monthly income of…" Again, the blinking green light distracted her from her presentation.

She wanted to the reject the call again when Mark said, "Why don't you take the call, could be something very important. If not, why would that Anne keep calling, right?"

Embarrassed yet annoyed by this turn of events with a prospective client, Carol sighed, smiled and picked up Anne's call. "Hi Anne, this is Carol, what do you need?"

Everything became a blur as her world came crashing down around her, along with that heavy sinking in her chest. It was as if the earth had opened up, and harlots of hell grabbed her by her torso as she was being dragged into hell.

"…income…of…between two thousand to three thousand dollars depending on which plan you choose, for as long as you are unable to work," Carol stammered, her voice trailing as she looked out the window of the conference room on the thirty-fourth floor. Other voices and sounds all seemed to fade into a mind-numbing buzz of a dying wasp, and even her vision became clouded and murky. And all Carol could hear were the words, "Through me you pass into the city of woe. Through me you pass into eternal pain. Through me among the people lost for aye…All hope abandon ye who enter here." Those words on repeat said in an ominous voice in her head as she felt a serpentine dread coiling inside of her, constricting her just enough to make her suffer, but not enough to kill her.

Then, as if carried by and goaded on by an invisible force, Carol stood up, walked out of the conference room, out the glass doors of the office, and into the elevator down. She didn't care about her things that she had left behind in the office. Her power blazer draped over the chair she was sitting on, her briefcase left gaping open, forlorn on the floor, her laptop still running the interactive office program left on the table, her tablet folded on the desk next to the laptop, her documents strewn all over her desk, water bottle, all the trappings of her identity as a financial consultant, all left behind in the office and the conference room. Her mobile phone in her hand, and her trusty handbag with all the cash she needed for the week, her cards, whatever clothes she had left on her back, she stumbled out of the office building in a daze, swaying in the wind aimlessly, with a glazed look in her eyes.

She got into a taxi just outside the office lobby, and said, "Drive" to the taxi driver and nothing else. She felt nothing, she could hear nothing as she felt like being pulled apart in many different directions while a dark cloud descended on her. She felt like drowning but was unable to struggle for breath. Unable to fight for life. A malevolent, invisible hand gripped her, and coupled with that serpentine dread coiling inside of her, she could do nothing but be carried off into the darkness. When pressed by the taxi driver as to where he needed to drive to, Carol limply threw her identity card into the front seat of the cab where her home address was printed on the back. Annoyed by the perceived rudeness, the taxi driver rolled his eyes, uttered a swear word from under his breath and drove on. Carol was too occupied to care.

Nothing mattered now.

Not even the eighteen missed calls that she received from her colleagues, manager and boss. She looked out the window and saw nothing but blackness and these words swirling in the air and booming in her ears:

*Accents of anger, words of agony*

*Forever in that air forever black,*

When out of the blue, as if that malevolent hand gripping her being released her bit by bit, she burst into tears and bawled her eyes out. The taxi driver, concerned, asked if she was okay, but she ignored him as she continued to weep. That black hand of grief released her vocal chords, and she let out a long, heart-wrenching wail of grief and despair, and she flailed about in the backseat of the taxi as if she was a rag doll being tossed about by that malevolent hand. The taxi driver, confused and unsure what to do, kept his eyes on the road, muttered a prayer under his breath and focused on getting Carol home, even as she was a woman overcome by grief and helplessness. Carol doubled over in the backseat, planted her face into the fabric of the seat and beat her fists in regret at the back rest of the taxi, causing more alarm for the taxi driver.

"Fuck!" were the first words she stammered out in between her guttural cries of despair. And those were the only words she could say. It was barely a month ago when she made her birthday wish to spend more time with Aunt Rachel, and to bring her happiness and colour in her days. But she would no longer be able to do that now and that thought and that regret was the malevolent hand gripping her in darkness.

"Miss, are you okay? Do you need anything?" the taxi driver asked her cautiously.

"No, keep going," Carol said as she let out a faint whimper, a frail voice hidden behind a thick layer of grief and regret.

Carol did manage to eventually compose herself. She sat up straight, wiped herself with the tissue papers offered to her by the kind elderly taxi driver and sat in silence as the taxi moved across the island closer to her home. There were no words she could think of, no words she could say, nothing that she wanted to say, so even as the taxi driver tried to make small talk with her, all she could muster was a feeble grunt as she teetered on the edge of reason and composure, barely hanging on so that she didn't break down. She looked out the window to see the world going past, moving on despite the tragedy. She had half expected the world to stop for her in this time of need, but that was not to be so. Not for her. Not for anyone. The sun was shining down hard, and the colours of the world seemed bright, but all Carol could see were the dullness and insipid shapes in a world that no longer harboured Aunt Rachel.

When she finally got back to her apartment, it felt smaller than usual, and her legs were heavier than normal. All she wanted to do was to sink into the couch and stay there until everything got better and colourful again as they were before. Shoulders slumped, she dropped her handbag on the floor, dragged her feet across the hall into the shower and, without taking her clothes off, she turned the shower on. A cold blast of water slapped her across her face and smacked her head as she closed her eyes. Her knees buckled as she crumbled onto the floor, cold water beating down on her, and she felt comfortably numb. She stared into the nothingness that surrounded her and peed and shit all over herself as she lay there broken on the bathroom floor, slumped against the cold grey wall. The cold cement floor did little to encourage her to get up and gather herself as she slid further into the floor; it was as if she no longer had the bones to hold up a body that no longer had the will to live. She found herself in a full foetal position, in her own urine and filth with cold water beating down on her, with a trail of brown water flowing from between her legs into the shower gully trap, as if punishing herself for always putting off spending time with Aunt Rachel. A guttural wail of pain and regret was unleashed from her throat as another bout of guilt and grief hit her hard on the chest, and she writhed like a rag doll tossed hard on a ship in a tempest. As she lay on the cold floor, her cries were now a series of broken gasps, punctuated by a childlike whimpering, and in her mind, she allowed those few moments to wallow in her sadness and grief. She lay there wallowing for a good ten minutes before finally straightening herself up, ripping her clothes and underwear off and throwing them out the bathroom near the indoor rubbish chute and washed herself clean.

If only she could wash herself clean of the guilt and regret.

She closed her eyes as she cleansed herself, and all she could see now was Aunt Rachel, her back facing her, arms in the air, hips swaying seductively, her tattoos crawling out from her jeans across her lower back, swaying dangerously to the chorus of 'Pour Some Sugar On Me'.

Aunt Rachel then turned to look at her, smiled and said, "Music is life, Carol, remember that," hips still swaying without skipping a beat.

Carol cleaned herself thoroughly and washed every nook and cranny she could reach. Using her exfoliating bath gloves, she scrubbed herself red and scratched her skull clean with shampoo. She stood under her rain shower to rinse off the lather on her body and hair. She took a series of deep breaths and grunts and like an athlete psyching herself up before the finals, wiped her grief from her eyes and off her shoulders as she prepared to face what was outside her bathroom. Cold water still fell on her head, and sometimes she felt as if she was drowning on her feet and she felt like breathing in the water into her lungs, her wet hair falling across her face, covering her eyes. The sounds of the bathroom and her world slowly returned as her ears slowly recovered from the grief, and she could clearly hear the gush of water smashing the bathroom floor and flowing down into the gully trap. Bits of dark faecal matter still clung to the white cover of the gully trap as she cringed in disgust at what she did just moments before. Still naked, she quickly got on her hands and knees to clean the gully trap with an unused toothbrush, ensuring that her faecal matter was washed down and the gully trap cover cleaned and pristine white as before. She got onto her feet and scanned around the bathroom floor to see if there were any more bits of faecal matter swimming about and flushed the underwear she wore earlier with how badly she had stained them. It was bad enough for her to decide to throw them out without thinking of how much it cost her. She felt a surge of urgency in her to pull everything together and to stop falling apart. It was what Aunt Rachel would have wanted her to do. She stood under the running water for a while longer, steeled herself into action and turned off the shower.

Once the water turned off, her skin immediately felt the cool air latching on now that she was no longer protected by the running water. She shuddered as goosebumps began to form on her skin when she realised that she had to run out of the bathroom naked to get to her towel. In a series of quick and efficient moves, she was soon dried, warm and toasty from the shower as her flat was plunged into a darkness brought by the dark gathering of clouds outside. They looked exactly how she felt. Fishing out something comfortable and conservative, she put on minimal makeup, got dressed, booked a taxi and was at Aunt Rachel's house for her wake. Many of her relatives were already there milling about in a very sombre ambience. She rushed to find and hug her mum tight and buried her face in her shoulder. She found that she was out of tears and all cried out, yet the heavy sinking feeling in her chest still weighed her down. Carol's mum, knowing how close she had been to Rachel, whispered in her ear, "She is in a better place now, darling, don't be sad, okay?"

Carol closed her eyes and hugged her mum tighter and could only afford a pained grunt. Because there were no words to describe what she was feeling at that point.

After what felt like an eternity, Carol found herself in a daze as she mingled around the very modest, almost spartan home, randomly nodding her head to acknowledge her relatives. She didn't recognise a lot of the people there, but they seemed to recognise her, Carol, the daughter that Rachel loved like her own. All were there waiting to receive the body from the hospital so that they could begin their own funeral rites. As far as Carol knew, Aunt Rachel did not believe in the rites of religion. Her religion was a life of rock and roll rebellion. Even in her last days, she always asked Carol to play her songs from the "eighties rawk" playlist and would talk about the memories she had attached to every song that came on.

How 'Black Dog' reminded her of her first date with some guy named Andrew.

How 'Livin On A Prayer' reminded her of her time at the shop with Sam.

Carol wanted to reach for the radio sitting forlorn in the corner, pop in a Slaughter CD and play 'Fly To The Angels,' a fitting song about death and dying, but Carol did not want to cause offence and an uproar. She preferred to sit on Aunt Rachel's worn out olive-green fabric couch and keep her memory alive in her.

So she sang to herself, swaying back and forth the wailing vocals of Mark Slaughter belting into the chorus.

Suddenly, there was a flurry of activity as people began to rush out the front door in anticipation of something. Carol figured that the body had finally arrived, and it filled her with a dread of a thousand years. She opened her eyes and caught a glimpse of the cold metal coffin being unloaded from the hearse, and Carol broke down, not in tears, but a fit of shivers. Chills ran down her spine, and it was as if a cold claw gripped her and tossed her about like a rag doll. She fell into the old musty couch in an uncontrollable fit, unable to breathe. Once again, everything faded into a muted buzz while colours dissolved into a blur of grey and black and she felt like she was floating in a space between life and death, when she felt a strong tug which snapped her back into reality. She saw that her dad pulled her off the couch, gave her a bear hug, which calmed her as they usually did. She stopped shaking and composed herself, ready to look upon Aunt Rachel's face for one last time.

Her dad was speaking to her, but she couldn't hear a word he was saying. Carol was psyching herself up to see Aunt Rachel's body when she noticed a shadow in the distance with piercing eyes staring at her. She focused her eyes and saw that it was Shaun, a family friend who grew up next door to Aunt Rachel. He was about Carol's age, maybe younger, or could be that he was just smaller. But dressed in black, he seemed to have cleaned up okay. They acknowledged each other with a sombre nod as she looked back into her father's sorrowful eyes.

Carol spent the rest of the day avoiding any contact with her relatives and explaining to her boss and colleagues what happened. "Carol, I am sorry that happened, but she is not your immediate family, she is your aunt, so we cannot give you more than two days of compassionate leave. The fact is that you have to serve over fifteen clients over this period…" was the last thing she heard from her boss as she hung up the phone. And with that, she quit her job. She threw the phone on the bed and walked out of the room to finally mingle with the relatives and to see Aunt Rachel. Many tried to make small talk with her, but she just shut them up with a smile and a grunt. And in a small apartment, it was getting very tedious to keep doing that to relatives. It wasn't that Carol was being rude, but she just wanted to be alone.

Her favourite person just passed.

She just quit her job.

That was a lot to happen in a day, let alone a few hours. So many changes, so little preparation and barely time to react.

Like how, out of the blue, she felt her mum's hand grabbing hers and bringing her into Aunt Rachel's room where her body had been washed and prepared for the wake. Carol gasped as she saw the bulge on the bed covered in a traditional floral funeral shroud. She closed her face with her hands and wanted to leave, but her mum grabbed her by the shoulders telling her that this was something she had to do.

And she was right.

Carol took a deep breath; a stale musk of old sheets and mothballs mixed in with a whiff of lavender and lemongrass aromatherapy oil lingered in the air. The room didn't smell like death at all. It smelled just like how she remembered Aunt Rachel. She stared at the white bulge on the bed and asked to be left alone with the body for a few minutes. She sat at the edge of the bed facing away from the body at first before twisting her torso to turn and look at Aunt Rachel. Carol reached for the top of the shroud and pulled it down to reveal Aunt Rachel's face.

She looked like she was sleeping, and Carol half expected her to open her eyes and smile that sweet, crooked smile at her. Carol ran her fingers through Aunt Rachel's hair, putting them in place and running her fingers over her face. She felt her cool skin, smooth and pale, almost sanded down. Carol had expected to weep and wail, but she had no more tears left. Not for now anyway. Carol moved closer to look at Aunt Rachel. She wanted to say a prayer but was never a believer, and she was at a loss for words.

All she could say was, "I'm sorry. I'm sorry for not spending time with you at the hospital. I'm sorry for not being there when you passed. I'm sorry for not calling you enough."

Carol felt that she should cry at this moment but felt bad that she couldn't. Even as she sat there apologising to the body, even as the sadness shrouded her body like the shroud around Aunt Rachel, she could not cry. To an observer, she appeared to be someone just going through the motions, like muscle memory. But what they couldn't see was the weight of guilt and regret that was weighing on Carol's shoulders. She caressed Aunt Rachel's cold cheeks with her thumb running softly below her eye, she planted a kiss on Aunt Rachel's forehead and finally said goodbye.

She twisted the knob that felt ancient in her hand as she opened the door to a bevy of relatives crowding outside Aunt Rachel's bedroom, all clamouring to say their final goodbye to the rebel Aunt Rachel. The same aunt who was always the subject of everyone's rumour-mongering.

That she was a lesbian.

That she couldn't give birth to children and that was why no man wanted her.

That she was a bossy and domineering dragon-lady no man wanted.

Carol never paid attention to the rumours even as they flew about viciously in the family. And neither did Aunt Rachel. To Carol, Aunt Rachel was a woman who lived life on her own terms and did things her way. Her way, which rubbed many the wrong way, but she didn't care. But try as she might, she could not remember a single shred of advice that Aunt Rachel gave her despite her dispensing what had to be thousands since Carol was a child. The only thing that she could recall and replay in her mind was when Aunt Rachel said,

"Music is life." That was because her entire life was an example for Carol.

To live on your own terms.

Always.

All around Carol, people were talking in hushed tones, arms folded in front of them, and Carol felt stifled, like a noose was slowly tightening around her neck and she couldn't breathe. She pushed her way out of the cramped apartment, knocked her shin on the edge of the worn coffee table and stormed out the front door into the yard and let out an almighty gasp and instantly felt better. Still, everything seemed to be muffled to a dull buzz around her, the colours muted yet the brightness of the day blinding. She felt like a vampire being out in daylight for the first time, squinting and shielding her eyes in sensory overload. Carol felt someone grabbing her arm, and it transported her back from her headspace and she saw Shaun, with arms around her back, squeezing her bicep in an effort to console her. Carol smiled and grunted at him, but that did not deter him from speaking to her. Carol saw his mouth moving, yet no words came out of it, no sound. It was still a dull, muffled buzz, and her temples were starting to ache.

Her vision flitted between a blurry mass of grey matter to a clear focus of reality, both of which weighed her down heavily with melancholy. The tiny voices floated by endlessly, some swirling around her face, but all were a fool's speech that slept in her ears. She would feel someone occasionally holding her arm and squeezing it gently as if consoling her, and she actually enjoyed it. Once in a while, there would be a soft caress running up and down her shoulder and back. In her daze, she didn't really care who did it, because it did comfort her a little bit, and she would periodically nod at nothing really, she just felt it was an appropriate thing to do at some point. She felt like she was floating when a rising cacophony of distant voices echoed her name that brought her back to Aunt Rachel's wake, snapping her back to reality.

She realised that Shaun had been talking to her all this time, talking to her and touching her. Not that she minded, but it now felt weird that someone she barely knew was touching her like that, even if it was to console.

His touches felt loaded with intent.

So she focused.

"So what do you say, Carol? You wanna go grab that coffee and scone later after the wake?" Shaun's voice reverberated in her face, and she realised how close Shaun was standing to her and she could feel his body heat and his hot coffee breath. She could almost hear the wheezing in his nose as he breathed and the dull sludge of his muscles from under his skin stretching and tensing.

"Wait, what?" Carol asked. And then it hit her. "Did you just ask me out on a date?"

Shaun nodded his head, smiled bashfully and tremulously caressed her arm.

She pulled away from him and said, "You. Asked. Me. Out on a date. At Aunt Rachel's wake?"

Shaun, unable to sense the incredulous tone of Carol's voice, continued to smile and took a step closer to Carol to touch her hand.

Carol slapped his hand away.

"Why are you doing this? I have always liked you, Carol, and I thought if not now, when?" Shaun whispered to her in an effort to not cause a scene.

"When? How about last week? How about when we were twenty-one? How about never?" she hissed.

"But why, is it because I'm not rich? Is it because I live in a tiny apartment with my parents?" Shaun asked.

Carol looked at him in disbelief. There they were, at a melancholic event, dripping with mourning and regret, and all he could think of was why *he* got rejected. Carol scanned the room looking for her mum or dad but found neither. She felt an inhuman rage rising in her, overpowering her and taking control of her. Looking at that now very creepy smile, she wanted to rip Shaun a new ass, she wanted to give him a tongue lashing.

His hands moved down to her waist and pulled her closer to him as he said, "So, how bout it, darling, shall we?"

Inflamed with rage, she threw her hands across his face, making contact with a loud splat of skin and flesh on soft cheekbone. Her hand connected so sweetly with his face that it hurt, but she was sure that he was hurting much more. However she couldn't be sure because Shaun's face had turned away by the sheer force of her slap, and he walked away even before recovering from it. Eyes bored into the two of them in disbelief as a sullen hush fell over the house.

Carol saw her mum and walked to her. She hugged her and buried her face in her shoulder and, this time, bawled her eyes out. Shaking, all she could say was, "Mummy." She could hear distant voices once again swirling around her, and this time, the words warmed her heart.

"Wow, she is just like Rachel."

# 23.

Alex clicked on the link in Sammyboy and read a very familiar line. "Frida, a 23-year-old Polish mix, smooth like silk, sex like tiger, and teacher grade BBBJ." He saw a blonde, long-haired treat shining in high definition through his forty-four-inch television. She was in red and very undersized lingerie recycled from the last whore. Arms raised, armpits in their full glory, legs apart and lips pouting.

*Haha.*

*These fellas never change their marketing tagline, huh?*

*I remember this from when Lyna was whoring here.*

He almost fell for it though, just like he did with Lyna. This Frida was even staged the same way as he remembered Lyna, in the soft, retro filter, with toned armpits and her pasty white skin. He was visiting the online brothel, a throwback from his whoring days and wanted to see how things had changed there.

*Just a quick peek. No harm, no foul.*

*I don't feel like banging anyway.*

So he clicked on the thread in the forum to read about her statistics, service and what they termed 'field reports' on the lady. There were no reviews on her, but her statistics ignited a slight tingle in his groin.

*No, not today.*

*I don't feel like having sex anyway.*

He hadn't been feeling like having sex in a while now, which was strange for him. He lazily scrolled down the page looking at the different but same pictures of this Frida and reminisced of the conversations he had with the digital pimp creatively named Mr Pimp, to whom he paid a hundred and sixty dollars for a forty-five-minute session with Frida. He was surprised nevertheless that he was nostalgic about Mr Pimp and not so much about Lyna.

*I must be moving on from her nicely.*

He stuck to his guns and did not call Mr Pimp for a session with this Frida, but he decided to send him a text anyway. Just a slight probe, nothing to it.

"Hi bro, it's me Hungry. I was on Dome 3 again and saw the new 'Frida.' Haha. Nice nice. I do miss the old Frida though." Click send.

It was a matter of minutes before Mr Pimp replied, "Haha, yeah she was one of the good ones. You interested in this one?"

"No not really, but if you do bring in the original Frida, I for sure will take a session. So that is a hint for you bro, to bring her back in." Alex sent the message.

"Yeah, man. You call on her to make a comeback tour here," Mr Pimp replied.

"No, I can't call her, we didn't exchange contacts back then,", he lied. "Thought you would have her contact details. Just curious though, are you in touch with the old Frida?" Alex asked.

"I have her original contact number, but I am not in touch with her. Why?" Mr Pimp's reply came.

"Oh, nothing really."

More lies.

"Just wondering if I can get in touch with her. I was quite close to her that time."

"Yeah, I remember you seeing her almost every week!" Mr Pimp quipped. "Okay, here you go, this is the number I got in touch with her with. Not sure if she is still using this number, because I tried messaging her but no reply. But I am sure this number is being used because it is being read. Maybe you will have better luck getting in touch with her, and if it is indeed her, please ask her to come work for me again, she was my best girl and she made me rich!"

*Oh wow, this actually worked!*

"Oh wow, thanks bro! Sure, I will ask her if she wants to do a comeback tour. But so you know, if she does, I will be her main and regular customer," Alex typed and sent the message to Mr Pimp.

Mr Pimp send the laughing emoticon followed by, "No worries and good luck!"

Alex could feel his heart bursting through his chest from sheer ecstasy. This was the moment he had been pining for.

*To hell with getting over, to hades with moving on!*

*This might just work!*

He pictured his happy place with Lyna fully restored in the soft sepia-filtered scene smiling at him once again.

*I have worked so hard to try to get over her — is this the way to go from here?*

*Well, maybe this is my reward for the penance I have been inflicting on myself.*

*But relax, this number might not even be the right one.*

*What has Mr Pimp to gain from giving me her number?*

*Maybe he's just trolling me, like how I myself would troll other lonely, sad fuckers.*

Alex stared at the empty message window on his phone, not knowing what message to write, doubts swirling in his head. He ignored the other messages that were flying into his mailbox and the notifications that kept popping up on his phone screen as he was lost in his own doubt. Limp as his penis had been of late, it seemed to have awaken from its slumber and was stirring in his crotch as he adjusted himself uncomfortably in his seat. Still staring into the blank message window on his phone as the day slowly turned dark and dusk crawled into the air, he sat there in the dark, his face illuminated by the backlight of his fast-draining mobile phone, still swimming in a sea of confusion and diffidence.

*Okay, I need to stop this.*

*Man alive, I am hungry as fuck!*

*Okay, I'll go get dinner first.*

*Let's take a walk to get food and kill this boner for a while.*

Alex got up from the sofa, stubbed his toe on the coffee table in the dark, and cursed out loud as he fished around for his keys to leave the house, now bathed in a suburban darkness. A kind of darkness that was punctuated by the relentless glare of the street lights, a darkness that was broken by the fluorescent lights bleeding out of his neighbours' windows.

*Is it really a good idea to message her?*

*What is the worst that could happen?*

*There'd be no reply, and that will be a sure indication that I can totally move on.*

*There'd be no reply even after the message is being read, which will tell me that she is no longer into me.*

*Heartbreak.*

*Is that what's going to happen?*

*Am I headed for heartbreak?*

Alex hummed that song as he trudged along the path, eyes fixed on the ground, dragging his leaden feet along as he continued to be consumed by doubt and now hunger. He could hear the squeaking of his feet rubbing against his cheap rubber slippers as he walked, not really knowing where to go and what to eat. With the world hurtling past him at the breakneck pace of a big city, he felt like the weeds at the bottom of the river, its roots hanging tenuously to the riverbed, doing its best to not be carried away by the currents. He had one hand in his pocket, fiddling with the keys as he walked along, ignoring the sea of faces that unknowingly floated past.

Finally he came upon a cafe named Route 66, and he was suddenly overcome with a craving for fish and chips, mainly because he saw it on the blackboard menu placed strategically outside the cafe. He walked into the neo-retro themed cafe and placed his takeaway order with a cute but too young wait staff. He was the only customer there at that time, and as he stood there whistling and waiting for his food, he was again lost in his own thoughts.

*So what is the best-case scenario then?*

*She replies, tells me where she is, I come to her, we meet up, fuck and live happily ever after?*

*That sounds like a glorious piece of fried gold.*

*And what if it doesn't work out?*

*What if all this time you've pined for Lyna, and then you find out that you can't stand to be with her for more than three days?*

"Here you go, sir, your order of fish and chips with vinegar and extra tartar sauce," a voice interrupted his thoughts.

Alex paid for the meal and sauntered home with his bag of piping hot fish and chips rubbing against the sides of his calves along the path as people stepped out of their way so he could pass through. The sounds of suburbia ringing loud in his ears and despite the cacophony of sounds and voices, he felt strangely alienated, as if he was a leper making his way home to the leper colony. He finally got home, still unable to shake off the feelings of alienation, and he tore into his fish and chips with a vengeance.

Halfway through his meal, while chewing bits of fish and batter, he picked up his phone, and with his oily fingers, went to what might be Lyna's contact number and opened a message window. This time, he steeled himself and typed and sent a simple, "Hi Lyna, it's me Alex, remember me?" He then threw the phone into the sofa and went about devouring his dinner, trying very hard to take his mind off his mobile phone. He found that he stole glances at the phone to see if the notification light was blinking and that he had to consciously stop his hands from automatically reaching out to grab the phone. The smartphone sat there in the corner of the sofa, as if taunting him, and like a junkie trying to get off drugs, Alex felt the pain in him as he consciously stayed away from his phone. Even the slightest hint of a blinking light would see him snap his head to look at his phone.

*Okay, I have to stop looking for the phone.*

*I need to stop being so attached to it and hoping for a miracle.*

*If it is indeed her number, then good.*

*If she replies, then better.*

*If it's none of the above, then too bad, a little bit sad, but we know that is a strong possibility anyway.*

It was hours later when the notification light finally blinked, and it was a message from his colleagues about work. Alex opened the conversation window between him and possibly Lyna, and saw that the message was not delivered yet, which could be good or bad.

*Maybe this is not such a bad thing after all.*

He already had himself and the house washed and cleaned and was getting ready for bed with one last look at the conversation window.

*Still not delivered.*

Alex drifted off to a dreamless sleep and woke up to get ready for work five minutes before his 5 a.m. alarm went off. Eyes barely open, with slumber still hanging heavily on his eyelids, he searched in the darkness for his mobile phone. His eyes were blinded by the sudden burst of the smartphone backlight and saw no reply to his message. It was, however, delivered and read.

*Okay, so someone has read it.*

*Mean's the number is still working.*

*Hope it's her, but if it's not, then, no worries.*

He went about the day as usual, navigating the bureaucracy, traumatising teenagers, attending pointless meetings and making house visits to negligent parents. All in a day's work. It was Wednesday, his usual heavy day, so he didn't even have time to be fiddling about with his phone. Finally, at 4 p.m., he fished out the phone from his backpack and saw the WhatsApp notification light blinking and the message bar telling him of the three hundred twenty-six messages he received since eight in the morning. Most of them were work-related, several from the group chats with his friends, others from his friends and some other random messages he had been ignoring for months. As he scrolled down the interface, he saw that he had indeed received a message from Lyna.

*Oh, shit.*

*She replied!*

*What if I open it and it's something bad?*

*Idiot, what if it's something good?*

He took a moment to compose himself and tapped the screen to open the WhatsApp chat window and read the message.

"Hi. Yes, I do remember. Sorry, I just got off work when I finally saw your message last night. How the fuck did you get this number?" the message read.

*The message was sent a few hours ago in the afternoon.*

*Maybe it was her lunch break.*

*Is she an office lady now?*

*Wait what time zone is she in that she just got off work at 8 p.m.?*

*Could she be in a similar time zone?*

Alex leaned back in his chair, feet up on his desk and let it sink in that the love of his life was finally back. He began to play several scenarios in his head, all of them ending up with the both of them living happily ever after. Short of planning the entire wedding in his head, Alex began to prematurely plot out the events of the next few years involving Lyna and him.

"I got your number from that Mr Pimp, that's how the fuck I got your number, I have been missing you a lot since you left."

He clicked send, and it was delivered, received and read in an instant, and he could immediately see that Lyna was typing a reply.

"That bastard. Haha. Yeah, this app only identifies my old number even after I changed numbers."

Alex saw her typing another message.

"Yeah, I missed you too. But I not sure. And then it got too long, and I thought you would be seeing someone else, so I decided to forget it. But I am glad you messaged me, it's, like, perfect timing." Smiling emoji.

"I'm now very happy to be in touch with you again, darling. Where are you now? Let's meet up and talk about this. About us, the future and all that." Alex typed the message as he walked out of the office for some privacy, ignoring the students who plied him with greetings and colleagues who said goodbye to him.

"I am now working in Perth, Australia, quite near you, I work nights though, so it is best if you come that we meet after two a.m." The reply came attached with a selfie of Lyna, bare-faced, long blonde hair, and clearly just rolled out of bed.

Alex felt an explosion of unbridled joy in him as he finally saw the face that he longed for flash brightly on his smart phone screen.

Or maybe he came in his pants.

Nevertheless it was all that he could do to control himself as he responded with a selfie of his own, white shirt, tie and face covered in work grime, with a message that said, "Okay, I know Perth. I know it very well, I will be there, and we will be together finally."

"Okay. I got to make breakfast now and prepare for work, darling. Message you later, okay?"

Kiss face emoji.

And with that, everything seemed to fall into place once again, and all was right in his world. He couldn't help but smile a goofy smile, the kind one had when he was in love.

Alex saw the world in a whole new light and with a renewed drive and direction. He walked back to the staff office, plonked himself down on his chair. He breathed in the cold, musty air of the staff room, and saw how his desk reflected his state of mind. Cluttered, and a mess. So he set out to clean up his desk for the next hour, and clean it up he did. He was surprised at how he was hanging on to random shards and scraps of paper from years ago, unmarked bits of assignments from students who had since graduated from university and were working at their first jobs. And in an hour, he began to see the shiny, smooth brown top of his desk, a sight he hadn't seen in years. His desk had been cleared up in no time, and he felt spiritually cleansed, with a massive weight being lifted off his chest, shoulders and head. His colleagues remarked on how uncharacteristically clean and tidy his desk was and joked how he even appeared to look like a whole different person.

Alex enjoyed the brief attention he received, but not as much as he enjoyed texting and video-messaging Lyna over the next few days, weeks and months. There was now a spring in his step, more strength in his deadlifts, as he discovered his why.

He finally had six hours of uninterrupted sleep at night, and his random and nocturnal boners came back with the force and fury only matched by Mother Nature herself as he looked forward to receiving Lyna's texts or video messages. It was the first thing he looked out for when he woke up and the last thing he did before going to bed.

Alex began a countdown before his date of departure by taking note of and crossing out the mini milestones that came by. Aside from that, he also had a payday countdown before his departure and was constantly reminding himself and Lyna about it.

*Ah, great. Three more paydays before D-Day.*

*So let's do this!*

*This is actually happening!*

However, there were days when doubt would creep into him and paralyse him. And he would spend days and weeks with doubt swirling in his head, as he got tossed about in a sea of confusion. As much as this was something he had been hoping for since they both went their separate ways, Alex felt more comfortable in playing the victim and pining for her.

*Do I really want to travel halfway across the world just for that chance to be with her?*

*Am I coming across as desperate and needy?*

*I think I am the only one who wants this to happen.*

*She seems to be nonchalant about this whole thing.*

*What if she has moved on from me?*

*I have been obsessing about moving on from her; I never even thought about how she could have moved on from me.*

*What if she is just entertaining me as a former client?*

*Or what if that is her intention? That I am her side hustle?*

*What if I am only going there to have my heart torn out?*

*Shit.*

*Why, why why am I such a sappy loser?*

He went through that mentally debilitating monologue on a daily basis as he allowed for doubt to creep into his being. It was unlike him as much as it was typical of him, and this dichotomy of character had often landed him in hot water many a time. Nevertheless, something in him had changed, even before Lyna came back into his life.

*Maybe all this casual is not doing me much good.*

*What I need is an anchor.*

*I honestly thought Bobo could be one, but she was just like the rest.*

*Why do I treat myself like that?*

*Why do I allow women to treat me like that? Like a fun whore.*

*I need to stop.*

*Self-pity is not a colour that looks good on you.*

And therein lay the trauma Alex suffered from this luscious Ukrainian trollop. As much as he returned to who he was before, it was a different person than the one he knew of. There was a disconnect between who he was now and who he had been with Lyna before, and that was causing the endless internal conflict in him. And the constant second-guessing, doubt and uncertainty on top of the Lyna-shaped hole of a loss that he never really got over, they all scarred him internally, but instead of strengthening him, the scar tissue made him weaker. He didn't care for all that though, the symptoms of breaking down, the cracks and fault-lines forming around his soul, because the euphoria he felt at meeting Lyna and fucking her again papered over the cracks as he focused on saving money, being on the ketogenic diet and getting in shape for what he imagined to be a fuck fest.

And before he knew it, the days had flown by and there were no more paydays left to count as he found himself all packed, ready to go, and in line at the airport counter to check-in for his flight out to Perth. He stood in line like a stone amidst the sea of families with unruly children, confused parents and tired airport staff. However, none of them had a clue of the anxiety that was ripping him to pieces on the inside as he mentally fidgeted and fussed about, replaying the different scenarios that could happen in Perth and repeating the words he had planned to say in every scenario.

*Okay, so if all goes well, we will fuck.*

*If she needs more time, then unlatch yourself for a while and see where it takes you.*

*If she is not interested, well at least you get a holiday out of it.*

*But still, try to see if you can fuck one last time.*

*What if she's already seeing someone else?*

*Oh God, what if she already has a kid with some guy, and she needs to tell me face to face?*

*What if she is dying?*

So on top of that, his mind was also abuzz with random, confusing and debilitating thoughts that dragged him deeper and deeper under this tumultuous sea of uncertainty. He could feel a weight hanging in his chest, pulling him down further into the watery abyss, where soon there was no light shining from the sun, just a deep, lonesome blue darkness that swallowed him. He felt a tight squeezing of his heart, like a serpent coiling around its victim squeezing every ounce of life out of him as it desperately tried to maintain a beat and rhythm. His breathing became very laboured, short and shallow and he could feel some form of an attack coming on, but he could not tell what kind of attack it was. It could be a panic attack, or a heart attack, and he had no way to tell. He could feel the cold fear gripping his entire being as beads of cold sweat trickled down his back and forehead. His soul trembled in cold fear. It started with a tingle in his feet, which then took control and weakened his legs as he came perilously close to falling to his knees. He tried very hard to calm himself down and took a series of deep breaths, and it was all that he could do to not fall over the edge of this anxiety and uncertainty. It took a near gargantuan mental effort to keep himself together in a series of mental reassurances and deep breaths, and that was when he caught a whiff of a familiar scent.

Chanel's Mademoiselle.

Aside from setting fire to his loins, the scent always calmed him down, and it snapped him out of the stormy sea of anxiety. His heart stopped racing and settled into a comfortable rhythm. His breaths became longer and more relaxed as the thin film sweat that had formed around his face dissipated in thin air. He transformed into a lusty bloodhound as he snapped his head about, looking around for someone who might be wearing the scent. He was sniffing the air like a bloodhound hunting for its prey when his eyes fell on the sight of a sinewy arm, muscles ripped through its almost translucent skin. Alex, leading with his nose, followed the scent toward that arm. An arm that began to slowly turn to face him.

He was at Changi Airport.

And it was the Mademoiselle at the airport.

# 24.

It had been months, and Carol had been existing instead of living. She had been an unthinking creature, functioning mainly on instinct and muscle memory. A rumble in the belly meant hunger, and hunger meant getting her keys, holding it up to ensure that she was holding them before closing the door and locking the gates, then forty-three steps to the elevator, a hundred and three steps to her usual food stall, a regular nod of the head, and then retraced her steps back. Repeat this three times daily, and that had been her life. In between meals, all she did was sit on her couch, stare into space, with nary a thought running in and around her head. Phone calls were generally missed – as she would only entertain calls from her family – her letters piled up in her mailbox, dirty laundry stewed and marinated with each other in the washer. Even showers were mostly an afterthought as opposed to a necessity before the Doom, as she has termed it. Bills and mortgage were all debited directly from her bank account so that were things off her mind. Plus, she had been working hard for the past decade, so she could afford a year or so of wallowing.

She revelled in the squalor and the darkness that had descended on her and never thought she would see the light at the end of the darkness. Dark clouds circled around her head and in her mind with the sound of distant, rolling thunder echoing constantly, the threat of a tempest looming large.

Slouching on the couch, she slid further in an abyss of loneliness and regret, with the dark clouds tracking her every move. She basked in her self-pity in her oversized AC/DC T-shirt and well-worn boxer shorts that had not touched detergent in a while. Carol flitted in and out of sleep, between her bed and couch all day, every day. But what she really wished for was to sleep for the next few months, or even years. Music from the eighties rock playlist oozed and bled out of her home surround sound system, painting the walls with a deep hue of melancholy. The songs of her youth, but most importantly, the songs that reminded her of Aunt Rachel, hung heavily in the air, tight like a stained funeral shroud wrapped around a corpse. Nevertheless, these songs were the only connection she had with Aunt Rachel, and Carol was adamant that Aunt Rachel be kept alive in all the songs as picture perfect memories scattered all over the floor of her mind, pictures of Aunt Rachel and her, some actual memories, some made up, as she wondered if she would ever get past this.

Once, in a concerted effort to kick herself out of this funk, she went to the extent of renting a car and drove around in silence. She would get on the highway and space out, relying on pure muscle memory as she came to just as she got to the end of the highway, not remembering how she got there in the first place. It wasn't long before she gave up on that and decided it was safer on the couch. Charmaine dropped by after work every now and then to see if she was okay and to try to talk Carol out of her funk, but she could see that Carol was in too deep in this funk and that she would only get out of it when she was truly ready. For now, what was best for Carol was to allow her to wallow and ensure that she was fed, washed and got some sun once in a while. Carol had run out of tears and was all cried out, so the random bouts of uncontrolled weeping had passed, which in itself was progress.

Another shot of whiskey, another glass of wine. Another packet of food, another song sung. Cold water on her face, warm water flowed down her back. Disembodied voices howled and whined every now and then, all of which moulded into a blurred vignette of her life.

And it was one day when she was rolling on the couch, freshly washed, and ready for hours of more wallowing when a song that had been out of rotation on her playlist came on. It was a different sound that came out of her speakers; instead of the heavy, slow pluck of the guitars backed by keyboards and other effects, this was a happy, almost hopeful pluck of two acoustic guitars whose notes seemed to dance together in perfect choreographed harmony. The guitar sounds were almost shimmery, and it shone a ray of light on her that could chase away the dark clouds haunting her the past few months. It was like a cool breeze flitted by providing her with a cool respite from a scorching hot day as Carol closed her eyes and allowed for the cool air to settle on her skin.

It was 'Dust In The Wind' by Kansas, a song that is a meditation on mortality and the inevitability of death.

She looked up, and something in her seemed to click into gear. What it was, she did not know. But as soon as those lyrics were sung, something spoke to her, wordlessly, and it was as if new life had taken root and began to sprout from within her. It was as if a drought had been lifted in the parched valley of death that was now beginning to be showered with rain and growing some green.

As the melodious voice of Steve Walsh carries her emotions higher, she felt like a drop of water in an endless sea of hope

The darkness seemed to be slowly but surely drifting away as colour started to return to her sight. The fog of melancholy and distress was slowly lifting as she began to feel some warmth creeping into her soul once again. Carol felt like it was Aunt Rachel's spirit who had come to comfort her and to chase the blues away. She could almost feel her warm hands caressing her in a comforting embrace that drained all sorrow away. Mostly, she felt that Aunt Rachel was sending her a message.

That Carol shouldn't worry, nor be sad. Because all we are IS dust in the wind

Carol felt overwhelmed with emotion; it was not of sadness but of joy as she bopped her head to the haunting yet hopeful melody of the song. In her darkened stupor, as she felt she lay beyond the grace of God, she must have clicked something on the app which had the song playing on repeat. Or it could be something supernatural at work, she knew not. And soon, she caught a hint of a fragrant smell of flowers and incense wafting through the cool evening air, a smell vaguely familiar, but something she could not put her finger on. A sense of calm now washed over her as a smile began to slowly be painted across her face. There was soon no doubt in her mind that the spirit of Aunt Rachel visited her in her time of need to bring her comfort, to assure her that it was okay for Carol to move on. And even though she had felt that she was all cried out before, she began to break down. However, there was a difference this time. There were no regrets, nor was she weighed down by crippling melancholy. In between broken gasps and fresh tears rolling down her cheek, Carol managed to say, "Sorry" and a "Goodbye" in a shivery whimper to what she felt was the spirit of Aunt Rachel. She felt at peace, as a weight was lifted off her shoulders along with the darkness that had been plaguing. She got off the couch, took a very long shower, washing off her guilt, remorse and regret. Naked as the day she was born, Carol looked out the window at the clear azure sky, occasionally broken by small patches of white clouds passing by.

Her tears washed away. Carol felt born again, with the slow breeze caressing her face, and she looked forward to a new day. She then did something she hadn't done in a while, which was to go into lockdown, as she methodically closed and locked her doors and windows before retiring into her bedroom and drifting off to a long, restful, dreamless slumber.

Carol smiled the moment her eyes opened the next day, and in the cold, harsh darkness of her bedroom, she felt a peace she hadn't felt in months. She even felt the embers of heat stirring in her loins as she imagined a nice, warm, hard dick in her mouth. Some things hadn't changed, but Carol had fundamentally changed. She felt a change in her but was unable to put her finger on what it was exactly. That change felt to her like a bad word bleeped, a wink that was too quick to notice, an imperceptible nod, and a subtle shiver. Even her lust for flesh seemed to have been displaced slightly. She lay in bed a while longer to find her bearings once again before jumping out to stretch her now stiff joints and muscles. The months of depression she slipped into had taken its toll on her body as she felt the aches and pains of a grizzled and grumpy senior citizen cursing at imaginary beings outside her home. She groaned and grunted as her bones creaked and muscles unwillingly flexed and relaxed. Carol felt shooting pains going across her body like multiple shooting stars streaking across the night sky, leaving behind in her a trail of pain that she had never felt before.

She willed herself to go through this routine of stretching followed by a run before a healthy breakfast where she would usually plan for her day. But since she was unceremoniously fired from her job after months of avoiding her bosses, she realised she now had the time to do anything she wanted. She hunched over the kitchen island where she inhaled her breakfast smoothie as she crunched the numbers, and soon realised that she could afford to travel comfortably for a whole year before she would need to come back and take another six months to look for a job. She felt a renewed vigour coursing through her veins as she looked at a map of the world, running her fingers over the smooth tablet screen, pinching in to zoom in on specific countries and cities, scrolling across land masses and oceans, and zooming out. The world was now her playground, and she found herself planning flights, crunching more numbers, looking at global weather patterns, checking modes of transports across continents. And for the next few days, these were the only things she got up to with an almost alarming level of obsession and fervour. And rightly so, because taking time off for an epic trip around the world needed to be done properly without landing into trouble the moment her bags were unpacked back home. She needed to make plans for the home as well – would she want to find a tenant to rent the apartment or cut the electricity and utilities, leaving it vacant for the next year or so?

So, the normally tedious process of preparing for a break of global proportions went on in earnest, getting more intense as the days and weeks went by. She had decided to put up her apartment on the rental market, and now the process of sieving out prospective tenants had well and truly begun. Carol had to go through way too many weirdos to find the right ones who responded to her ad online.

The first to respond to her ad was Yenny, a young, pretty twenty-year-old girl from Miri in Sarawak, who had left her home country for the first time and was living in a foreign country for the first time for her first job. On her own, she could not afford the rental Carol had wanted, but she intended to bring in two of her friends to contribute. Carol suggested she bring them along for the interview. They agreed to set the appointment, but they did not show up on the day and ghosted Carol, something which the new Carol dismissed as youthful folly.

The next prospective tenant was the yuppie Abishek, a mid-level manager of a large multi-national bank, in his late twenties. He ticked the few boxes Carol had for a prospective tenant, loved the house and wanted a long-term lease. He visited the apartment, resplendent in his work garb – a crisp white shirt, sleeves folded, pants that fit his strong legs well – and Carol was smitten, if only for a while. The old Carol would have flirted shamelessly with him, but the new Carol was showing much restraint, even as Abishek began to turn on the charm in order to be the one she chose to be the tenant. Carol enjoyed his subtle flirting and felt like she was flexing another muscle that hadn't been working since the Doom. A wink and nod and a subtle touch on her skin, and she was close to making him her tenant, but she had others who wanted to view the apartment. Plus, she didn't really feel comfortable with Abishek and felt that he would turn the apartment into a debauched whorehouse of interns, secretaries and receptionists, all of whom would be coming and going. So she kept his application on ice.

She then hosted a heavily tattooed couple. The husband, Leroy, was a chef, and the wife, Annie, worked in a clinic in Simei, and both were predictably keen to move in immediately. The couple was very polite, almost freakishly polite, which made her uncomfortable. Nevertheless, she looked past that and was seriously considering them to be her tenants until they let it slip that they would also have the wife's little brother to move into the other room that she had been using for storage. Carol felt uncomfortable having a living, breathing human in that space, but mostly because she could not find any strength in her to clean out that room. So she asserted to them that the room was to be kept empty, or at least, for temporary guests. They wore their disappointment heavily on their faces as they left the apartment.

Another one in the keep-in-view (KIV) file for possible consideration later on.

The next one who came to view the apartment was Jasper, another yuppie who was a party frat fuckboy who said the words "bruh" and "like" way too many times for her liking. Plus, he didn't seem to be too reliable when it came to making payments, and the last thing she wanted was for her apartment to turn into a frat house with broken furniture and a pile of cushions in the middle of everything. He did, however, make a very clumsy attempt to flirt with her by taking her hand and caressing her fingers gently with the hope of either closing the deal for the house, or at the very least, with her. It was something which she mildly appreciated but ultimately didn't care for, so fuckboy was kicked out of contention early on.

So it was for the next few weeks, Carol hosted many visits by prospective tenants, all of whom were very keen to stay at her house. And rightly so, because she had it decorated in what was termed then as the Scan-dustrial style of home décor. It was a portmanteau of "Scandinavian" and "industrial", a fusion of home décor trends that she found to compliment her cold, harsh yet colourful character, the furniture carefully curated and bought to match and complement her décor with a smattering of standout, conversation-starter pieces that turned her house into a museum of past and present. A vintage typewriter from the eighties perched comfortably on top of the upcycled console table next to the forty-six-inch smart TV, exposed wiring and bare lightbulbs hanging from the ceiling, with window frames and gates painted matte black. The house stood out from the cookie cutter apartments that lined the corridor on every floor of the block, making it a popular spot for opportunists who trawled the old estate looking for a photo opportunity.

She was close to giving up when she realised that she had one final appointment for the day with a lady named Myra. There was still some time, so she cracked open a can of cold beer and took a time-out before she had to launch into her now well-rehearsed script about the house and its features. Myra came knocking on the front door with a chubby but pretty little trollop of a girl hanging off her arm.

Myra was dressed in a white shirt that hung loosely below her waist and boot-cut ripped jeans, a throwback to fashion in the nineties. Her long hair hung lazily, unkempt across her shoulders. She looked like she had a deep distrust in every-thing, like a jaded cynic who wanted to be a recluse forced to be out in the world. She had this intense, critical look in her eyes, not unlike the one Carol was wont to give every now and then.

"Hi, Carol?" Myra asked in a deep and no-nonsense tone.

"Yes, I'm Carol. You must be Myra. Come on in."

"Yes, I am, thank you. This is my partner, Nymeria"

Nymeria (actually spelt Namirah) smiled and looked like an overgrown teenager in her skate shorts, colourful and pris-tine kicks and punk band T-shirt that screamed "Against All Authority." She looked high that day, with lazy desert eyes and was very laid back and docile. She had an easy smile about her that was bright and innocent, emphasized by the very faint freckles that were littered across her cherubic face. Her pixie-cut curls were a hustle and bustle of brown that ran riotously across her head. She only muttered a hello to Carol, but Carol noted how her voice was soothing, as if it came from high in the mountains where the air was crisp and the breeze fresh. Or just that she was high as a kite, she wasn't

332

sure. Carol smiled at the both of them and felt at ease with them in no time.

They shook hands and exchanged pleasantries before Carol launched into her script about the apartment. This was the easiest part of the viewing, with the litmus test being the way they were able to communicate with each other. Carol felt as if she was interviewing for prospective partners – minus the flirting – instead of tenants, but it was important for her to find reliable tenants who were not going to fuck things up for her, the house and her plans while she was off gallivanting across the globe.

But there was something about Myra that she liked but could not put her finger on. It could have been Myra's intensity in her look and demeanour or that easy-going character hiding behind that intensity. It could also be the way Carol saw herself in Myra, how kindred spirits were often drawn to and identified with each other. Carol had pretty much decided to let Myra be her tenant, but she just needed to get to know Myra a little bit more before deciding. So she invited both Myra and Nymeria out for drinks just across the road to find out more about their situation and what they were like after a few drinks. And it was at the grubby, gritty old-man coffee shop that they all realised how much they had in common, from friends to interests, lifestyle and beliefs. But Carol just needed to hear one thing from them: that they were a lesbian couple. It was just something she wanted to hear because couples renting a place usually meant stability, reliability and most importantly, consistency in making rental payments. And for it to be a same-sex couple, the stability and reliability increased tenfold because for them to commit to each other and to co-habitate, it told her that their commitment to each other and the living space was ironclad. In between cheap, watered-down beer and roasted peanuts, the music that soothed Carol's ears came in the form of Myra and Nymeria professing their love for each other, and how they felt it getting stronger even after ten years together.

The trio's chemistry was undeniable, and they appeared to be friends catching up from where they left off years ago and, despite being the only prospective tenants to ask for a lower rental price, Carol was happy to offer them the lease to her place, right there and then. She went as far as to accede to any of their requests regarding move-in dates and what to do with the remaining furniture. Carol was convinced these two lovebirds were what she wanted, so she pretty much okay-ed all their requests. The fact that all she wanted to do was to leave it all behind and go for her adventure never played in her head.

And so it was for the next few weeks, Carol kept herself busy with planning for the trip of her lifetime whilst getting her house ready for her tenants. Soon enough, she finalised her travel plans, which was to land in her spiritual home ground – Perth, Australia – before crossing the Nullabor to the eastern cities of Melbourne and Sydney, a pit stop in Auckland before making her way up north to Tokyo for a quick look-see before heading to Vancouver, British Columbia where her trek in North America would begin. From there, she planned to make her way down to Central America and maybe Cuba, and if she still had or could find ways to earn money, she would be gallivanting around Europe as well. Should be easy. As a toned, beautiful Asian woman in North America, she could make easy money working as a stripper maybe, if she chose to play up her exoticism. Or find some rich, old sugar daddy in Florida who had yellow fever to fund her trips in return for company and a chance for him to rewrite history.

But those were plans kept deep in the KIV file, still tempting nevertheless.

Her affairs were soon sorted cleanly, and all that was left was for her to go to the airport for her flight. She made her rounds to say her cursory goodbyes to family and friends, assured those closer to her that she was and would be alright. None asked why she was doing this because they all understood why. The Doom had affected them too. But it wasn't like they needed to be assured because they all knew who Carol really was deep down, and she could take good care of herself and hold her own anywhere in the world. Nevertheless, it was a sudden and ballsy move to drop everything and travel the world, regardless of the circumstances surrounding it.

She stayed at her mum's house before her departure and spent her days trying to please her mum, who in turn spent the whole time guilt-tripping Carol. Carol just smiled through gritted teeth and took it all in stride knowing that all this would end the moment she got on board the plane. She even volunteered to do chores and cook for her mum, just to ease the hard time she was getting from the aging matriarch. Lying in her childhood bed at night, she took leisurely strolls down memory lane as she reminisced about her time in Perth and made mental notes of the things she wanted to do elsewhere on her travels. To get tattooed in every city she stayed in, which would be her first step towards emulating Aunt Rachel. She also planned to indulge in a spot of daytime drinking, meet people from all over the world at travellers' events and hostels, people with different perspectives who would keep her on her toes mentally. Who knew, she might even have her travel fuck if any of them should be so lucky. Sometimes, she would go on Google Maps and virtually walk the streets of Perth and almost fetishistically scour through pictures of ever bar, tattoo parlours and places of interest she planned to go to just so that she could feel like she was there already, and not in her childhood bedroom, dreaming of flying on wings of steel.

She was also not one for shopping; she was mostly keen on new experiences and was looking forward to what Australia, North and Central America could offer her wandering soul. Even with her elderly mum nagging in her ears about practically anything, her mind was already wandering about as she imagined azure skies, fluffy white clouds gently rumbling past, clear blue oceans crashing on the shore, white water foaming and hissing on the sand. She could almost smell the salt in the oceans, the fresh figs and eucalyptus in the crisp Aussie air and hear the jangly Aussie twang speaking to her. She imagined getting into a spot of bother at the American customs with their strict border and visa laws but ultimately clearing immigration without having to be subjected to a cavity search, although it would be a cool funny story to tell if she did have one performed on her. She imagined the hostility she might receive amidst the sea of friendly faces and nonchalant, easy-going attitudes with the occasional rudeness breaking the monotony.

So when the day of her departure arrived, she was massively relieved as she got dressed in her most comfortable bedroom best: sweatpants, well-worn running shoes, her stretched out muscle tee and a hoodie from her late teens punk rock days tied around her waist. She was dressed for comfort on what was to be a fairly long flight and had no problem looking like a hobo. But what she had a problem with was smelling like one, so she liberally but carefully spritzed her favourite Chanel's Mademoiselle on both skin and clothes. With a ninety-litre backpack strapped on her shoulders and hanging off her hips, she was ready to take on most of what the world could throw at her. With Aunt Rachel's indomitable spirit guiding her and pushing her on, Carol felt invincible and was going to take the world by the scruff of its neck and dry hump it raw.

Carol loved being at Changi Airport. She loved the hustle and bustle of the terminals, the smell of luggage, coffee and the chatter of disembodied voices that floated comfortably in the air. She especially loved airports when she was the one travelling, and with a smile on her face, a spring in her step, she floated on clouds to the check-in counter, even the twenty-plus kilogram backpack failed to weigh her spirits down. Dumping it on the carpeted floor, she stood, body weight resting on one leg, her sinuous arms akimbo and foot tapping to an invisible beat as she waited in the check-in line. Staring into space and not looking at anything in particular and moving along with the queue, she felt a brief moment of peace when suddenly she felt a weight bearing on her back, as if the backpack she had been carrying was put there again by an invisible force. She felt the discomfort of eyes boring holes into the back of her head, as if trying to look deep into her soul. She gingerly scanned around to see what was happening but was unable to focus on anything or anyone. Carol tried to brush it off and focused on the road that lay ahead, but that feeling of being stalked and watched soon crawled all over her skin like a wet tongue accompanied by hot breath on her back, making her shiver in fear and delight. She closed her eyes and took a deep breath to calm her flesh, and to not get horny in an inappropriate public place, when a familiar melody jumped in her head and clung onto her soul with a vice-like grip.

It was a beautiful melody.

It was a familiar melody.

It was one that comforted her yet also one that surprised her.

*Time*

*It needs time*

*To win back your love again.*

*I will be there.*

*I will be there.*

Once again, she turned to look, and this time, instead of a blurred flurry of activity in a sea of nameless people and disembodied voices, someone came into her field of vision, an image sharp as a knife, clear as crystal, filled with danger.

It was the man.

Just standing there.

The man with the biceps.

The man who made her sing 'Still Loving You.'

The man in the maroon shirt, just standing there, with a hunger etched across his face, looking deep into her soul.

She stood there rooted to the ground, as was he, just drinking the sight of each other as 'Still Loving You' rang loud in her head, and all she could think of was, what song was playing in his head right now?

# 25.

*(1)*

Time seemed to have slowed to a crawl, the universe moving simultaneously at a snail's pace and at the speed of light as the once-disembodied voices and ambient noise faded and melted into a slimy sludge that hummed a long, sorrowful dirge from a time of the ancients. Alex felt as if his feet were encased in lead, his shoulders burdened with an unseen weight and his mind blank.

*It's the Mademoiselle!*

*Wait, it is her, right?*

*The Mademoiselle at the airport, here with me again, at the airport.*

*The Mademoiselle with the arms with veins popping up from underneath her skin.*

*Her arms do look strong, but it is hard to tell from here.*

*The Mademoiselle who had the ponytail and was in the deep red dress.*

They locked eyes with each other, and it felt to him like a meeting of souls, a meeting that would forge a bond that would never break nor end. A clash right in the breathing room between pleasure and pain.

*The Mademoiselle humming one of my faves: 'Still Loving You.'*

*And how the Mademoiselle is still bathed in Chanel's Mademoiselle.*

*Even now I absolutely adore her poise and posture, like a statue masterfully carved in alabaster by God's divine hands.*

*I can see her dominating me and yet being submissive when she wants to be, and only to those who are worthy of her time.*

*I am pretty sure that I am, though.*

*And I am sure she will come out strong, arms swinging, fighting in disgust too.*

*We will become a horrific mating ball of loathing and disgust, swimming in a pristine and warm pool of pleasure.*

*I should say something to her, right?*

(2)

Carol stood there, transfixed in his eyes. His powerful gaze, coming from a pair of sad eyes, like an abused dog struggling with crippling fear and consumed with anger, which ultimately left it confused. She could see the conflict in his eyes between the intense need to be validated and loved, and the almost mindless pursuit of rapture. It took a while for Carol to gather her senses, with just enough time to drink the sight of his biceps, seemingly having minds of their own, calling her name.

Or did they have her name written all over them?

Either way, Carol claimed ownership of those bronzed biceps, even if it was for one second.

Because it was a second that rang through forever and a day.

'Still Loving You' rang loud in her ears as she tried to drown it out and focus on how to conduct herself. Floating on a cloud of nonchalance surrounded by a shield of mystery, but with eyes swimming in captivation and, in a certain light, awe. A wry smirk crawled across her face as she ran her fingers across her forehead, pushing her hair aside as if to present to him her best face. It was as if her gesture was a come-hither gesture, like a queen beckoning her courtly subjects to come forth bearing gifts of pleasure and mirth. Her weight shifted to one leg, her hips cocked outwards suggestively, one arm akimbo, the other hanging loosely by her side, she stood.

Waiting for something.

Waiting for him.

Like a stone.

Unmoving.

She felt that she had been waiting for him all her life, and she felt as if she had known him for a lifetime and more despite having spoken no words to him and knowing nothing about him. All she had were the lyrics of 'Still Loving You.' But she was ready. As ready as she would ever be, for an approach by Mr Still Loving You. In fact, she welcomed it. She did not suffer through these bouts of insecurity and doubt just for her to be ignored by the man who literally made her sing a love song.

She maintained her field of vision, and she could see how comically he seemed to be making his approach, bold yet hesitating. There she stood, waiting, anticipating. With every new moment that passed, another moment froze, and she felt as though there was no longer a past, nor a future. Carol felt like the past, present and future had melted into a bowl of primordial soup and where everything boiled down to an essence of a sensation that had already been devoured by the past. Time stood painfully still for Carol, perched at the edge of a memory staring into an abyss. A memory so fragile that all it would take was a whisper of the wind to make it crumble into dust.

*And 'Still Loving You' still rings loud in her head, and it was all that Carol can do to not sing it out loud.*

(3)

Alright, Alex. Time to gussy up, harden that boner and enter like a hot dick.

*Yeah. Talking like that helps. Real nice, Alex.*

*Shut up.*

*This is going to happen.*

Alex did not understand the source of the crippling doubt consuming him, but it was something that he had to address.

*Just go up to her and say something.*

*Anything.*

He stood there unmoving, not even in a poetic sense. It was as if he stood in a chasm of space and time that was quickly filling up with a thick, heavy sludge of anxiety.

*It doesn't have to be words, just say something!*

His shoulders slumped, and it was as if his heart had melted in the searing heat of the blaze burning his self-esteem and buried his confidence under mounds of ash.

*Why are you still here?*

He seemed to be shrivelled and retreating, swaying in the breeze, just waiting to be trampled on by the raging horde of migrating beasts in the Serengeti.

*This is the longest that anyone hasn't moved from one spot.*

His head hanging limp on his shoulders, his heart, his will shrinking and his self-esteem bruised, his ego drowning in his awkward insecurity and doubt. It was all that he could do to not cower and be overawed by all that he was feeling at that moment.

*What are you – statuesque?*

But a melody began to ring in his ears. It almost seemed like the airport public announcement system was playing it, and it was getting louder. The familiar tune easing itself into his consciousness like a hard dick sliding into a warm and moist mound of pink glistening flesh. A hint of a smile slowly carved itself across his face as that familiar melody breathed new life to his fading loins. His shoulders perked up, his crooked smile now plastered across his face like a stray brushstroke on an art piece that was an out-of-place flourish to finish the piece. His spirit seemed to be lifted as the winter chill passed and his bruised ego miraculously healed.

*Alright, I am going to talk to her.*

He began to mentally stretch and warm up. He ran conversational scenarios in his head and mentally practiced his approach. He ran lines in his head like an actor rehearsing a monologue.

*No no no. Not a monologue.*

*Dialogue, yes. Monologue, no.*

*What am I doing?*

*You idiot.*

*Have you seen a lion limbering up and stretching before he takes down a gazelle?*

It used to be instinct for him. Second nature. Muscle memory. But like a stroke victim relearning how to use his limbs again, he was finding this process to be cumbersome and excruciatingly painful mentally.

*I wish it was as easy as getting a whore. Just show up and pay.*

*But whores are cheap, you idiot.*

That familiar melody again asserted itself in his mind. Now instead of hanging on to his ears and latching itself on his brain, the melody, the tune, seemed to be taking a life on its own in his body. Its jangly crisp guitar chords ran through his veins, the subtle and shimmery harmony of the second guitar filling the void in him, lifting him up higher than he had felt in years. Alex took a deep breath, buoyed by a sudden wave of fortitude, made tentative strides towards the Mademoiselle first. Two steps forward, and one step back.

It was as if Klaus Meine was singing about Alex when he sang about how he will fight to win her love.

Another three steps forward, his body now entering its fight or flight mode, trying to cripple itself with anxiety and fear.

Here a verse 'Still Loving You' played again in his head that whispered to him of a love that can break down anything.

He could feel his feet shaking as if stepping on a ground that was unstable and breaking in an earthquake. An earthquake that was inside him. A tempest raging. A new normal fighting his previously learned instincts.

His heart was bursting in his chest, his breath quickened and he felt as if the fitness tracker was working hard and was about to congratulate him for a good workout. His vision blurred and his hands were shaking as a cloud of anxiety fell hard on him.

He stopped dead in his tracks to gather his wits. He could see the Mademoiselle standing there, her weight resting on one hip, tapping her feet, waiting to see what would happen next. Would he black out from this battle stress he was feeling? Or would he overcome it?

All this while, 'Still Loving You' is still playing in the air.

Alex ran his trembling fingers through his hair, and he could feel a thin layer of sweat forming on his scalp as his sense of inferiority weighed heavily on him. Time seemed to stand still, and while everything else slowed down to a low drone, a hum and a murmur, the song in him still sang loud.

*This can't be the end...*

(4)

Carol stood uncomfortably in line as she waited for something to happen. She had hoped that she had not done anything that would deter him, but she still needed to maintain a certain level of nonchalance. Her furtive glances at this awkward mess of a man seemingly in a weird dance of forwards and backwards was at least entertaining to her. She stifled a smile at the awkwardness of it all as she adjusted her hair, gently combing it behind her ears and fixing her fringe for what must have been for the thousandth time just in the past few minutes. She cocked her hip and tapped her feet to the beat of the song floating in the air around her.

She could see him.

The man with the biceps slowly, tentatively walking towards her, and in her mind, he looked like a penis that was being reluctantly turned on and kept hard against its will. He looked puffed up and full of confidence, engorged with blood flowing rapidly in its veins, its flesh throbbing and pulsating at the slightest touch. But in the next minute, he had the wind out of his sails, where he looked limp and flaccid, shrinking and retreating deep into himself, shy and recoiling in an unfounded fear of the deep. He looked as if spring and winter came and went in an instant with summer and autumn absent in between, in this bizarre passage of the sun.

Carol tried to find every which way to distract herself from the unfolding physical comedy in front of her. He seemed to be running more than one conversation with himself, or himselves. One seemed to be giving him uplifting, encouraging and positive messages, and another seemed to be a harbinger of doom lobbing grenades to eviscerate his confidence to shreds, and Carol could also see another that seemed to be singing to him and getting him to forget about what seemed to be the gargantuan task ahead of him. Like an experienced childcare teacher distracting her crying charges with song and dance.

*I see you still.*

Soon, he was close enough for her to smell him. But it was more like he was close enough to sniff the air around her, which he did, not so subtly. But true to the form he had been exhibiting in the past few minutes that really felt like hours for Carol, he retreated four steps back just as he seemed close enough to talk to. Carol heaved an uncomfortable sigh of resignation as she subconsciously scratched her cheeks in irritation. She could feel her face aflame with annoyance and having scratched her cheeks too hard, but she was glad that he was oblivious to her annoyance. He seemed to be in his worlds of fear and self-loathing, and another of cocky confidence and positivity.

*All you need is to say hello.*

Amidst the hustle and bustle of airline passengers, tourists and the humdrum of people taking photos and the mechanical voice on the public announcement speakers, Carol could hear a soft, subtle melody. At first, it lay just underneath the elevator music that droned endlessly around the airport. They moved in time and harmony together before it began to slowly drown out the monotonous drone of the soulless airport music. It became more prominent, and Carol recognised its unmistakable melody. She felt as if her body was sinking in a soft mattress as she watched the events unfold in front of her, as that familiar melody cradled her consciousness and comforted her soul.

*This can't be the end....*

(5)

Alex had ventured close enough to the sun to have felt his wings melting in the searing heat of the Mademoiselle. Yet it was the melody that kept him afloat in the face of the vast source of light and warmth for the universe. And he really did feel like a dick as he paced back and forth in his approach to the Mademoiselle. He stopped at an arm's length to compose himself. He took a deep breath, and soon the floral musk of orange and patchouli, the unmistakable scent of Chanel's Mademoiselle, flooded his senses, which in turn restored his vitality and fervour. He felt the hot sliver of potent life force flowing through his veins once again, with his confidence somewhat restored, like a plant basking in the bright glow of the afternoon sun after the rain.

He felt nourished.

His crooked smile carved across his face as his eyes met with the Mademoiselle. Alex took another deep breath, strode forward purposefully into what he perceived to be the darkness, and with the nonchalance and the devil-may-care attitude he carried on his back in the days of yore, he tilted his head, smiled cheekily at the Mademoiselle and nodded his head in acknowledgement of her presence. A hint of a smile crept across the Mademoiselle's face, and his confidence boosted.

"Hi, I'm Alex," he introduced himself.

"Hi, I'm Carol," she said nonchalantly.

"I believe we have met, somewhere, sometime," he continued.

Carol nodded and said, "I believe so."

"I think it was at the airport sometime ago," Alex said.

"I think so too," Carol replied.

"If I remember correctly, it was months ago, also at the departure hall. But you weren't leaving; I think you were meeting someone. Were you?" Alex recalled.

"Yes, I was actually on a date," Carol replied, trying her best to be indifferent.

"So how'd that turn out?" Alex asked with a playful smile on his face.

"Not well."

"How come?"

"Well, at the end of that first date, he had a forty-seven-slide PowerPoint presentation for a planned holiday in New Zealand for just the two of us. And when I rejected, he offered to buy me dessert and wanted to fuck me at some cheap fuckshop."

"You thought that was bad? At least you didn't go to bed with your date and found out that she had an olive oil fetish and wants you to roll about in a tub full of it —"

"Well, that was interesting," Carol interrupted.

"That's not the only fetish she had, as I found out another super gross one the next day," Alex said, careful not to scare Carol off with a scatty story the first time they met.

"Hahaha, ooohhh, tell me more," Carol replied, half in jest, and a more solid half very interested and curious.

"No, not yet, maybe when we get more comfortable with each other, then I can tell that story and many more!" Alex said.

"Well, I look forward to that and to swapping war stories with you," Carol replied encouragingly.

Alex could not take his eyes off the Mademoiselle's and spent the next few minutes captivated by everything about her. It almost felt like he knew her well enough to feel her skin on his, to run his fingers through her hair. Alex was well aware of what the Mademoiselle smelled like, and he wanted to run his nose over every inch of her skin and take a deep breath of her scent, her essence, of her being. He wanted to trace her lips gently with his finger, all while looking deep into her eyes, not saying a word to her, because none was needed.

Other than…

*This can't be the end, I'm still loving you.*

(6)

She wanted him to trace her lips gently with his finger, all while looking deep into her eyes, not saying a word to her, because none was needed.

Other than…

*This can't be the end, I'm still loving you.*

# Author bio

Sharyl Lidzhan is a Literature, History and English teacher from Singapore with a Master's degree in mass communications, and a magnet for all things, people and experiences that are strange and bizarre. His first novel is described as "witty" with "a contagious sense of humour" when "portraying unapologetically flawed characters", and not from his mum. When not throwing hissy fits at surly teenagers, he is often found moping around Singapore with keroncong or power metal in his ears, looking for carbs, dessert and bourbon. He has spent 20 years trying to get in shape and is always on the lookout for public toilets with attached bidets. He also has a weakness for Mexican food and needs near-constant adult supervision.